THE
LOST
TOMB

THE LOST TOMB

N.J. CROFT

Entangled Publishing, LLC
2614 South Timberline Road
Suite 105, PMB 159
Fort Collins, CO 80525
rights@entangledpublishing.com

Edited by Liz Pelletier and Heather Howland
Cover design by Bree Archer
Cover photography by
bukitdamansara, AlexStar, and pniesen/GettyImages
Andrey_Kuzmin/Shutterstock
SergeyNivens/iStock

ISBN 978-1-64063-916-4

Manufactured in the United States of America

First Edition March 2020

ALSO BY N.J. CROFT

The Lost Spear
The Wall
Disease X

"With Heaven's aid I have conquered for you a huge empire. But my life was too short to achieve the conquest of the world. That task is left for you." ~ Genghis Khan on his deathbed

CHAPTER ONE

Noah Blakeley revved his Harley and pulled out in front of the two riders flanking him. Behind them, the huge truck lumbered. Otherwise, the road was quiet, the way ahead lit only by their headlights, a narrow tunnel of light through the darkness. They hadn't seen another vehicle since they'd turned off the freeway.

Might as well have been the road to fucking nowhere.

The knot tightened in his gut. The one he always got before a fight. Though if everything went to plan, then there would be no actual fighting tonight. That wasn't on the agenda. He was almost sorry.

He'd know soon enough if things would go down as intended. They'd better. Otherwise, he'd wasted three months of his life on this deal.

As they rounded a curve in the road, the lights of the checkpoint shone up ahead. Noah eased back on the throttle, and the bike slowed. His muscles tensed. If they were stopped, it was over; something had gone wrong. But as they approached, the metal gates swung open. He didn't see anyone as they drove through. The checkpoint appeared unmanned, though maybe they were just staying out of sight.

Through the gates, a long, straight road led into more darkness.

This was a military storage facility. One that had officially closed six months ago. Finally, a light flashed three times—that was the signal—and a huge warehouse structure loomed out of the darkness.

He peeled off the main track and headed to the right, pulling up outside the open double doors. The light flashed again as he switched off his engine and swung his leg over the bike. Beside him, Rick and Steve did the same.

Rick swaggered over, a big grin on his ugly face. "Hey, looks like we're in business. I never thought we'd be making a deal with the fucking army, but Christ, these days, anyone can be bought."

So it appeared.

Noah pulled off his helmet and rested it on the bike seat, running his hand over his shaved head. He checked the pistol stuffed down the back of his pants as two guys jumped down from the cab of the truck.

"Man, this could be the start of something big," Rick said. "We already have a buyer for this stuff, and they'll take anything we can get. You did good, bro."

"Good enough that you'll let me in on the

deal?"

Rick's eyes narrowed, and for a moment, Noah wondered if he'd pushed too far. He had been with the Brothers of Jesus three months, and while he was useful, they didn't entirely trust him yet. "We'll see. Anyway, we don't have the goods yet. Where the hell are they?"

As he spoke, two figures appeared in the doorway, both in army fatigues. A corporal and a sergeant. Damn. It was unlikely they were anywhere near the top of the food chain. He'd been hoping they would be dealing with someone a little farther up the ladder.

He and Rick walked up, side by side. "You have the stuff?" Noah asked.

The sergeant stepped forward. "You have the money?"

Rick turned and nodded to the man at the back of the group. Jace hurried up. He carried a laptop. "I'm ready to make the transfer as soon as we have confirmation of the goods."

Noah almost smiled. That was sophisticated stuff for a bunch of bikers.

"Then come this way." The sergeant swung around and headed into the warehouse. Dim lights flickered to life, revealing a cavernous room, empty except for a pile of crates against the far wall.

They stopped beside them, and Noah whistled.

The crates had been opened to reveal the contents. There were enough guns to start their own personal war. He pulled a paper out of his pocket and checked the weapons against the list. The buyers had been specific about what they wanted. They could cause all sorts of mayhem with what they had here.

But that part wasn't his problem.

It took half an hour to go through the lot. Turning, he gave Rick a nod. "It's all here."

He moved off to the side as the payment was made, his eyes searching the building. Nothing was out of place. If this went down clean, they could move to the next stage, and things might just get interesting.

Finally, the deal was completed, and Jace headed back to the truck. The headlights came on, and it rolled slowly into the warehouse.

As it came to a halt beside them, all hell broke loose. Lights flashed on, and the sound of booted feet approached, together with engines heading their way.

Shading his eyes from the blinding lights, Noah stepped back behind the nearest crate.

"What the fuck?" Rick crouched down beside him.

Exactly Noah's sentiments. This wasn't the way it was supposed to go down.

Three months he'd been undercover with the

Brothers of Jesus. Three fucking months with a load of fucking assholes. And it looked like he'd wasted every second of that time.

The Brothers were merely a link in the chain, and it was the parties on either side Noah wanted to nail—namely, whoever in the military was dealing arms and then the terrorists who would ultimately use them. Tonight was supposed to have put him on the path to discovering both.

His mind raced. Could they still salvage the night's work? Get out of there? They needed the goddamn merchandise. He peered around the crate and assessed the situation. His eyes were still adjusting to the light, and things didn't look good. A line of soldiers were strung out across the doorway, all in full combat gear and pointing their weapons in his direction.

The blood fizzed in his veins, and he came instantly alive. His body told him that maybe he was going to get that fight after all. His head told him otherwise. No way could they win this. All the same, his gaze flicked to the crate in front of him—they would have no shortage of guns.

"Toss your weapons and come out with your hands behind your head. You have one minute."

Time slowed. He looked at Rick, his eyebrows raised in question, though he already knew the answer.

"I say we go for it," Rick said.

Jesus, but he'd always known the man was an asshole. "What? You want us to go up against the whole fucking U.S. Army?"

Rick grinned. "They're pussies compared to the Brothers."

Actually, he might be right. Most of the brothers had military backgrounds. They were also tough as shit, and they liked a fight. But they were outnumbered ten to one, and Noah wasn't ready to die just yet.

"Come on, bro." Rick grinned. "Let's go down fighting."

I don't think so.

Noah glanced around, assessing the situation. The corporal and the sergeant had vanished—had they been part of the take down? He had to presume so. Jace was nowhere to be seen. He must have been picked off at the truck. That left two of their guys in play. He spotted them behind a crate a few feet down. He could just see the edge of their leathers.

Rick had already pulled his pistol. Was he bat-shit crazy?

Easing his own weapon out from the back of his pants, Noah held it at his side, his brain frantically scrambling for any way out of this that wouldn't be considered a total failure.

"Your time is up."

Something shot over his head, landing just

behind him with a *pfft*. Clouds of dense gray smoke billowed out, and his nostrils clogged with the distinctive acrid stench of a gas grenade, his lungs already tightening with the need for oxygen. His eyeballs were on fire, melting from the inside out. He could barely see through the thickening air, but he could hear the booted feet heading toward them.

Time to get the hell out of there.

"You ready?" he mouthed at Rick.

Rick gave a maniacal grin.

Yup. Crazy.

As Rick stepped forward, Noah lunged to the side, raised the pistol, and crashed it down on the side of the other man's skull. Rick's eyes widened. Noah whirled and kicked out, and Rick crashed to the floor. He made to get up, and Noah stepped on the arm holding the pistol, heard the crack of bone.

"What the fuck?" Rick growled.

"I just saved your goddamn life," he said. "Say thank you." He clipped the other man on the forehead, and he went down and out.

Noah tossed his pistol out beyond the crates. "I'm unarmed, and I'm coming out!"

His skin prickled. This was a dodgy moment. There was always a chance they would shoot him anyway or the Brothers would take a pot shot at him from behind. But they also came out, hands in the air, coughing and choking.

As he stepped forward, men ran at him from all directions, gas masks covering their faces. Someone kicked his legs out from under him, and he swore as he crashed forward onto his face, his nose slamming into the floor with a grinding crunch. Blood flooded his mouth as his hands were yanked behind him and cuffs snapped on. He rolled his head to the side, watching as they dragged Rick, still unconscious, from behind the crate and cuffed his hands behind his back.

Someone yanked Noah roughly to his feet. He stood, impassive, while another man patted him down. His mind searched furiously, but he couldn't see a way to make this work in his favor.

What the hell had happened? Had someone snitched?

The place was emptying out. The other three Brothers were hauled away.

He blinked, trying to clear his vision. Then someone came up behind him, and the cuffs were unlocked. A man in uniform stopped in front of him. Noah recognized the face behind the mask, just as he pulled it off and grinned. Captain Alex Breyer, Noah's second-in-command.

"Welcome back, Major. Love the leathers. Suits you."

"Fuck off," Noah growled.

"The general wants to see you."

Fucking great.

Noah had lost the ability to relax in the last three months, always sleeping with one eye open, listening for anything that might be a threat. Now he recognized bone-deep exhaustion. He'd probably sleep for a week once he found out what the hell had fucked up his mission.

So far, he hadn't been able to find anything. All Alex knew was that the unit had been ordered to intercept the deal at the warehouse, not the reason why. That was the army for you.

Now he was in the back of a vehicle driving to D.C., where General Peter Blakeley, Noah's commanding officer—and also, incidentally, his uncle—was based. That likely meant that his cover had been irreparably compromised and he was heading for debriefing.

He'd volunteered for a position in Project Arachnid, the new anti-terrorist initiative, just over two years ago when it had come into being. Before that, he'd been working as a military liaison with the CIA. At first, his uncle had refused to consider him, but it hardly qualified as nepotism. There weren't that many people volunteering seeing as how it was unlikely to be an advantageous career move.

Noah had wanted to be someplace he would make a difference, and for him, terrorism was where the current war was happening. All around them. If he could be instrumental in slowing the spread down, then he would be doing something worthwhile with his life.

Going after the bad guys.

His ex-wife, Eve, had always said he saw things as too black and white. For Noah, that's the way they'd always been.

Eventually, he fell into a light doze, only waking when the car pulled up outside the Pentagon.

Alex had handed him his ID back at the warehouse, but he still got some strange looks walking through the building. They had given him an escort at the first checkpoint. "Sorry, sir, but I don't think you'll get very far otherwise."

He supposed there weren't too many six-foot-four guys with shaved heads wearing gang leathers strolling through the Pentagon. Especially at this time of night. It was around four in the morning.

"Good God," Peter said as he opened the door and waved Noah in. "You look…"

"Like an asshole," Noah finished for him.

Peter grinned. "I was going to say you look the part." He studied him, head cocked to one side, eyes narrowed. "And you do. More than look it, actually. I can feel the menace oozing off you. You're good at this."

Noah shrugged. "It's a matter of getting inside

their heads." He'd always been able to do that. Maybe he should have been an actor.

"And your nose is broken." Peter waved him to a seat and took the one on the opposite side of the big desk. He opened a drawer in the desk and pulled out a bottle of scotch and a couple of glasses. "You also look tired," he said, pouring them both a glass and pushing one toward Noah.

He picked it up, swallowing the contents in one go, then placed it back on the table. Peter raised an eyebrow but refilled it. Noah blew out his breath and slumped back in the chair. "I didn't realize how tired I am until I was on my way here. I haven't been sleeping too well."

"I can imagine."

He took a sip of scotch this time, holding it in his mouth and savoring the peaty flavor—it was a shit ton better than the cheap stuff he'd been drinking the last few months. "So what the hell went wrong? Why the raid? That wasn't the plan. I was supposed to stay under. Follow the trail."

Since he'd started working with the unit, he'd begun to see patterns. Before that, he'd always believed that terrorism was basically random. Perpetrated to cause chaos and terror, but with no long-term strategy involved. Now he wasn't so sure. He had a theory that there was some sort of global plan, someone choreographing all the larger terrorist groups. To what end, he couldn't see.

Once he'd seen the pattern, he'd started to predict where and when the attacks might take place. That had led him to the Brothers, and he'd gone undercover, found the military connection. They were supposed to let the deal go through and he'd follow it along the chain while his team went after the military angle, found out just how far up the corruption went, and cut it out.

"There was a leak somewhere," Peter said. "They knew about you. The soldiers were going to reveal your identity once the product had been loaded. They would have taken you out. So we made the decision to rescue you first."

"Thanks," he said drily.

"Well, you were no further use in your present position. And I do have a slight fondness for you."

"You wouldn't have done the same for anyone?"

"Of course. I am sorry, though—this mission was three months of your life. Anyway, at least we have some leads to follow. The two soldiers."

"I'd like to question them myself, sir."

Peter placed his empty glass on the desk. "I love it when you want something and call me 'sir.' But it's not going to happen. You're dead on your feet. You're going to take a couple of weeks leave, and then we'll regroup and decide where to go next."

"We have to get them."

"I know."

"And I enjoy my job."

Peter snorted. "Sometimes too much."

What the hell did that mean? When they were married, Eve used to say something similar—that he enjoyed the danger. He rubbed a hand over the stubble on his cheek. "I just want to put an end to this. Terrorism is bad enough, but at least the people believe in what they're doing. This, on the other hand, is pure evil."

"You don't think all terrorism is evil?" Peter asked.

Did he? While he would never condone the use of terror, he could understand why a person might resort to it to change an economic, social, or political system they considered unjust. "Come on, Peter. Both you and I know that one person's terrorist is another's freedom fighter." Or government. Christ, there were governments his country dealt with that committed far worse atrocities than the average terrorist on the street. "What defines terrorism isn't what's done but who does it."

"You've always been able to see both sides," Peter mused. "That's a strength and a weakness, though you've never believed the end justifies the means, which I've always found a contradiction."

He didn't ask if Peter believed the same. Some

of the things their own government had done would hardly bear close scrutiny. "I will never agree with the means, but I can still understand the motivations."

Peter studied him for a moment. "Maybe you've been undercover too much. You shouldn't identify with these people."

"I do not, nor will I ever, identify with the Brothers of Jesus." Noah pressed his fingers into the back of his neck, trying to ease the pressure. "But right now, someone out there is taking advantage of the fact that there are people born into societies that consider terror a viable option for changing the world. Now they're being used and manipulated for a purpose they know nothing about and certainly don't believe in."

"You don't consider people have free choice?" Peter asked. It was an argument they'd had many times.

"If they know what their choices are, sure. It feels like most terrorists are products of their upbringing, unable to break free of the chains that are wrapped around them from the moment they're born and that tighten every second they spend in their environments."

"For a small minority, maybe, but I believe most of us can choose the paths we take." Peter smiled. "Maybe you don't believe that because you're a product of an upbringing *you* can't let go."

He studied Noah for a moment. "When was the last time you spoke to your mother?"

Noah frowned. "What the hell does my mother have to do with global terrorism?" Probably more than she knew. He smiled at the thought, but Peter just gave him a look. Noah sighed. "Fine. It's been a while, but we're not talking about me."

"You don't believe you're a product of your upbringing? It didn't affect you at all?"

"Fuck off."

"I hope you're speaking to your uncle and not your superior officer."

"Of course."

"She called a few times while you were away," Peter said. "I said you'd call back as soon as you were able."

Noah gave a humorless laugh. "Was she sober?"

"I think so. You know, you have to forgive her one day."

"There's nothing to forgive."

"Hah. Anyway, call her and get her off my back."

He'd think about it. "Anything else?"

"Eve called a couple of nights ago. She was trying to get ahold of you. She sounded a little… worried."

"Worried? About what?" It could be one of many things.

"I'm not sure. She said she was just in need of a familiar voice. The call came from Russia somewhere."

Noah frowned. What the hell was Eve doing in Russia? Presumably this related to her job, but as far as he was aware, she hadn't done field work since before they'd met, twelve years ago. She had a very civilized job these days, as a lecturer in archeology at Cambridge University in England. And he couldn't blame her for wanting that, not after what she'd been through. She suffered from PTSD, and she hated flying. Or, rather, she was *terrified* of flying. He didn't think she'd been on a plane since she'd left him and gone back to the UK, five years ago. So what had dragged her out of her comfort zone?

He glanced at his watch. It would be mid-morning in Europe. He waved a hand at the phone on Peter's desk. "Can I?"

"Go ahead."

He punched in the number from memory. The call went through, but he just got a weird beeping. He tried again and got the same thing. He sat back and thought for a moment, then put in the number for Eve's parents. The kids would have been staying there if Eve was away.

It picked up after a few rings but no one responded. "Hello?"

"*Noah*," he heard Eve's mother, Stacey, sob on

the other side of the line. What the hell was going on?

"Stacey, what's happening?"

"It's Eve. She's dead."

CHAPTER TWO

Noah closed his eyes as they lowered the coffin into the ground.

Christ, he hated this.

He was angry. Such a waste of life. But if he was honest, most of his anger was aimed at Eve. What the hell was she doing in fucking Russia? She had three children.

So do you, asshole.

He could almost hear her words in his head.

Time to step up.

It wasn't as though he had a choice. And that thought made him the asshole she'd no doubt considered him to be.

To his left, Eve's mother stood sobbing quietly. Maybe he should try and comfort her, but he'd never been good with crying, and he had no clue what he could say to make things better.

It had been two weeks since he'd gotten the news of his wife's death and his life was changed forever.

They'd been divorced for five years, but despite having three children together, he'd not played a huge part in her life. Or that of the children. He'd believed they were all better off without him. Obviously, Eve had thought that as well or she wouldn't have left him in the first place. It wasn't as though she didn't know who and what he was from the start. They'd met when he'd been part of a military rescue mission sent into Iraq. A group of archaeologists, including Eve, had been taken hostage by terrorists.

His team had managed to free them, though a couple had died in captivity and they'd all been tortured. Eve had been in bad shape physically—she'd taken a bullet in the shoulder during the kidnapping, which had gone untreated—but in worse shape mentally.

Even filthy and hurt and scared, she'd been beautiful. Blonde hair, blue eyes, and tiny. She'd made him feel protective. He'd fallen hard and looked her up afterward, needing to check whether she was okay. He'd never thought further than a fling. He didn't do relationships. After the example of his mom and dad, it was hardly surprising.

Then Eve had gotten pregnant.

Neither of them believed abortion was an option without a really good reason, which they didn't have. And so they'd ended up married. It had happened fast.

The truth was they loved each other—hell, he loved her even now—but love was never enough. In fact, love might have been the problem. If he'd cared less, he might have coped with marriage better. In the end, it drove them apart.

The second time she'd gotten pregnant, it was on purpose. A deliberate attempt to tie him to them as a family. Instead, it had driven him away. He was shit-scared of emotional connection, according to Eve. She'd known him so well.

For the last three months of her life, he hadn't even spoken to her. He'd been undercover and the risk was too high. Playing his little games, Eve would have said. And she was probably right. In the end it made no difference, and the truth was he'd never been there for her. And now she was dead and he'd never get the chance to say he was sorry.

A small hand slipped into his and squeezed. He looked down at Lucy, his youngest daughter, who was gazing up at him with her big blue eyes. She was six years old and looked exactly as he imagined Eve would have looked at that age.

"Don't be sad, Daddy. Grandma said mommy went to heaven and one day we'll see her again."

Noah managed to hold back his snort of disbelief. His eldest daughter, Harper, standing rigidly on his other side, was not so self-controlled. "Don't be an idiot, Luce. Heaven doesn't exist. And anyway, Mommy was an atheist. She didn't believe in that crap. So if she's gone anywhere, it won't be Heaven."

Harper was holding onto the hand of Lucy's

twin brother, Daniel. Daniel reminded him so much of Noah's little brother, Ben, that sometimes it hurt to look at him. Ben had died when he was not much older than Daniel, a long time ago.

Whereas Lucy and Daniel had been clingy since he arrived, shadowing him as though they were scared he'd disappear, Harper had been distant and also a little disdainful. She was eleven and old enough to realize what a crap father he'd been. Now she held his gaze, her expression challenging. "Do you believe in Heaven, *Daddy?*"

Hell, no.

That probably wasn't the best answer. "If your grandma believes, then that's good enough for me. Your grandma knows everything."

Harper snorted. "Good answer, but a total cop out."

She was bright, though not nearly as tough as she wanted to appear. Her eyes were red from crying, even though there was no sign of tears now. She'd gotten her looks from him, which he was betting pissed her off. She was tall for her age, thin, with shoulder-length black hair and gray eyes.

She didn't trust him. Probably believed both her parents had let her down.

Because, in the end, Eve hadn't been so different from him. She'd been off chasing some dream of her own when she died. Why? What had changed for her? She'd sworn she would never do field work again—and he was sure she would never have the nerve—so why had she been in Russia?

The vicar was talking, and Noah let the words wash over him while Lucy hugged his leg.

Eve had died in a plane crash—ironic when he considered how scared she had been of flying, how she'd avoided it when she could—her body burned beyond recognition and only identified by DNA records. Which meant they hadn't had the closure of seeing a body. Not that he would have allowed the children to see. But somehow, the lack of definitive proof made her death seem unreal. He kept expecting her to appear in the cemetery.

He was aware of a lot of attention on him and not particularly *friendly* attention. But then, most people here didn't know him. He hadn't been part of this life, and he didn't fit in.

He ran a hand over his scalp where his hair was just starting to grow. The funeral had been arranged by Eve's parents. She was an only child, born to them late in life, and her death had turned them even older. He'd been staying with them and the children since he'd arrived in the U.K., but they'd never been close. He'd always suspected they didn't think he was good enough for Eve, and they were no doubt right. They were the real thing, the fucking aristocracy. Five hundredth in line to the throne or some bullshit. They lived in a stately home, and there was plenty of room, but he didn't feel comfortable, and he was going to have to make some decisions soon.

No doubt they were hoping he would leave the children with them and disappear back where he came from, and that would be the easy option. And maybe the sensible one. They would be better off without him. And what was he supposed to do if he stayed here? The army was his life.

Eve's parents were too old to take on young children, though, no matter what they believed. Her father was close to eighty, her mother in her seventies. And while they could afford staff, did he really want his children brought up by paid help?

Christ, it was a mess.

Of course, none of his family was here. Peter would have come, but he was caught up with something that he refused to talk about. Probably the aftermath of Noah's last mission.

He'd spoken to his father and briefly told him the news. Asked him to speak to his brother and sister. They'd never been close, and he preferred not to have to listen to their false condolences. They'd never even met Eve.

A prickle ran down his spine, and he turned his head slowly to look around. Off to the right, a woman stood alone in a stand of trees. He was sure he'd never seen her before; he would have remembered. Striking, she was tall with short black hair, longer on one side than the other. She wore black, though he suspected it wasn't for the funeral, as she had a goth look about her. Dark eyes and lips, black jeans, tears in the knees, a black T-shirt, and a studded belt. For a moment, she caught his gaze and held his stare, her eyes narrowing on him. Then she gave a small nod and stepped back into the shadows of the trees. He stared after her for a long time.

Who was she?

A passing stranger? Or had she known Eve in some way? Why hadn't she joined them at the graveside?

At last, the service was over. He just had the reception back at the house to get through and then the rest of his life. He picked up Lucy—she wrapped her arms tight around his neck—and gave the grave a final glance.

As he headed back to the cars, a woman walked toward them from the gate. Noah recognized her, and his steps slowed, a frown forming on his face. He stopped and waited. Tall with dark red hair, pale skin, and pale green eyes, she was flanked by two men in dark suits. Bodyguards? Secret service, maybe—they had that look. They fell back as she approached Noah, coming to a halt in front of him and holding out her hand. Noah hesitated for a moment then placed Lucy on the ground. He glanced at Harper. "Take your sister and brother to the car. I'll meet you there."

She opened her mouth, probably to argue, but then gave a quick nod, held out her free hand to Lucy, and just about dragged her away. Lucy stared at him over her shoulder the whole time, and he felt the now-familiar stirrings of guilt. He shook off the feeling, turned back to the woman in front of him, and held out his hand. "Senator."

Her handshake was firm.

Michaela Clayton, Senator for Washington and also head of the oversight committee that had given the go ahead for Project Arachnid. While Noah had never met the woman, he'd seen a few pictures. Not many—she kept a low profile for a senator. Apparently, she was a good friend of the president, and his uncle had once mentioned that she was a woman to watch. Would probably be in the White House one day.

"I'm sorry for your loss, Major Blakeley," she said.

Noah kept his face expressionless. He had no clue what the senator was doing here. "Thank you."

"I'm sorry to barge in on you at this sad time, but I'm only in the country for the day, and I wanted to meet you in person."

He glanced toward the gate. The cars were

moving away. Harper stood beside the last one, watching him, her arms folded over her chest in a position that so reminded him of her mother. She was probably tapping her foot as well. "You did?"

She smiled. "To offer my condolences, but also I have a proposition you may be interested in. I've been impressed with your work. Very impressed. Though the last mission was…unfortunate."

Translate that into a total fuck up. "Very," he said drily.

"Dad?" Harper came up beside them. "Are we going yet?"

"In a moment." He turned back to the senator. "This is my daughter, Harper."

The senator held out her hand, and Harper took it somewhat suspiciously. "Your mother was a wonderful woman, and I'm so sorry you lost her."

Harper mumbled something and tugged her hand back.

"You don't want to come back to the house?" Noah asked.

"I'm sorry, I'm flying home this afternoon. I just wanted to pay my respects and also meet you. Your uncle speaks very highly of you."

"He is my uncle, after all."

"He's also a good judge of character. And he believes we have a lot in common. You probably haven't decided what your next move is. This has all been so sudden. But your circumstances have changed, and I'm guessing that you might decide that military life is no longer…suitable."

Noah cast a sideways glance at Harper. She raised an eyebrow. "I haven't decided yet. As you said, it's all been sudden."

"Well, if you do decide to leave the army, I may have a position in my organization for you. Along similar lines to your current work but perhaps without the inherent risks." She cast a smile at Harper. "I won't go into the details now."

Noah was intrigued, but the senator was right. Now wasn't the time. He nodded. "It was good to meet you, and I'll look forward to hearing more."

"I'll get my assistant to schedule a meeting. I hope we talk again soon."

"I like her," Harper said as she walked away, her bodyguards falling into place behind her.

"You do?"

"She's sort of…charismatic."

"Good word." And she was right. The senator had an air of authority and an easy charm.

And a proposition.

"I'm sorry you got stuck with us," Harper said. "I know it's not what you wanted."

He didn't bother to deny it. She was too bright to be taken in by platitudes. "Let's not worry about it now. We've still got the rest of the morning to get through. Then we'll worry. Right now, we'll go see what your granny has cooked up for us."

She giggled at that. "'Granny' doesn't cook."

"Okay, what cook has cooked up for us."

• • •

Sara watched from the shadow of the trees, tugging at the heavy silver cross hanging from her left ear.

She'd wanted to get a look at Noah Blakeley to try and decide whether she should approach him or maintain her distance. He was army, which probably meant he would do things by the book. Was that good or bad?

She wasn't a by-the-book person herself; more of a do-what-was-needed-and-throw-the-book-out-the-window person. Not that there would be anything in the book about this sort of situation.

He was tall and attractive in a conventional sort of way. Handsome and brave-looking in his uniform. Black hair and gray eyes, a lean face with a big, bony nose and a little scar that ran down his right cheek. A knife wound from a hand-to-hand combat incident ten years ago. She'd hacked into his file.

His gaze had clashed with hers, and she'd seen a flicker of interest. Again, was that good or bad? Could she use it?

Sara doubted she was his type. Eve had been

blonde and beautiful. A typical English rose. Sara was anything but.

She tugged at the earring again. She'd never been nervous before, and the experience was new, unexpected, and not particularly pleasant.

She'd almost been on the verge of going forward and introducing herself...until the senator arrived.

In her high heels, the senator was not much shorter than Blakeley, and both had a presence. She was too far away to hear what they were saying and couldn't tell whether they knew each other or not, but they both seemed at ease.

She wished she could hear their conversation.

With one last look, she headed back to where she'd parked her van. She'd just keep watching him until she decided if he was ready to hear the truth about his wife's death.

Or whether he already knew.

CHAPTER THREE

Noah came back from his run to chaos.

He'd rented an apartment in North London, less than a mile from the tube so he could get to work easily but also close to Hampstead Heath to give the kids some semblance of countryside.

Lucy was desperate for a puppy. Christ, this was his nightmare come true. A goddamn puppy. And three kids. And a job in the city.

He suspected the children hadn't been entirely happy with leaving their grandparents' house. Except, strangely, Harper, who claimed their granddad was a "bloated plutocrat" and that their grandmother was trying to turn her into a Princess Diana clone.

The girl was too smart for her own good.

He'd enrolled them in private schools not too far from their new home. At least he could afford to pay for it. With his new salary—about four times what he'd been earning as a major in the U.S. Army—he could probably afford to pay for boarding school. That was a tempting idea.

It was just as well his pay was good. Rent in London was astronomical, and he had to fork out for a live-in nanny. The one their grandparents had employed had agreed to come along, but he didn't like the woman, and he suspected she liked him just as little. If he'd believed she was the best choice for the children, he would have put up with her, but she was too strict. He would pay her off and get someone younger once the children were more settled. Most nights, Lucy and Daniel still woke up crying for their mother.

As he opened the front door, a shrill scream filled the air. He broke into a run and charged through the door into the kitchen just as Ms. Pierson slapped Daniel across the face. Noah stopped abruptly, and everyone turned to face him.

"I think you should leave," he said quietly.

"But I—"

"Just go. Now." He waited until she had left the room then looked around him. "What happened?"

"Daniel wouldn't eat his breakfast," Lucy said. "And then he said he wouldn't go to school. And then he screamed."

"In Ms. Pierson's defense," Harper put in, "he was being really annoying. I might have slapped him myself if she hadn't gotten there first."

"You're allowed to slap him. You're his sister."

"Really?" She sounded delighted. He had to start thinking before he said anything to Harper.

He closed the space between him and Danny and hunkered down close to the little boy. He was so goddamn cute. It was hard to believe he was

Noah's son. He was sucking his thumb, a habit Eve had told him he'd grown out of. Until Eve's death. Now it was never out of his mouth. "You okay?"

Danny nodded.

"How about I take you to school?"

He nodded again.

Noah glanced at his watch. They should have left by now. They'd be late. He'd be late. For his first day at his new job. He blew out his breath and wished he was going somewhere he could shoot someone. "Give me one minute."

In the end, he hadn't had to think too hard about Senator Clayton's proposition.

If he couldn't go back in the army, then he figured this was as good as it got. Plus, he'd spoken to his uncle about the senator, and he had sung her praises. In fact, he'd never heard Peter sound so enthusiastic about anyone before.

His official title was Head of Security for Clayton Industries. That was the umbrella organization for the senator's family business, a huge, multinational conglomerate with companies in every line and most countries. He hadn't realized the senator was so wealthy. It didn't show in her lifestyle, which was a plus in her favor. However, while he would eventually—once he had gotten up to speed—have an overall say in strategy for the company's security division, his real job was threat analysis.

Apparently, the company had an information-gathering system set up. Intel flooded in from all corners of the globe, including information pertaining to terrorist organizations and terrorist acts either past or considered likely. He'd had a conference call with the senator. She'd explained her thinking on the matter, and it was so close to Noah's, it was uncanny. She had also seen an escalating pattern, a coalescing of groups and actions, and believed there was a plan behind all the seemingly random acts of terror. And if there was a plan, then there was also a planner. Someone at the center of it all, pulling the strings.

Noah's ultimate job was to identify the planner or planners. The senator believed it was a group of powerful people who had come together for a cause. Unravel the cause, the motivations, and that would lead to the people involved. In the meantime, he was to produce threat level reports for all the countries where Clayton Industries functioned. Which was just about them all.

They had a building in the city close to Liverpool street, a huge glass and steel structure. A uniformed doorman opened the glass doors as he approached and gave Noah a nod as he walked through. "Can I help you, sir?"

At a guess, the man was ex-military, and Noah's appearance was somewhat different from the usual people passing though those doors. He

hadn't bothered with a suit; he wasn't dealing with
clients, and suits weren't his thing. He was in dark
pants and a white shirt. At least his hair had grown
another half-inch, so it was now about the length
it had been when he was on normal active duty.

He pulled his ID out of his pocket and handed
it to the man whose name was Jerry, according to
the badge on his chest. Noah gave him an easy
smile—the man was just doing his job. "First day."

He didn't get a smile in return. "Follow me, sir."

He followed to a desk with a security sign on
the front. "Just a moment." Jerry pulled out his
phone and turned away.

Noah looked around. It was just after nine,
making him half an hour late. Way to make a good
first impression. The place was busy, lots of people
in thousand-dollar suits—or he supposed
thousand-pound suits here in London—looking
busy and important. He leaned against the desk
and folded his arms across his chest. Jerry turned
back, his eyes wide, his lips pulled down in a
frown. He shoved the phone back in his belt.

Noah supposed he was the man's boss a long
way up the chain. He was guessing Jerry had just
found that out. He looked like he wanted to
salute.

"Sir. I apologize for the delay, sir. I was told to
expect you but…"

Noah took pity on the man. "But I'm not what

you were expecting?"

"No, sir. I mean, yes…"

"At ease, soldier."

"Yes, sir. Your assistant is on his way down, sir. He'll sort out your security clearance."

"What's your background, Jerry?"

"Sergeant in the Paratroopers, sir. Injured out, sir."

"Iraq?"

"Yes, sir." A look of relief passed over his features. "There's Mr. Shipley," he said. "Your assistant."

He hadn't even known he had an assistant. Obviously, he had a lot to learn. He studied the man hurrying toward them. Mid-twenties, tall, light brown hair cut short at the sides, longer on top. This one definitely wasn't ex-military.

He stopped in front of them and held out his hand. Noah shook it.

"Pleased to meet you, major."

"Not a major anymore. Call me Noah."

"I'm Tom Shipley. I've been assigned to work with you, show you around, make sure you have everything you need. If you'll follow me, I'll take you to your office."

He led the way to an elevator around the corner. "This just serves the top two floors. All the senior management have their offices up there." He flashed the card across a panel beside the elevator, and the doors slid open. "Your security card will access the elevator, but the doors on the top floor are all activated by retinal scan. We'll get all that sorted for you later this morning."

The security seemed a little excessive. What the hell were they doing up there? "Very high tech."

"All the head offices are installed with retinal scans now."

"Have you worked here long?" Noah asked as they stepped out of the elevator into what looked like another reception area. A man sat behind a desk in a security uniform. He nodded but didn't speak as they went past. Tom lowered his head to the scanner by another door, and it opened, revealing a large corner office.

Noah whistled. "Who did you have to toss out to give me this?"

"It was used by the senator when she visited."

So Clayton had given up her office for him. He walked across to the window and stared down at the city of London spread out below him. It was impressive, but he'd always preferred the wide-open spaces to the city. Back in the U.S., he had a cabin in the Virginia mountains that he always visited when he had down time. Here, he could feel the walls closing around him. He shook off the feeling. This was his new reality, at least for the foreseeable future. He had to make the best of it.

He blew out his breath and turned to survey

his new office. It was just as impressive as the view. He sat in the big leather chair in front of the steel desk. The expanse was shiny and completely clear. No computer in sight.

"Do you have a security background, Tom?"

"No, sir. I'm a systems analyst and information technician. I'll be getting you up to speed on the systems you'll be using and making sure you have access to whatever you need."

"Sounds good. Do I get a computer?"

Tom grinned. "Yes, sir." He swiped a hand over the desk, and a screen rose up out of the steel. A smooth keyboard appeared on the flat surface. Tom leaned over the desk, pressed a key, and the screen came to life. He typed in a few words and then stepped back. "That gives you access to your work emails and so on. Again, it will be all protected by scans as soon as we've completed the procedure. I'll go and check on that now. And leave you to…" He shrugged. "Whatever." He waved a hand to a door at the back of the room. "Bathroom." And then at the cabinet opposite. "Coffee. You want anything else, just call 100."

"Tom," Noah called out as the other man reached the door.

He turned. "Yes?"

"Is there a shooting range around here?"

Tom's eyes widened, and Noah had to bite back a laugh. What the hell had they been told about him? He'd wait a few days before he asked.

"Actually, there's one in the basement. I'll make sure you have clearance for that as well." And he was gone.

Noah sat back in the chair and surveyed his new domain. He got up and walked around, got a coffee — he hadn't had time for one that morning — sat back at his desk, and felt a little lost. Noah wasn't the type to sit around. He needed something to do. Something that would kickstart his stagnant mind. Problem was, while he knew the broad scope of what his job entailed and that there should be a wealth of information at his fingertips, he wasn't yet sure how to go about doing anything.

There was an email icon on the screen, and he tapped on it. He had ten new emails.

The first one was from the senator, welcoming him and scheduling a call for the following day. Good. Maybe he could get started after he spoke to her. He scanned down the rest of the list and didn't recognize any of the names. He'd read them in a moment, but his gaze snagged on an email halfway down. The subject line just said, "Eve."

His gut tightened as he opened the email, then he sat staring at the screen.

Your wife did not die in an accident. She was murdered.

CHAPTER FOUR

What the fuck?

He read the email again, then his gaze flicked to the sender line. It was empty.

He sat back in his chair, his body going unnervingly numb. He'd blindly accepted Eve's cause of death because, really, there was no reason not to believe his ex-wife had died in a freak accident. Eve didn't live the kind of life he did. Even the kidnapping that had led to their initial meeting twelve years ago had not concerned her specifically. She'd just been in the wrong place at the wrong time. And as far as he knew, she had no enemies to speak of.

Could Eve have been murdered? And if so, why?

And why would someone send him an anonymous message about it *now*?

Was this some sort of warning? Or maybe a threat?

For the first time since Eve's death, his brain clicked into gear, turning over the pieces, trying to find a pattern the way he'd always worked best.

And still, he came up with nothing.

Was someone trying to mess with his head?

If so, they were succeeding.

He wanted to punch something. Maybe he *had* spent too long with the Brothers if physical violence was his first inclination. Regardless, whether the email was true or not, there was a reason someone had contacted him. He needed to find out who and why.

He had contacts from his old life, IT experts, who could likely trace the sender. He'd start there.

Then he needed everything he could get on Eve's accident. All Noah knew was that Eve had been on a private plane traveling from Irkutsk in Russia to Ulaanbaatar, the capital city of Mongolia. The plane had gone down only ten minutes into the journey. The brief report he'd seen had concluded that the most likely explanation was a bird crashing into one of the engines. The pilot had died along with his only passenger. Eve. There had to be more. Presumably the Russian police must have investigated and likely the Aviation Authority.

The fact that she was in Russia at all had niggled at his mind since he'd heard of her death. Something had changed, something so important that she had overcome her fears and left her children.

That thought brought him up short.

Could the children be in danger?

Jesus.

He needed to organize some security, but they

were just getting back into a normal routine. How would he explain it?

Gather the intel, then make an informed decision.

But fast.

He was still staring at the email when Tom reappeared at the door. "Security is ready for you," he said.

After one last look at the message, he swiped the screen to clear it and rose to his feet. "Tell me," he said, "can someone send an anonymous email through the internal system?"

Tom gave him a strange look. "No. It's not possible. All emails have a sender. As far as I'm aware, there's no way to block it."

Noah glanced down at the blank screen. He could have argued, but he didn't know how much he wanted to reveal to Tom. Whether he trusted the other man. Or not.

They rode the elevator down to the security department in the basement, where they took his fingerprints, retinal scans, voice prints. There hadn't been this much security in the army. Through it all, his mind kept returning to the anonymous email.

He returned to his office as soon as he was finished and reread the message.

Why would anyone want to murder Eve? That's where he was stuck. She'd been an archaeologist who spent her life teaching and searching for really old things that no one else cared about anymore. Certainly not enough to kill for. At least, that's what he'd always believed, but then the past had never interested him. Just the present and the future.

Now, he needed to find out everything about her work and try and figure out why anyone would have taken her out. To stop her finding something?

He also couldn't ignore the possibility that the email had nothing to do with Eve's work and everything to do with his.

While his work with Project Arachnid had mainly been undercover, he had no doubt he'd made enemies over the years. Eve's death might be some sort of revenge, though if that was the case, he would have expected whoever had done it to claim responsibility. Otherwise, what was the point? All the same, he would make a list of the groups and individuals he had worked with or against who might feel the need to make him suffer.

The only other possibility was that the email was nothing but a prank. Maybe someone didn't like the idea of him taking this job, wanted to unsettle him. Or, worse, distract him. Was there something he wasn't meant to find and someone feared he'd be able to do just that in his new position?

Drumming his fingers on the desk, he stared into space. Then, without giving himself time to think it was a bad idea, he picked up the phone and glanced at the time. It would be six o'clock in the morning in D.C. He punched in the number for Peter's office. His uncle was usually at his desk by now, and sure enough, the man picked up on the second ring. "General Blakeley."

"Peter, it's Noah."

"What is it?"

He hesitated as second thoughts crept through him. Maybe he should find out more before he involved anyone else.

"Noah?"

The fact was, Peter had access to information no longer available to him, and Noah needed answers fast. "Do you know of anything that might have suggested Eve's death was not an accident?" By virtue of Noah's position in Project Arachnid, any suspicious deaths close to him would have been routinely investigated.

"Why are you asking?"

Peter was Noah's father's younger brother, and Noah had known him all his life. There were only ten years between them, and they'd always been close. Peter had made the effort to spend time with him whenever he was in the country, and after Ben had died and everything turned to crap, he'd been the one person Noah had felt he could rely on. It was because of Peter that he'd asked his father if he could go to military school—the same one Peter had attended—and because of Peter that he'd joined the army. It was all he'd ever wanted.

Father figure, role model, and later his mentor—Peter was the one person he trusted implicitly.

"I received an anonymous email saying that Eve was murdered."

"Jesus, Noah." There was a minute's silence, no doubt while Peter processed the information. "There was nothing in the reports to suggest foul play."

"Who carried out the investigation?"

"Exactly who you'd expect. The local police in conjunction with the Russian civil aviation authority. The plane was still over Russia when it went down."

Yeah, Noah figured as much. "Can I see whatever files you have?"

"Do you think that's a good idea?"

He pressed a finger to his forehead. "I don't think I have a choice. I can't ignore this."

"No, you're right. I'll send them through. But my immediate thought is that you're being manipulated. I just can't see how. Or why. You're out of Arachnid. Why would anyone come after you? Maybe revenge? But it seems a very odd way to go about it."

"I know. I've been sitting here trying to work out the possible motives and coming up with... nothing."

"Have you told anyone else about this?"

"Not yet."

"Then I'd keep it to yourself. In the meantime, forward me the email. I'll get one of our people to look into it, though I doubt we'll find anything. Maybe it's just someone trying to mess with your head."

"I've considered that." He sent the email to Peter's secure account. "Could it be something to do with my new job?"

"Why do you ask that?"

"The email came through on my new work account. Could be significant."

"Or not. You're reaching. How are the children?"

Noah blew out a breath and ran his hand over his short hair. "Harper is channeling her inner bitch. Luce thinks I'm going to die if I leave her sight. Daniel has decided screaming is the best way to get what he wants. Oh, and I fired the nanny this morning." That reminded him—he needed to find someone to watch the children. And fast. He didn't think any of them would survive too long if he was their sole carer.

"That good, huh?" The amusement in Peter's voice came through loud and clear.

"Yeah, that good. The Brothers were a breeze compared to this. Anyway, let me know if you find anything. And send those reports."

"Will do."

After the call ended, he pressed 100 and asked Tom to come in.

"Tom, I need a nanny. Urgently."

The man raised an eyebrow. "Aren't you a little old? Or is this some sort of fetish?"

"I'm serious. Find me the perfect nanny who can start today by four o'clock or you're fired."

Tom grinned. "I do like a challenge."

CHAPTER FIVE

As Noah hesitated outside the door of Cranfields, a private club in the city, a black SUV drove past. He tracked its movements, taking a mental note of the license plate. The vehicle didn't slow, just kept on moving, disappearing around the corner. He couldn't shake the feeling that he'd seen it before, though.

Best case scenario, he was being paranoid. After all, black SUVs were hardly uncommon on the streets of London. Maybe he *wanted* there to be something suspicious about Eve's death. Maybe he was incapable of living an ordinary life and was hunting for anything to drag him out of the quagmire of boring domesticity. Maybe the part of him that still loved Eve was still struggling to let her go.

But the email had been real.

It was eight in the evening, and he should be at home, spending time with his children. He was all they had now—or so Harper had informed him that morning as he'd hurried out the door.

Poor fucking kids.

With a last glance down the road, he pushed open the door to the club.

Stepping inside was like traveling back in time.

The place reeked of cigar smoke and old leather. The walls were dark oak paneling, the curtains crimson velvet—a cross between an old-fashioned library and a bordello, or so Noah imagined. He knew nothing about either such places. The few occupants looked about as old as the furniture. He hadn't even known gentlemen's clubs still existed, yet here he was.

Professor Donald Ramsey had been Eve's tutor at Oxford where she'd gotten her undergraduate degree and started her post-grad research. He'd been at their wedding. He was also Harper's godfather. Noah liked the man, though they'd never been close.

He found Don sitting in an armchair in the bar, drinking whiskey. He must have been in his sixties, but he looked fit and too young to be in this place, his face brown from the sun. He'd been on a dig in Africa and hadn't been able to come to Eve's funeral service, but he had called, and Noah knew he felt genuine sadness over Eve's passing. As Noah approached, he stood up and then waved him to the chair opposite.

"I'm so sorry about Eve," he said. "She was a wonderful woman and a great archaeologist. We'll all miss her."

"Thank you." He sat down, and Don held up two fingers at the barman. The man immediately came over with the drinks then left with a smile and no words.

"Good service," Noah said, picking up his whiskey.

Don gave a wry smile. "You're probably wondering what I'm doing in a place like this."

"It did occur to me."

"My father got me a membership when I was twenty-one. I've been coming here ever since. It's somewhere to stay when I'm in town. You said you needed to talk. How can I help you?"

Noah took a sip of whiskey. Single malt and smoky in his mouth. Appreciation of good scotch was something Peter had taught him at an early age when he'd given a twelve-year-old Noah his first shot of single malt. "I just wanted to understand Eve's work better. We never spoke of it much."

"A little late now, isn't it?"

Was there censure in the words? Probably.

"Maybe. But she was on a…job when she was killed. She hadn't been out in the field since the kidnapping. I guess I just want to make sense of it, understand the whys and maybe a little of what motivated her."

Don studied him for a moment, his head cocked to one side, and Noah resisted the urge to squirm. "Are you passionate about anything, Noah?"

The question wasn't what he'd been expecting.

"Terrorism," he said. "I'm passionate about stopping it."

"Interesting. Well, then maybe you can understand a little of how Eve felt about her work. She was passionate about archaeology. Perhaps the most passionate woman I've ever met. She loved the hunt and the chase, searching out the secrets of the past."

A part of him wished he had gotten to know that side of her while she was still alive. He'd always been so wrapped up in his own work, believed it to be more important, more relevant.

"What was she passionate about in the last few years?" he asked. Since the divorce, they'd stopped talking about anything personal and stuck to conversations about the children. "What was she working on when she died?"

"She was searching for the lost tomb of Genghis Khan. She'd been involved all her academic life. She wrote her thesis on it." Don gave him a look that clearly said Noah should've already known this. He wasn't wrong.

A pang of guilt hit him low in the stomach. "In Mongolia?"

"Eve worked from the university. She never got over what happened in Iraq and couldn't face fieldwork. But the advances in archaeological techniques over the last few years have made it easier to carry out research from the comfort of your own office. Also, it's not easy to get permission to visit Mongolian sites, especially anything related to Khan."

"Why is that?"

"I suspect they don't want the tomb found and desecrated. Mongolians don't treat death in the same way as most westerners. Anyway, shortly after she came back to the U.K., Eve got funding from an organization that I gather has a lot of influence."

"Do you know who?"

"The Mongolian Historical Society. I have to admit I'd never heard of them, but the techniques Eve uses — used — do not come cheap. So presumably they had money."

"But why would anyone really care?"

Don sipped the last of his drink then set the empty glass down. "What do you know about Genghis Khan?"

They'd studied him in the military academy, but some guy on a pony eight hundred years ago hadn't seemed particularly relevant to Noah at the time. This was in the aftermath of 9/11. He'd believed they'd had bigger things to think about. "Not a lot."

"I'm surprised, considering your interest in terrorism. Some people say Genghis Khan was the most successful terrorist who ever lived, so he should be right up your alley. He was also a brutal and successful warrior who came from humble beginnings to conquer a vast area across the Middle East and Europe."

"If I remember correctly, he killed a lot of people. Raped a lot of women." The killing Noah could get over. The rape not so much.

"Many think he was a tyrant, but if you measure him by the rules of his day, then he was no worse than most leaders and better than many. He was a liberal in a time of intolerance—he allowed all religions to flourish. And he was an egalitarian in an age when bloodlines meant everything. All you needed to progress in Khan's army was to be brave and be loyal."

"So why is his tomb so hard to find? I would have thought a big guy like that would have had a great fancy burial plot."

"You would think so." Don smiled. "All this talking is making me thirsty." He raised his hand to the barman again, and they were quiet while he brought over the bottle. "You can leave it," Don told the man, who nodded and left while Don filled their glasses. "There are lots of stories about how Genghis Khan died. One is that he was assassinated by an Indian princess who he had taken as plunder from a defeated city. That's my favorite. But the most likely is that he died as a result of an arrow in his knee while on his last campaign against the Tangut nation, along the

Yellow River. His body was brought back to Mongolia for burial, most believe somewhere on the sacred mountain of Burkhan Khaldun. But Genghis Khan did not want his burial site to be known."

"Why?"

"No one really knows, though there are other rumors which we'll get to later. Anyway, legend has it that his body was taken back to Mongolia by an escort of soldiers who killed any onlookers they met on the way. Then once the burial was completed, all the slaves, laborers, and mourners were murdered. And after that, the soldiers of the escort were also killed. Some say they drove a herd of a thousand horses over the site to hide the location of the grave, others that they diverted the course of a river. Whatever they did, it was effective—the burial site has never been located, though others have been. Many of his descendants were also buried in the area. In secret. It's believed that his grandson Kublai Khan had twenty thousand men killed following his burial."

"That's a little paranoid."

"Perhaps. And then there are the Darkhats."

"The Darkhats?"

"On Genghis Khan's death, fifty loyal families were appointed guardians of the area to keep the secret of the tomb. It's believed their descendants live there even now and will kill anyone who gets close. The area is known as the Great Taboo."

Was that the answer? Had these Darkhats killed Eve because she was about to find out the location of the tomb? It seemed a little unbelievable.

"But that's just a legend," Don said.

There was something else he didn't understand. "She was in Russia when she died. Why? When the tomb is supposed to be in Mongolia."

"Archeology has changed a lot over recent years. It used to be a lot of digging and finding nothing, so you'd move on and dig somewhere else, until eventually you struck lucky and actually found something."

"The good old days," Noah said. Actually, it sounded pretty boring to him.

Don grinned. "Yes. The good old days. But things have changed. Today, archaeology is more like being a private investigator. You may get to do a little digging at the end, but first you have a lot of information to sift through. And, most recently, satellite images to study. Thousands of them, looking for some minute thing out of place that might indicate there is something interesting underground."

"So that's what Eve was looking for in Russia? Seems a long way to go. Why not just get them sent or shared?"

"I don't know for sure what she was doing

there—we hadn't spoken for a while—but I doubt she was looking at satellite images. Maybe at military records, not related directly to the tomb but to another artifact: The Spirit Banner of Genghis Khan."

He sighed. "Okay, so what's a Spirit Banner?"

"The Mongolian warriors created them by tying horsehair around the shaft of their spears just below the blade. Genghis Khan had two, a white one for times of peace and a black one he carried into battle. The Mongolians believe that the warrior and the spirit banner become so entwined that on his death his spirit passes into the spear and it becomes the embodiment of the warrior on Earth."

"So Eve was looking for these spirit banners?"

"The white one disappeared after Khan's death, maybe buried with him. But for centuries, the black spear was kept in a monastery in central Mongolia, guarded by the monks. Then in the 1930s, Mongolia was overrun by the henchmen of Stalin. Over thirty thousand people were killed in a series of campaigns to stamp out the Mongolian religion. Stalin was a real tyrant."

"And they took this banner?"

"No. It was apparently whisked away to safety but never seen again. I suspect Eve was following the trail of the Spirit Banner. She spoke about it briefly the last time we met. Here, actually. A couple of months before she died."

"Wouldn't she have told someone if she'd found it? If it was such a big deal."

"Maybe. Maybe she didn't get the chance. Or it was found but they haven't made the announcement yet. Not everyone does this for the fame and fortune." He emptied his glass and looked across the table, eyes narrowed as if he could see into Noah's head. "Now are you going to tell me what this sudden interest in your ex-wife's work is really all about?"

Noah made a snap decision. "I received an anonymous email claiming Eve was murdered."

Don was silent for a minute, staring into his glass. "And what do you believe?"

"I have no clue. But she tried to get ahold of me the night before she died. She left a message but didn't say what was bothering her. And the next day, she was dead." He put down his glass and pressed the spot between his eyes, trying to make sense of everything, to see a pattern in the pieces. "I just don't get it. Why would anyone kill over a grave of some guy who's been dead for nearly a thousand fucking years? Treasure?"

Don shrugged. "Genghis Khan looted his way across the world, amassing great wealth. So I suppose it could be treasure. But I suspect something else, and you're not going to like it."

Noah snorted. He didn't like any of this. "You'd

better tell me then, so I can get used to the idea."

"There's another legend, not so widely known or believed, that Khan's success was not just down to his prowess as a warrior and leader but that he had some sort of secret weapon, a magical talisman that he took into battle, carried between two black stallions, so powerful and dangerous that, when he died, he wanted it hidden forever. Or maybe not forever but until a worthy successor came along. Only someone destined to become the ruler of the world would be able to find the Talisman and use it."

Noah blinked. "Shit. Magic? *Really*?"

Don chuckled. "Your expression says it all. I take it you don't believe in magic?"

"Hell, no."

"I don't believe in magic, either, but there are those who do. And perhaps something doesn't have to be real for people to believe. Look at religion."

He was right, of course. Most of the terrorist attacks that took place had some tie to religion. There were plenty of people willing to die for beliefs Noah found totally incomprehensible. Though in his experience, many times religion was just a cover for a political or power-based agenda.

Still, he couldn't believe that Eve had been killed because of some magic talisman buried eight hundred years ago.

He'd told himself to keep an open mind. But open to magic?

Never going to happen.

He'd follow through on all the leads—he had no alternative—until he uncovered the truth, be it magic or revenge. But now it was time to change the subject, finish his drink, and go home to his children.

As he left the building fifteen minutes later, his gaze automatically searched the roads.

There was no black SUV.

• • •

Sara stood in the cover of a deep doorway across the street and watched Noah Blakeley leave the club. The daylight was fading, and the streetlights were coming on. In the dim light, he appeared preoccupied.

From her research, she was beginning to believe that Noah actually was that rare specimen—a genuinely good man. Maybe he could help her or they could help each other. She just had to work out the best way to approach him.

She was about to step out and follow when a black SUV crawled out of the alley beside the building he'd just exited. She went still as she memorized the license plate. The same vehicle had passed as he entered.

Was someone else following him?

Friend or foe?

She'd better find out and soon, because she didn't want to lose him now.

CHAPTER SIX

Noah's heart missed a beat each time he opened up his computer, but so far, there were no more emails.

It was frustrating. He felt like his life was on hold, unable to move on.

Now he sat, staring at the envelope Tom had dropped on his desk before he left for the evening. It was from Peter and no doubt contained the promised reports on Eve's accident. He hesitated to open it. While he'd seen death many times — often the results of terrorist attacks, and bombs were a messy way to die — nothing could prepare you for the death of someone close to you. Especially if that death was violent.

Taking a deep breath, he ran his finger under the flap and tipped out the contents onto his desk. Three pieces of paper and a bunch of photos.

Leaving the photos until last, he read through the reports, but they contained nothing he didn't already know. No surprises. The last paper was a handwritten note from Peter saying he'd asked around and gotten no hint there was more to Eve's death than the official police reports contained and that the tech experts had so far been unable to find the IP address for the sender of the email, which suggested whoever had sent it had access to some very impressive technology.

He flipped over the photos. The first showed a plane standing on a runway. Medium-sized with seating for ten or so people. A company insignia painted on the side—Blue Sky. He'd never heard of them. The second showed the site of the accident and the burned-out wreck of the plane. The crash had happened so early into the flight the plane would have still held plenty of fuel to burn. Likely, it went down quickly—there had been one brief message from the pilot, stating he had engine trouble and was turning back. After that, nothing. If he'd had time, he would have dumped the fuel. Not that there was any chance of landing safely. They'd crashed on a rocky mountainside.

Had Eve been aware she was about to die?

He hoped not.

He turned the last picture over slowly, knowing what it would show. A corpse on a slab in a morgue. But staring at the photo, he felt nothing. The body was unrecognizable, the flesh burned away, the bones blackened. It could have been anyone. In a way, he was glad, though part of him needed to see her one last time. He still found it hard to imagine her gone.

He tucked the reports and pictures back in the envelope and shoved them in a drawer.

What did he have?

A dead ex-wife.

An anonymous email.

And what sounded like a secret organization searching for the tomb of Genghis Khan and a magic talisman, because they wanted to take over the world. Which was where things fell apart, because whoever it was would have no reason to kill Eve and every reason to want her alive.

He circled back around to this being related to him and his past. He'd made a list of possible individuals and organizations that might want revenge. Alex, who had taken over command of Project Arachnid, was pulling the files for him and would flag anything of interest. But Noah had checked that morning, and so far nothing had come up.

He needed more information.

He eyed the computer in front of him. Maybe he should divert some company resources.

Drumming his fingers on the steel desktop, Noah considered the possible consequences. Worst-case scenario: he'd be killed by whoever had murdered Eve—if she had been murdered—and his kids would be orphans. But a more likely outcome would be finding himself out of a job, and he needed his salary to pay for the new nanny. Who was—praise the Lord—working out fantastically. Just as well, because after a slow start, he'd gained access to everything he needed and was up to his ears in work.

The information had started coming in. Anything terrorist-related ended up on Noah's desk. The scope of the senator's organization was huge, spanning the globe. He'd never had access to resources like this in the army. There were reports from the police, military—how the hell did they get hold of those?—even conversations overheard in bars and churches and mosques around the world.

The extent was frightening in a way, that a private company should have access to this amount of information.

His phone rang. He picked it up. "Senator Clayton is on her way up, sir."

"Thank you."

Michaela Clayton had flown into the country that morning for official meetings but managed to fit in some time with him before she returned to the States later that night. She'd said she wanted to talk face to face. Just checking in with him. Making sure Noah had everything he needed. And hopefully giving him a clearer view of exactly what his role was. What she expected him to do with the information. How he was supposed to justify his exorbitant salary.

He was looking forward to the meeting.

• • •

As the elevator took her up to the top floor, Michaela Clayton closed her eyes and cleared her mind. It had been a long day full of meetings, but she would hopefully manage a few hours to sleep on the flight back.

First, she wanted to meet with Noah Blakeley. It was time to assess his usefulness and his commitment.

While he possessed the qualities she needed, Tom had some doubts as to whether it would work out. Not whether Noah was up to the job, but more as to whether he would be comfortable utilizing the resources available and embracing the overall long-term strategy of the company.

She was hopeful, because the fact was they both wanted the same things — an end to terrorism. An end to the people and organizations that held the world to ransom.

The building was quiet as she stepped out of the elevator and crossed the carpeted floor. She didn't bother to knock, just pushed open the door. Noah was seated behind his desk but stood as she entered.

The similarity to his uncle was amazing, and she felt herself softening toward him. Peter had been a good friend over the years. Though dressed in jeans and an open-necked shirt, Noah was a far more casual figure than his uncle.

He walked around the desk, coming to a halt in front of her, his hand held out. She took it, and his grasp was firm.

He glanced behind her. "No secret service tonight?"

"I left them in reception. I presume I'm safe with you."

"Perfectly."

"Good. So how are you? I'm thinking London must be a big change from what you're used to."

"The English are an alien species, ma'am."

"They are indeed. And please, call me Michaela." She smiled. "I don't suppose you have anything to drink? It's been a long day."

"Scotch?"

"Wonderful." Peter always kept scotch in his office—another similarity.

She crossed over to the cream leather sofa and sank down while he went back to his desk and pulled a bottle and two glasses out of the drawer. After pouring them both a measure, he sat on the opposite end of the sofa.

She raised her glass. "Welcome to Clayton Industries."

He raised his own glass and took a swallow of scotch. "Thank you. I'm grateful for the opportunity."

"How are you settling into the job?"

"Fine." He relaxed back in the seat. "Although

I could do with a little more information as to what you're looking for, specifically. What you'd like me to achieve here."

"A similar role to the one you performed in Project Arachnid, but without the actual active duty — we'll pass that on to someone else." She studied him over her glass, trying to determine the best approach. "Perhaps if I explain a little about why I offered you the job, it might give an insight as to what I'm expecting of you."

He raised a brow. "Should I be worried?"

She gave a short laugh. She liked his attitude. Polite but not intimidated. "You have a reputation for being able to get into the minds of terrorists."

"I'm not sure that's a compliment."

"Maybe not, but it's a useful ability and enables you to see patterns. I've spoken to people, and all the breakthroughs on Project Arachnid were down to your insights. I'd like you to do the same for me, but with slightly more resources at your disposal."

"To what end…Michaela?"

"Twofold. Firstly, I'm a businesswoman as well as a politician. I'm sure you've looked closely into the structure of Clayton Industries and must be aware that we have branches all over the world. Information regarding terrorism can be very useful. In some countries, the effects on the economies after a big attack can be devastating.

We would like advance warning if possible."

"I'm not sure it is—reliably, at least—but I'll see what I can do."

"Excellent. There's also a bigger picture. I strongly believe the world is teetering on the edge of the abyss." She watched his face as she spoke, but he gave little away. "It will take very little for the balance to shift, and we'll be plummeting into hell. I'd like to prevent that. While there's a lot I can do within the governmental structures, there are limitations and barriers to the free flow of information. With the resources of Clayton Industries at your disposal, you have access to far more. Over the years, we have built up a network of information sources unrivaled by any organization, private or public. Make use of it."

He was silent for a moment, at a guess trying to decide whether to ask something.

"If you have any concerns, Noah, ask now."

"I've been...impressed with the level of information available. It's staggering. I suppose I'm wondering—is it...sanctioned?"

"You mean is it legal? Let me ask you something first—does it matter? We're fighting a war here. We need to use whatever weapons we have at our disposal or we *will* fail."

He nodded. "I guess I've been part of the system for too long. So while I understand what you're saying and agree to some extent, at the same time, I'm not willing to use any means; there are lines I won't cross." He shook his head, his expression rueful. "I'm just not quite sure where they are yet."

A good answer—probably as good as she could hope for at the moment. "That, of course, is a decision you need to come to yourself. But you have the opportunity to make a real difference here. How much of a difference is up to you. Take a little time and consider where your lines are. In the meantime, it shouldn't affect your usefulness." Though it could become an issue, and she needed to put some safeguards in place, just in case.

He blew out his breath. "That's good. I'm looking forward to getting to work."

"I'm guessing you're going to need help. Have a word with Tom—he can get you whatever resources you require."

"I'll do that."

"I'm flying back tonight, but please let me know if there's anything you need. Any questions you want answered. I look forward to seeing what you come up with."

She placed her empty glass on the table and rose to her feet, smoothing down her skirt. She caught him watching her—was there a glimpse of male appreciation there? Perhaps.

They walked side by side. At the door, she turned and held out her hand. "How is your family?" she asked as he took it. "How are the children coping with losing their mother?"

"Truth? I don't know. We don't communicate very well."

She gave his hand a squeeze before releasing her hold. "It will take time. But you'll get there."

"Maybe." He frowned, and she got the impression he was considering saying something further but hadn't decided.

"There's something else on your mind?" she asked.

"You're very perceptive." He exhaled. "I received an anonymous email. It claimed my ex-wife was murdered."

She pursed her lips. "And you believe it?"

"Hell, I don't know. It seems crazy. And so far, I've not come up with any evidence to support it."

"You've been looking into it?"

"Of course. Crazy or not, it isn't something I can ignore. I need to know one way or the other. If Eve was a target, maybe the children are in danger as well."

She rested a hand on his arm. "Of course. Reallocate some of our security to your children. Then you must use the company resources to conduct your research—they're at your disposal. And I'll let Tom know you're to have any help you need."

"Thank you."

"It's not entirely altruistic. You'll work better if this is resolved." What *had* happened to Eve Blakeley? She'd love to know. Perhaps Noah would discover the truth. She took a step back, looked up into his face. "Change is coming, Noah. Make no mistake. And we are all going to have to decide where we stand and what sort of world we live in on the other side."

And she turned and left.

The meeting had gone well. She liked him.

But she was in no way sure of him.

• • •

Noah went back to the sofa, poured himself another scotch, and sat back in his seat. He had the resources of the company at his disposal. That was incredibly generous, and he'd use what he could. And he'd function better knowing the children were safe.

He needed to decide how best to move forward, but his mind kept straying to the rest of the meeting. He had a real chance to make a difference here. Do something useful in his life without the restrictions that had chafed so much during his time with the military.

An alluring thought.

And dangerous.

Rules and laws existed for a reason. You didn't just bypass them because you could and you had the money to make it possible.

Or was he being naïve? Maybe that's the way the world had always worked. And it could in fact be used as a force for good. As Michaela suggested, he'd spend some time and see where he was comfortable drawing his lines. How things worked out. He glanced out of the window to darkness; he hadn't realized how late it was.

He picked up the phone and punched in his home number. "Jenny, it's Noah. I wanted to check on the children."

"It's past eleven o'clock, Noah. They're children, and they're in bed asleep."

Shit. Really? "Sorry, I got caught up in something at work."

"No problem. Harper was disappointed you didn't make it to dinner, but I let her watch an extra half hour of TV to make up for it. I suspect she thought it was a good deal."

"I bet."

"I'm going to bed myself now."

"I'll try not to wake you when I get home."

"Good night."

He finished his drink and headed back to his desk. So much information at his disposal, even if he hadn't yet decided whether to use it. He'd gotten lucky with this job. At least one thing in his life was going in his favor.

As for the rest? He wasn't so sure.

CHAPTER SEVEN

In the week since the meeting with Michaela, Noah felt like he hadn't stopped moving. His brain bulged with the sheer quantity of information pushed into it. At the same time, he was thinking with a clarity he hadn't experienced in a long time.

He'd worked out the key words and phrases he was interested in. And, deeper than that, the concepts he was looking for. Subtle indications in the chatter. In turn, he'd developed filters that helped flag information that might be of interest. He now had a team of twenty people working for him, analyzing the information as it was reported. He'd interviewed the people Tom had brought along himself. It wasn't merely intelligence he was looking for but intuition. They had to be extensions of Noah's own mind.

He'd hardly seen the children in that time. Usually, he left before they got up in the morning and wasn't home until after they were asleep.

He'd taken Michaela at her word and arranged for two of the Clayton Industries security employees, a man and a woman, both ex-military, to watch the children. Jenny knew; the kids didn't. The last thing he wanted was for them to feel they were in any danger. And mostly he believed they weren't—all his inquiries had come up blank, and there had been no more emails. There was just that little niggle in his gut.

He'd learned to trust his gut a long time ago. He wasn't taking any chances. Not with their lives.

So far the security detail had seen nothing untoward, which was good. He didn't want to pull the kids from school. It would be summer break soon, and he planned to send them to their grandparents—they would be easier to watch unobtrusively there.

It was five-thirty in the morning, and the house was quiet, but when he pushed open the kitchen door, he came to a standstill. Harper was perched on a stool at the breakfast bar, dressed in red pajamas, a glass of milk in front of her.

"Morning, sweetheart," he said with forced cheerfulness.

She looked him over and pursed her lips, no doubt taking in his running gear, but she didn't speak.

He sidled to the fridge, grabbed the milk, and drank straight from the carton. She raised an eyebrow, and he cleared his throat. "I wanted to apologize," he said. "I know I haven't been around much lately." He gave a shrug. "I've been busy at work. New job…"

"No worries, Daddy." She smiled. "It's okay. Actually, it's pretty much like old times, except without the mom *or* the dad."

He winced. *Ouch*. But what could he say? She was right. He had an urge to hug her, promise he'd do better, but he was in no way sure he could. All the same, he made a mental note to free up some time at the weekend to spend with them.

He dropped the empty carton in the trash. "I have to go."

"I know you do. But Luce and Daniel don't understand. They're babies, and they miss Mom, and they need you."

Christ, how could an eleven-year-old make him feel like a complete bastard? Maybe because she was right.

He crossed to stand in front of her. "Look, there's some stuff going on right now. But I'll try and do better. Okay?" She nodded, but he wasn't sure she was convinced. "Talk to Luce and Daniel, decide what you'd all like to do this weekend."

"With you?" He could hear the disbelief in her voice.

"Yeah, with me. We can all go out. We can—" Hell, he had no clue. He shrugged. "We'll think of something. Hey, I'm still learning this kid stuff."

"I know." She drained her glass of milk and slid off the stool. "Have a good day at work."

"I'll try."

He was still feeling guilty as he let himself out of the building.

Since his first day on the job, he'd made it a habit to run the six miles into the office from home and back again in the evening. It took about forty minutes and was almost as quick as the tube—sometimes faster and far more pleasant. Plus, it was the only way he could fit in any exercise. He left clothes at the office and could shower in his private bathroom.

The streets were quiet this early in the morning. Although the sun wasn't yet up, it was already warm. As he spent most of the day in an air-conditioned office, he appreciated the heat.

He concentrated on the thud of his feet hitting the pavement but slowly became aware of a prickle down his spine. His inner radar was picking up something. Someone concentrating on him. His heart rate shifted up a notch, the muscles of his stomach contracting. He glanced over his shoulder as subtly as possible but could see no one. Then his gaze caught on a black SUV with tinted windows parked across the road. The license plate was different from the vehicle he had spotted the other night.

Easing down his pace, he peered inside the vehicle as he passed but could make nothing out. For a brief moment, he considered stopping, banging on the windows.

But he was unarmed—that was going to have to change—and he had no clue what he might be facing.

If he was facing anything at all.

An overactive imagination? He no longer believed that. The prickle persisted. He tensed, making a rapid review of his surroundings, his mind instantly identifying the available cover.

The parked vehicle disappeared behind him as he ran on, his shoulder blades twitching and sweat sliding down his back.

He needed to up his game. He'd gotten sloppy.

Jerry was on night duty. He opened the door as Noah approached and nodded. "Morning, sir."

"Morning."

Instead of heading for the private elevator that would take him up to his office, he veered off and took the door leading to the stairwell. He ran down a flight of stairs to the basement. A second security officer stood at the door to the shooting range. He looked like a Jerry clone, and Noah was guessing he was another ex-military. The man nodded and opened the door before Noah could get out his ID.

He'd been meaning to come down here but hadn't gotten around to it yet. He'd always found shooting…therapeutic. He'd taught Eve to shoot. He'd thought it might empower her, help her get over her fears. She'd been a natural. She'd also hated it. Maybe if she'd had a gun, she would still be alive.

What had she been scared of that night in Russia? She had tried to call him. Why?

An image of her burned body flashed in his mind.

He pushed it away and turned his attention back to the security guard. "I'd like to use the shooting range. Is that okay?"

"We have instructions to get you anything you need, sir."

"A gun?"

"Yes, sir. You need to register it with the local police if you plan to take it out of the building, but we can do that for you. What would you like?"

Noah smiled. "What do you have?"

The man grinned. "Follow me."

The place was a goddamn armory. They had more guns down here than the U.S. Army. The vault was lined with shelves of weapons. Mainly pistols but also some semi and automatic rifles.

He whistled.

What the hell did they need all this stuff for? Were they expecting World War Three?

He scanned the shelves. There was every type of pistol he could think of and a few he'd never come across before. He selected a Sig Sauer, tried it, but didn't like the feel. Tried another. And another. He found one he liked at number five. A Glock 19.

He spent half an hour on the shooting range

getting the feel of the pistol. It was a nice weapon, a 9mm, more compact than he was used to, but then it would have to somehow go under his running gear. That had never been a consideration before.

"Holsters?" he asked John.

"Through here, sir."

Tom was already at his desk when Noah walked through to his office still in his running gear, with the pistol in one hand and a couple of holsters in the other. The man raised a brow but didn't say anything.

"Give me ten minutes," Noah said.

He was showered and changed by the time Tom appeared, the gun locked in his desk drawer. And he'd only just opened his system. He stared at the email.

> *Your wife was murdered for information in her possession. You and your children are in danger. The people responsible will stop at nothing.*

He gritted his teeth. Always before it had been *his* life on the line. He'd been the one in danger. He'd been okay with that—hell, he'd thrived on it. This sick churning in his gut was something totally different. How the hell dare they threaten his children?

That was the thing with terrorists—they tended to target the innocents.

Was this a threat or a warning?

And what information? Had whoever supposedly killed Eve recovered it? If they were in danger, it seemed unlikely.

Tom cleared his throat, and Noah dragged his gaze from the screen to where the other man stood in the doorway.

"Is something wrong?" Tom asked.

He made a snap decision. "Yeah, something is wrong. Take a look at this."

Tom read the email over his shoulder. "Jesus. Who sent it?"

"I don't know. It's anonymous."

"Not possible. Do you mind?"

Noah scooted his chair back to give Tom more room. "Go ahead."

As his fingers flew over the keyboard, a frown formed on his face. "There's nothing. I would have sworn that couldn't be done. This isn't the first?"

"No. I received something similar on my first day."

"That's why you asked." He stared at the screen for a moment. "Are you okay with me asking our tech guys to have a look at this?"

He didn't need to think about it. His own

contacts hadn't been able to find shit. "Can you do it without giving them the actual contents of the email?"

"Of course."

"Then please do. As soon as possible."

Tom nodded. "Do you mind me asking—do you think it's true? Is that why you had the gun this morning?"

Hell, yes, he was starting to believe it was true. The emails alone maybe he could have discounted as someone messing with him, but combine them with the fact that he was under surveillance and they took on a more sinister tone. "It doesn't matter. Either way, I would very much like to know who sent them. When I find out, I'll decide what to do with the gun."

Tom raised a brow. "Right. I'll get on it."

Once he'd left, Noah sat back in his chair. Anger coiled in his gut. They'd threatened his goddamn family. He was ready to strike but had nowhere to aim.

What he needed was more data. He was sitting at the center of a veritable spiderweb of information networks. There had to be a way to harness that and dig out the truth.

He still couldn't believe that anyone would care enough about an eight-hundred-year-old grave to murder someone over it. So, right now, he was guessing that if someone had killed Eve, then it was more to do with *his* work than hers. He needed to find the motive. Revenge, maybe, or someone had wanted him out of Project Arachnid. If that was the motive for Eve's death, then it had worked miraculously well.

All the same, he couldn't discount Eve's work completely. He'd been trained not to disregard anything until it was proven to be of no worth.

Leaning forward, he sent off a quick email to Don asking if he knew the names of the other archaeologists Eve had been working with. Maybe he could find out more from them. At least what lead she'd followed to Russia.

The answer came back within minutes.

Have we got you hooked?

Here's what I know. There would likely have been others on the team, but the people she worked with regularly were a Russian archaeologist, Yuri Vasiliev, and a Mongolian scholar and expert on Genghis Khan, Tarkhan Ganbaatar.

Eve was also working with a space archaeologist, but that was unofficial. Most of them are. They don't live in the mainstream world. They're usually computer nerds, technicians, geeks who spend their whole lives staring at a screen, and they like to use code names. Eve referred to the woman she worked with as Star. That's all I know.

Professor Coffell, Eve's superior at the university, might be able to tell you more.

Bring the children to Oxford sometime soon.

Don.

Noah sat thinking for a moment then wrote an email to Professor Coffell, who he'd met and spoken briefly to at Eve's funeral, and asked for any information on Eve's trip to Russia. Why she had gone and with whom.

Then he opened up the company's security system, ran a search on the Russian first, and came up with a whole load of information. Born in Moscow in 1976. He'd been head-boy at his boarding school. What he ate for breakfast each Sunday morning. Jesus, how the hell did they know that? There was also a picture of a big, dark-haired, dark-eyed man. He looked Russian — whatever that meant — but Noah would have tagged him straight away.

He sifted through the information. Found a cell phone number and an email address. He tried the cell first and got no response, just a continuous beep, so he dropped the man an email, explaining who he was and that he'd like to talk, adding his cell number.

Vasiliev was a professor in Archeology at the University of Moscow, and Noah tried there next. He eventually got through to an admin who spoke passable English and who explained that Professor Vasiliev was away from Moscow at the moment, but they would give him a message next time he checked in. Noah asked when that would be, but she had no clue. Vasiliev had been out of contact for two weeks now.

Noah pressed his finger between his eyes. He was getting a bad feeling. These days, it was almost impossible for anyone to be out of contact.

He went through the whole process again with Tarkhan Ganbaatar with just as much success. Tarkhan was eighty-three years old and appeared to have vanished off the face of the planet. Noah left messages everywhere he could come up with. That bad feeling was still nudging at his mind.

Next he typed in "what is space archeology" and scanned through the results.

What is Space Archaeology? The use of underground or beneath the sea discovery techniques taken from the air. Such techniques include LIDAR, image interpretation (using ultraviolet, x-ray, light spectrum, etc.), Space Ground Penetrating Radar, and even simply studying Google Earth! All these techniques happen from the air with images or readings taken, with equipment transported, from a balloon, a drone, a plane, or satellite. ~ Andrew Barker.

He typed in "Star, Space Archaeologist" but came up with nothing he could use. He'd get Tom to allocate one of the analysts to dig deeper—if this Star was out there, they would find her. In the meantime, he had work to do. His salary to earn. Terrorists to stop.

By the end of the day, he had heard nothing from Eve's co-workers, but he had found something in the information flooding into his office. He tracked the last piece on the world map and sat staring at the screen.

There was his pattern. A global network of terrorist activity radiating out from a single point. Who was at the center? It was only a matter of time before he discovered the answer. In the meantime, he had a good idea where the next terrorist attack would happen. He sent an email to the senator. Then he put in a call to Peter, got his voicemail, and left a message.

"There will be an attack in Germany. Soon."

• • •

It was after midnight when he got home. The house was quiet, though Jenny had left the hall light on and some lasagna in the oven "in case he was hungry," according to the note on the table. He was starving, and he wolfed the food down straight out of the dish. Afterward, he placed it in the dishwasher—he was sort of learning to be domesticated—and headed up to his room.

As he was taking off the holster, a noise made him whirl around. He drew the pistol without conscious thought.

"Dad, I—" Harper stood in the doorway, mouth open, staring at the gun in his hand.

He dropped his arm to his side. Took a deep breath. "What is it, sweetheart?"

She frowned at the endearment. "Are we in danger, Dad?"

"Of course not."

Her eyes narrowed. Her lips tightened. "Then why do you have a gun?" Without waiting for an answer, she turned around and disappeared.

Shit.

CHAPTER EIGHT

Ex-MI6 agent, Zachary Martin, had a good idea of where the next attack was going to take place. He also had a good idea of what the end game was. Actually, the end game had given him the location of the attack.

In two weeks' time, there was to be a summit, hosted in Russia and attended by all the world's leaders. The Agenda: a unified global strategy to fight terrorism.

So far all the main countries were committed, except one—Germany.

Which was why Zach was sitting in a bar in Heathrow airport waiting for a flight to Berlin.

He needed to make someone listen, and fast. He reckoned he had a couple of days at the most and a list of contacts he needed to confront in person.

Unfortunately, the word had gone out. He was unreliable, the rumors said, not to mention unstable and not to be trusted. Apparently, he was seeing conspiracy theories where they didn't exist. Every call he made was met with the same questions. Why didn't he come in? Give himself up? Trust in the system?

He'd stopped trusting in the system a long time

ago.

The latest rumor he'd heard was that he was responsible for the death of his own partner. That one really pissed him off. Probably because they weren't far wrong. Lauren had died in a suicide bombing in Paris the day after they'd gone to their boss and told them Zach's theory about a centralized conspiracy to use terrorism to take over the world. Coincidence? Fuck that. Zach didn't believe in coincidences.

So while he hadn't actually killed her, Lauren's death had been down to him.

Now, Eve was dead as well. Also down to him.

He'd dragged her into this thing, and then he'd failed her.

He'd been pissed off at her. Their last meeting had been in a hospital room in Ulaanbaatar, where she'd been recovering from a bullet wound. He'd left her with strict instructions to get on a flight to the U.K. as soon as she was released. Instead, she'd slipped her bodyguards and vanished, only to call him from some obscure town in Russia the night before she died. She'd been panicking because she'd spotted John Chen loitering outside her hotel room. Last time she'd seen John Chen, he'd tried to kill her.

Zach had been too far away to be of any help, and most of his contacts were not returning his calls. In the end, he'd called Tarkhan, the

Mongolian scholar who had been with them on the hunt for the spear. He was the only person Zach could think of who might have the contacts to help. He'd promised to try, but after that, Zach had heard nothing. Until he got the report that Eve Blakeley was dead.

The news had been a gut punch.

He'd liked her. *More* than liked her.

So his next move was to hunt down that bastard John Chen and rip his fucking throat out.

Which he'd do as soon as he got somebody to listen to him.

They called his flight number, and he finished his beer and got to his feet. As he passed the bar, something on the TV screen caught his attention. A news flash.

Breaking News.

Reports are coming in of a terrorist attack in Berlin. The city's primary water source has been poisoned. Deaths are expected to be in the thousands.

He screwed up his boarding pass and tossed it on the floor.

He was too late.

CHAPTER NINE

It was close to midnight. Noah was heading for home, trying to shake off the sense of frustration gnawing at his insides. He'd heard nothing back from either the Russian or the Mongolian and was no closer to identifying Eve's space archaeologist, Star.

Tom had gotten Eve's phone records, but they showed nothing of use. There were a number of calls to the Russian's cell phone over the last months. Otherwise, the calls were to her parents and presumably the children. If she'd been in contact with Star, she'd been doing it by some other means. Maybe pay phones or hotel phones? It all seemed a little cloak and dagger for Eve.

The credit cards had given a little more. Eve had actually flown into Mongolia, not Russia. That had been a little over two weeks before she had died. What had she been doing in that time? No payment showed how she had made her way from Mongolia to Russia, though the credit card had been used to pay for the flight she had died on. He'd talked to the company, and the booking had been made over the phone by someone identifying themselves as Eve Blakeley.

Tomorrow he had his weekly scheduled call

with Michaela. He'd forwarded her the information on the suspected German attack. Even with his warning to Peter, they'd been too late to prevent it from happening. And it had been bad, with a death toll in the thousands and long-term repercussions that could last for years. By poisoning the water, the victims were totally random—men, women, children, old and young. All religions. No group had claimed responsibility. Tomorrow, he would let her know his theories on why it had happened. Germany, fearing more attacks, had immediately committed to attending the terrorism summit. Noah suspected that had been the goal.

The summit either needed to be canceled or the security increased.

He'd removed the children from school a week early. Jenny had taken them to their grandparents to stay, together with their bodyguards. He'd had to talk to Eve's mother about that—she hadn't been happy. She'd had a lot of questions, none of which he had answers to. It wasn't ideal, and he hoped he was overreacting, but he would function better if he knew they were safe.

Harper also wasn't happy. She hadn't spoken a word to him when he'd seen them off that morning. And Lucy had cried and asked him if he was going to Heaven like Mommy. He'd said he doubted it, but he didn't think the words had put her mind at rest. At least they would be on familiar ground with people they knew. And hopefully safe from any threat, real or imagined.

He was running through the empty city streets. Until he'd gotten to the bottom of whatever was going on, he would be safer driving, but part of him wanted whomever it was to come after him. To draw them out. To discover what was really going on.

As he turned a corner, it looked like he'd gotten his wish. His heart rate kicked up while his mind went crystal clear. The black SUV from the previous morning was parked at the edge of the road, the lights off and the engine dead. Noah looked around. He was in a quiet industrial street, the shops and businesses closed at this hour. No one was in sight.

Not changing his pace, he reached behind him, wrapped his fingers around the pistol in the back of his running shorts, and drew it slowly, letting it hang down at his side.

He waited for the engine to start up. Nothing. Up ahead, an alley led off the main road, and he headed down there and turned, pressed up against the wall, hidden in the shadows.

His gaze searched for any sign of movement, his stomach tingling, his muscles tightening. There was nothing from the vehicle, and the streets remained quiet.

After a couple of long minutes, he stepped out of the alley. He approached the SUV cautiously, his fingers tight around the pistol, expecting the doors to open at any moment. Nothing happened. He stopped just to the side and listened. There was no sound from inside the SUV. Had it been abandoned?

He reached for the door. It wasn't locked, and he opened it slowly, then faster as something pushed it from the inside.

Noah stepped back, raised the pistol, aimed it—

As the door widened, someone fell from the driver's seat to the pavement and lay face up, eyes open but seeing nothing. Noah waited a moment, and when nothing moved, he shifted closer and leaned down to peer into the vehicle. A second body slumped in the passenger seat, forehead resting on the console in front of him. The sharp metallic scent of blood filled his nostrils. Noah reached out a hand and checked the man's pulse. There was none, but his skin was warm to the touch. He hadn't been dead for long.

He turned his attention to the body at his feet.

The male was dressed in black, which didn't show the blood that must have drained from the bullet wound in the center of his forehead. There was zero point in checking for a pulse. While Noah didn't recognize the man, he had a feeling he'd seen him some place before. Hunkering down, he checked the pockets for ID, but there was nothing. Big surprise.

He pulled his phone from his pocket and hit 9-1-1, then realized he wasn't in the States, cleared the call, and pressed 9-9-9.

"This is the 9-9-9 operator. Which service do you require: ambulance, fire, police, or coast guard?"

"Police."

He waited, searching the area for any sign of movement. Everything was still. A light went on in an upstairs window then went out again a few seconds later.

"Metropolitan Police. Can you tell me the nature of your emergency?"

"I'm at a murder scene. Two dead bodies. Close to the junction of Haverstock Hill and Eton Road."

"Are you in any immediate danger, sir?"

How the hell was he supposed to know that? Probably. "There's no sign of anyone."

"Don't leave the scene of the crime, but if there is somewhere out of sight you can wait, then do so. We'll be with you in ten minutes. Stay on the line, sir."

"Okay. The bodies are with a black SUV, license number SE72 WKL, parked close to a church—" He glanced at the sign in front of the building. The place was floodlit. "Hampstead Seventh-Day Adventist."

"I know it."

"I'm going to wait in the alley on the opposite side of the road."

"You'll hear the sirens."

He could already hear them in the distance. Lights were going on up and down the road.

"Can you tell me a little about the murder? Do you know the names of the victims?"

"I've never seen them before in my life," he said. "I was running and came across the vehicle." He decided not to mention seeing the same vehicle yesterday morning.

"Running…as in jogging?"

"Yes."

"At midnight?"

"Yes. I was on my way home."

He looked around; the sirens were getting closer. Time to move to his bolt hole. As he stepped away from the vehicle, something shifted on the edge of his vision. Instinctively, he lunged to the side as gunfire shattered the relative silence of the street. A bullet caught him in the shoulder, spinning him around, and he slammed into the vehicle, his phone dropping from his hand and crashing to the ground. He could hear the man on the other end. "Sir? Sir?"

Gritting his teeth, he peered at his shoulder. It

was a bloody mess. He couldn't feel anything yet. That would come. And if he didn't get out of here soon, he'd likely go under from blood loss. It was streaming down his arm.

The shot had come from the other side of the road, an alley opposite where he'd taken cover earlier. His phone lay on the road. He'd have to leave the cover of the vehicle to pick it up, and right now that didn't seem like a good idea.

The sirens sounded so close now. Unfortunately, not close enough, and he was virtually out in the open for anyone to pick off. Another bullet hammered into the side of the vehicle. He had to get out of there.

At least he'd lost his phone and not his gun.

The pain was coming now, sharp and immediate, but he could deal with pain, zone it out. He took a deep breath, released it slowly, and planned his route. Over the small wall and into the church grounds. He studied the area for a moment, searching for the source of the floodlight. Then back at the alley, as a tall figure stepped out of the shadows. He wore dark clothing and some sort of mask over his face. Both arms were extended, a pistol in each hand.

Noah's gut clenched. Time to go.

He raised the Glock and shot toward the figure. Three shots. He just had the one magazine, so every bullet had to count. The figure ducked back into the alley, and Noah moved, spinning around, raising the pistol, and shooting out the floodlight. In the dim light, he dived for the wall and over. Fire streaked down his shoulder as he hit the ground, and he swallowed the scream. Then he was on his feet, the pistol still gripped in his hand, blood streaming down his arm. He ran, keeping close to the wall of the building until it ended and he was into the graveyard at the rear. He raced for the cover of a tall white angel with outstretched wings. Leaning back against the stone, he caught his breath then peered around. Bullets sent chips of marble flying through the air. The shooter was already in the graveyard. Or was there more than one? Noah sent out a couple of shots and then he was running again. He dived for the cover of a tomb and crouched, breathing hard. Lights danced in front of his eyes. He was losing too much blood, but he appeared to have lost his pursuer. He was heading in the opposite direction. Noah just needed to make his way back to the road where the police were no doubt already at the scene of the murder. Except the majority of police in London were not armed. Would his hunter balk at killing the police?

It was a risk he'd have to take. He wasn't going to last much longer; blackness edged his vision. He waited until the shooter was out of sight and then crept slowly back toward the church. The lights of the police cars flashed, so close. Then a figure stepped out of the shadow of the building, definitely not a police officer, their face lit up in the flashing blue light. Or rather the mask that covered the face. No way past.

Noah turned and headed back, staying low to the ground.

As he came out of the cover of a gravestone, something slammed into him from the side, hurling him against the hard stone, then lashing out, knocking his legs from under him so he crashed to the ground, his face buried in the grass. He rolled, kicking out, and his attacker grunted.

And then he was staring down the barrel of a pistol. This was it. He had a moment of regret— Harper was going to be so pissed at him. He raised his own pistol but knew he was out of time. And the Glock felt so heavy in his hands. The darkness was closing in. His assassin would be wasting his bullet.

Something smashed into the man from the side, and he went down under the blow. Noah rolled to the side, tried to push himself up, but his arms wouldn't hold him. He collapsed back, staring up at the sky.

Someone knelt beside him. He blinked, peered up. A woman with golden eyes. A tattoo of a star on the side of her neck. His mind focused on that one thing. A star. It should mean something, but his brain was slowing. Darkness was closing in on him, until his vision was reduced to a small pinprick.

Fingers touched his throat then withdrew.

He fought to stay conscious but was losing… everything moved away from him, the woman faded in and out of his vision, his eyes drifted closed.

Then water splashed on his face, and he blinked and gasped. A hand slapped his cheek.

"Stay awake," she grumbled. "We have to walk out of here—no way can I carry you."

"What…who…?"

"It doesn't matter. Shit, you're losing too much blood. Sit up. I need to get a bandage on you."

He gritted his teeth then pushed himself up onto his good elbow, pain shooting from his shoulder. He groaned, and her gaze shot to his face. She raised an eyebrow.

"Just do it," he ground out.

His heart raced, and he slowed his breathing, holding himself still as she pressed some sort of pad to his shoulder then wound a bandage tightly around, holding it in place. At least she seemed to know what she was doing.

She tied it off and sat back on her heels, tugging at her long silver earring while studying him. Maybe trying to decide whether he was worth the effort.

Who was she? How had she turned up at just

the right moment?

It didn't matter. He had no choice. He listened but could hear nothing. That wouldn't last. They had to get out of there. He nodded to the bottle of water by her side, and she unscrewed the top, slid a hand behind his head, and held the bottle to his lips. He swallowed convulsively then choked.

"Enough." He forced himself to sit upright. "We need to get out of here."

She got to her feet, stuffed her things back in her rucksack, and slung it over her shoulder.

She stared down at him, hands on her hips. "Then let's go. Before your new friends come back and finish you off."

His eyes narrowed, but he glanced around then reached out and grabbed the nearest gravestone with his good hand and heaved himself to his feet. He swayed then locked his legs in place. He paused as his gaze drifted over her face then lower, focusing on the tattoo on her neck. "Star?"

She nodded.

He swayed again, and she hurried toward him, wrapping her arm around his waist. She was a good six inches shorter and probably a hundred pounds lighter, and no way could she hold him up. Somehow, he steadied himself, and then they were moving. He concentrated on one step at a time, resting at each gravestone on the way.

It seemed to take an age, and he expected to

hear booted feet behind them, but all was silent.

By the time they reached the wrought iron gate at the back of the cemetery, his head was swimming, and he knew she was close to collapsing. The gate creaked as she kicked it open. Once out on the road, she paused, glancing around them, her breathing ragged. Noah was hanging from her arm, and the bandage she'd put on his shoulder was dark with blood. He took a deep breath and forced the strength into his legs. They were nearly there. A white van was parked only a few feet away.

"Come on, just a few more steps."

He focused on the van. One foot in front of the other, and finally, he collapsed against the side, arm cradled against his chest. She pulled herself free and opened the back door. He was just about unconscious as she tipped him into the back, and he curled his legs up so she could close the door.

The darkness was encroaching.

"Hope you're worth it," she muttered just before she slammed the door on him.

So did he.

Christ, he'd made a mess of things.

As the van rumbled into life, he closed his eyes and let the darkness take him.

Would he ever wake up?

Hell, yes. He wasn't dying without finding out what the fuck was going on.

CHAPTER TEN

Noah was lying in a bed.

Through his closed lids, he could tell that it was daylight, but his eyelids felt glued together, and he didn't have the energy to open them and face the day just yet.

Maybe it had all been a bad dream. Except his shoulder hurt like hell. And he didn't want to move because he knew, from experience, that it would hurt even more once he did. Instead, he lay there, on his back, eyes closed, and took stock of the situation.

There was a very good chance Eve had been murdered.

He was under surveillance and had been from shortly after he had started work at Clayton. At least, that was when he had first picked up the tail.

Then someone had murdered whoever was watching him. Had the killer or killers been following him as well? Fuck. There were a hell of a lot of people tailing him.

And then someone—either the same someone or a different someone—had tried to murder *him*.

If only he knew why.

His head hurt. At least that meant he was alive to feel the pain. Always better than the alternative.

The truth was he had come as close to dying last night, in the middle of London, as he ever had in any war zone. They—whoever they were— would have succeeded if the woman hadn't turned up at exactly the right moment. Coincidence?

Who was she? He'd seen her once before, at his ex-wife's funeral. She had a tattoo of a star on her neck. It looked like he'd found the space archaeologist Eve had been working with. Or rather she had found him.

A door opened and then closed, and soft footsteps approached the bed.

He forced his lids to open then shut them again—the light was too bright. He waited a minute and then squinted through his lashes. The same woman from last night. She was fiddling with something behind him, and he twisted his head to watch as she unhooked some sort of IV from a pole, which looked a lot like a lamp stand that had been adapted. Then she turned and bent over him. He felt a sting in his arm, and his eyes shot open. "Shit."

"Good morning, major."

He tried to decide what to say next, but his brain wasn't working properly. He had too many questions and couldn't decide which he wanted to ask first. Maybe he should start with something else. "Thank you for saving my life."

She straightened. "I'd like to say it was my

pleasure, but I think I might have sprained something lugging your heavy ass across that cemetery."

"I appreciate it. I would have been dead last night if you hadn't turned up when you did."

"Actually, the night before last—you've lost a day."

He frowned. "I've been unconscious for twenty-four hours?"

"More like thirty. You lost a lot of blood."

He'd lost a whole day. What the hell had happened in that time? Someone must be looking for him. "Where am I?"

"Still in London. I didn't want to move you until you were more stable. As I said, you lost a lot of blood. You nearly died."

"While I'm grateful for what you did, I'd love to know why you did it."

"Later. You need to eat something first—get your strength up so we can get out of here. Can you sit up?"

He bit back the questions. Mainly because his stomach rumbled and food sounded like a good idea. He suspected he wasn't in any imminent danger, and maybe his brain would function better with some fuel inside him. He dragged himself up, wincing as a flash of fire shot through his left shoulder and down his arm. Once he was upright, leaning against the wall, he twisted his head and peered at his shoulder. There was nothing to see, the wound covered with a clean white bandage. He prodded it with his other hand and winced again. It was tender.

"The bullet went right through. There's nothing important damaged. You'll be fine." She placed a tray on his knee and stepped back. "You need any help?"

Was she going to spoon feed him? "I'm good." He picked up the fork and looked at the food. Scrambled eggs and toast and coffee. His mouth watered. He concentrated on the food, then once his plate was empty, he picked up the coffee and relaxed back with a sigh. He was going to survive. Hopefully long enough to get some answers.

"You seem very well organized." He waved a hand toward the makeshift IV stand, and she shrugged.

"I have a…friend who works in an ER. They owed me a favor. I called it in."

She was moving about the room, clearing away the medical equipment, returning the lamp to its former usage. She was definitely the same woman from the funeral; she was very distinctive. Tall and slender, bordering on too skinny, emphasized by the skintight black jeans and black T-shirt she wore. Black lace-up Doc Martins. Her eyes had a slight tilt—definitely some Asian blood in there but mixed with something else—and were a deep golden brown. Black hair cut short, though longer—shoulder length—at one side, and silver and black earrings. She obviously liked black. And of course there was the tattoo, easily visible, on the side where her hair was shorter. On purpose at a guess.

Finally, she finished whatever it was she was doing and came back to stand over him, lips pursed. "I'm guessing you'd like to talk now."

"You're guessing right. Who are you? Were you following me? And if so, why?"

She picked up the tray from his lap and carried it over to the table then came back dragging a wooden upright chair, which she placed beside him and sat. "I'll answer your questions if you answer one of mine first."

It seemed fair enough. She had saved his life, but really it depended on what she asked. "I will if I can."

"Do you know who tried to kill you the other night?"

"No."

She raised a dark brow. "Really? You have no ideas?"

"Oh, I have plenty of ideas. I'm hoping you'll be able to cast some light on the matter. So who are you?"

"My name is Sara Riley."

He glanced at the tattoo. "But I'm guessing you

go by another name?"

"My online handle."

"My wife called you Star."

Something flashed in her eyes but was gone before he could identify the emotion. "Eve spoke about me?"

He shook his head. "No. Donald Ramsey—Eve's old professor—mentioned you. He just said someone was helping Eve collect information. Not officially on the team but some sort of computer expert, providing satellite imagery. He didn't know anything else."

Something occurred to him. If she was a computer expert, then maybe she was good enough to hack into the Clayton Industry systems and send an anonymous email. "Did you send emails telling me Eve was murdered?"

Her eyes narrowed, and then she gave a small shake of her head. "No." Then she frowned. "You got emails?"

"Later." He wanted to know more about her first, how she fit into this. "But you do think she was murdered?"

"I *know* she was."

"If you believe that, why not go to the police?"

"I don't trust the police."

"But you trust me?"

"I wasn't sure. Right now, I don't know who to trust," she said. "What I do know is I need help—I can't do this on my own, and Eve mentioned you were in the army. A major. You sounded as though you might be useful considering the circumstances."

"So you've been watching me. Trying to decide?"

She nodded then tugged on the long earring that dangled from her left ear. The right one had a stud in the shape of a skull.

"So maybe it's time to explain just what those circumstances are."

"Maybe."

He guessed that while she was in no way sure of him, she felt she had little choice. Other than that, he was getting nothing from her. "Come on, Star—why do you believe Eve was murdered?"

"Because the same freaking bastards tried to kill me."

"Who?"

"How the hell do I know?"

He'd have thrown his hands in the air if he hadn't known it'd hurt like a bitch. "So how do you know it was the same people or even that Eve was murdered? I've seen all the reports. There's nothing to indicate that it wasn't an accident."

She gave him a look of total disdain. "Are you really that naive?"

No. "Start from the beginning," he said. "Tell me everything. How you met Eve…*everything*."

She clasped her hands together on her lap and gazed straight ahead for a minute. Noah watched her but didn't speak again. She was gathering her thoughts; he could almost see her brain working, deciding where to start.

She appeared to be mid-twenties, maybe a little older. She wasn't beautiful in the conventional sense of the word. Too thin, too angular, all bones and sharp lines. No curves, just the hint of small breasts under the black T-shirt. She folded her arms across her chest, and he raised his gaze to her face. She was returning his look, eyes narrowed.

"Go on," he prompted.

She blew out her breath. "I've never actually met Eve, not face to face, anyway. But I'm a member of a number of online forums where people with similar interests meet and chat."

"You mean space archaeologists?"

"Yeah." She grinned. "I always loved that name, but then I always wanted to go into space."

"What do space archaeologists actually do?"

"We download images, usually from satellites—hence the name—and we study them to find out what they show. You can actually get paid for it—things like looking for indications of oil or mineral deposits. That's never interested me. I've always been fascinated by old stuff, things hidden beneath the ground. I'd been looking at images of Mongolia—"

"Where do you get these images?" he asked.

She looked away. Shifty. "All sorts of places."

"I'm guessing not all of them legal."

She shrugged. "I might have been known to hack into the odd satellite system. Maybe redirect a few. It's all part of the game."

"It's not a game."

"You don't think I'm realizing that now?" Her tone was sharp, then she sighed. "Anyway, I got into a discussion on a group about Genghis Khan. This other asshole said the tomb would never be found. I didn't agree. Eve joined the conversation, asked me a few questions, and it started from there. After that, we talked a lot. I liked her, and she offered to pay for my services. We don't often get paid, but she said money was no object, that some group was funding her. And she had all sorts of useful information and contacts. She was working with a Mongolian who'd spent his whole life studying a poem about Genghis—*The Secret History of the Mongols*—that contained clues and hints about where he was buried. I was able to redirect my searches."

"And you found it?"

"Maybe."

"Did you send something to Eve shortly before she died?"

Her eyes sharpened. "How did you know that?"

So she had sent something. "I didn't know for sure. But one of the emails I received implied that Eve had been murdered because of information in her possession."

She pushed back the chair and stood up then turned away and paced to the wall. Her whole figure was tense, hands fisted at her side. Finally, she came back, stood looking down at him, a line between her dark brows. "I sent a satellite image. To Russia."

"Do you know what she was doing in Russia?"

She shook her head.

"Was she alone?"

"I have no idea. She never mentioned anyone else." She sank onto the chair, hands clasped on her lap. She appeared to have gotten herself under control, her expression unreadable once more. "I know she had a team with her in Mongolia before that, but not whether they went with her to Russia."

"Do you know who was on the team?"

"No, but I got the impression there were a few of them."

He needed to find out who exactly was on that team. He hadn't heard back from Professor Coffell yet. He would have to chase that up. Something occurred to him. "Did you send copies to anyone else?"

"No. I worked only with Eve."

"And did she mention if she'd forwarded copies to anyone else?"

"No. But why would she?"

"Just to safeguard the information in case something happened to her."

"You mean like her plane going down and everything burning." She winced. "Sorry. That was insensitive. This must be painful for you. I know you were divorced, but I got the impression that Eve really cared about you."

"I felt the same. We just couldn't manage to live together." He thought for a moment. "Okay, so you sent her the image, but I still don't understand why you're so certain she was killed."

"I told you—because they tried to kill me as well."

"They clearly didn't succeed."

"Hey, the man's a detective." She rolled her eyes. "No, they didn't succeed, but only because Eve warned me. Like you, I thought she was being paranoid—this was a game to me. One I loved playing, but it wasn't dangerous. Well, there was always the chance someone might find I'd been playing with their satellites but not real in-your-face-trying-to-kill-you danger." She was tugging on the earring again, probably a nervous action. "But at the same time, she made me scared. She told me to go stay somewhere else just until I heard from her again. So I did. I spent the night in a hostel, and when I went back to my place the following day, it had been gutted by fire. These bastards obviously like burning things. The fire engines and the police were still there, but I waited until everyone had cleared out and went in. Everything was destroyed. All my equipment. Just gone. I was seriously pissed."

"And scared?" he asked.

"Yeah. I decided I was going to stay out of sight until I heard from Eve."

"But she never contacted you." Because she'd already been dead.

"No. After a week or so, I started looking. That's when I found out she had been killed—I had absolutely no doubt about that. I was terrified enough to stay holed up in a crappy hotel room with no computer for another five days. It was driving me crazy. Hell, I didn't have much of a life by most people's standards—I'm a computer nerd, but that was the way I liked it. And I wanted my life back, but no way was that happening until I'd worked out who killed Eve and why."

"So you came looking for me."

"I went to the funeral. I thought I'd just take a look at you. Eve thought you were an okay guy— well, maybe an okay asshole, but she liked you— and I didn't believe you could have anything to do with her death. And you were a soldier—that sounded like a good person to have on my side with people wanting me dead."

"But you never approached me."

"Maybe I'm getting paranoid as well, but there were too many people around. I'd gotten used to hiding and couldn't bring myself to step out of the shadows. Plus, it just didn't seem like the time. You seemed so…sad. And your kids were there—cute kids. So I took a look and then hid some more."

"You were following me *before* the funeral?" Why hadn't he spotted her? She was an amateur, and he was trained in these things.

"Yes. And I noticed that someone else seemed interested in you."

"The black SUV?"

"Yeah."

"So you were following me the night they were killed?"

"I was a long way behind. Then I heard the sirens and the shots."

"I'm glad you did." So that brought them up to date. He massaged the ache in his shoulder while he tried to assimilate the information, make sense of it, and decide on a way to move forward. First, he had to decide whether he believed Star's story.

She was gnawing on her fingernails, but as if sensing his focus, she glanced up and stared back. He decided that yes, he believed her, which meant Eve had definitely been murdered.

Don had said there was some group put in

place eight hundred years ago to protect the tomb, but that was mere legend. Noah dealt in facts. All the same, the timing made him suspicious. It lined up too well with the image Star had sent.

"Do you have copies of what you sent Eve?"

"I had everything on the computer in my place. They were destroyed."

"Not in the cloud?"

"I don't trust the cloud."

"Could you go in and get a new image?"

"No. I lost all the information Eve gave me. And she called me, so there are no emails or text messages for back up. I thought she was being paranoid again but obviously not." She frowned. "Do you really think that she was killed because of that image? It doesn't make sense."

No, it didn't. Unless it wasn't the image that was important, just that it had led someone to Eve. If they'd been monitoring Star at that point, they could have pinpointed Eve through the communications.

Could Eve have found out something else in Russia? Something someone didn't want out there? Maybe Genghis Khan was just a cover. Archaeologists often had access to places and people the intelligence community couldn't get close to. They were given permission to enter regions closed off to the military. Hell, Eve had been in Iraq when they first met. Could she have been approached by someone in the intelligence community, maybe recruited, and asked to collect information? Eve had hated the intelligence community, had always claimed they were anything *but* intelligent. They'd argued over his work all the time. All the same, the theory couldn't be dismissed. It certainly made more sense to him than she'd died because of an ancient grave.

"So what do you think?" Star asked.

"Honestly? As you said, it makes no sense."

"You know I was hoping for more. I've been thinking—maybe one of the other archeologists wanted all the glory and got Eve out of the way."

It was one theory. And actually, not a bad one. Except for the fact that everyone else had dropped out of sight, which hardly seemed to tie in with wanting all the limelight. "I've been trying to contact a couple of the people she worked with, but they're not answering their phones or emails, and no one's heard from them in a while."

"You mean since Eve's death? That's not good."

He was suddenly restless. "Do you know what's happening? Regarding the murders? Was there anything on the news?"

"The police are after you. You left the scene of a murder. Apparently, you're armed and dangerous. Or you're dead."

"Jesus, I need to contact someone, get word to

my family that I'm alive. My kids will be going crazy. They just lost their mother—they do not need to be hearing this stuff."

"You're right, but do you want to give yourself up to the police right now?"

No he didn't. He wanted to stay mobile, and there was a good chance he'd be taken into custody at least until they checked things out.

"I don't think you should tell anyone where you are. We don't know who we can trust."

She was almost right. But there was one man he would trust with his life. Peter. "I have an uncle. He's family. He'll get word to the kids that I'm okay."

"You're sure?" She sounded doubtful.

"I told you he's family." Though, really, what did that mean? He wouldn't trust the rest of his family as far as he could throw them. "Peter is different. I trust him."

She shrugged. "Your call."

Until Noah had answers to all of his questions, he was putting his family at risk. He couldn't go back to his old life.

He felt the familiar tightening in his gut, the tingle in his blood.

Eve had always told him he was addicted to danger. It was the main reason she had left him and taken the children. She'd said she wanted to distance themselves not only from the danger that followed him around, but also so that when he came to the inevitable bad end—as she was sure he must—it wouldn't hurt so much.

Now she was the one who had come to a bad end.

And he was going to find out why.

Decision made, he glanced across at where Star slumped in her chair, still chewing on her nails, a frown line between her brows. She wasn't his idea of a partner, but as she had said about him, she was all he had right now. While he wouldn't put anyone else in danger, she was already in the thick of it. Like him. Until they figured out what was going on, her life was on hold as well.

Noah would contact Tom first. With Clayton Industries' resources, the man should be able to find out who was with Eve in Mongolia—in case Professor Coffell didn't come through with the information. Then Noah would reach out to his contacts in the intelligence community, but he'd be careful. He didn't know who he could trust.

"So what next?" Star asked.

"We need to follow in Eve's footsteps, where she went, who she met."

"Who killed her?"

"Exactly."

CHAPTER ELEVEN

"Peter, it's Noah."

"Where the hell are you?"

Noah ran his hand down his face. "Still in London, but it's probably better you don't know more than that." He was using a new cell phone Star had assured him couldn't be traced, but he was feeling a little paranoid. Didn't want to say any more than he had to.

"What's going on? Are you aware that you're wanted for questioning with regards to murder? It's all over the news."

At least he wasn't a suspect. Yet. "Two guys, who I believe were following me, turned up dead. I called it in, but I'm guessing it was an ambush. I had to make a run for it before the police arrived because whoever killed them stuck around to kill me, too." He'd decided not to mention Star's involvement. It felt safer giving out information on a need-to-know basis, and Peter didn't need to know about Star just yet. He was sure his uncle would go along with whatever he asked, but there was always the small chance he would fall on the side of the law and set the police on them both. For Noah's own good, of course.

"So why not go to the police afterward? It

doesn't look good, Noah."

"Because I need to find out what's going on, and to do that, I can't risk being in police custody." He wasn't even sure he trusted the police. It had taken them a hell of a long time to come after him the other night. Could they have been involved? Dodgy cops were nothing new. Maybe they'd been paid to stay out of that cemetery until someone could finish the job on him.

"You think this is somehow related to Project Arachnid? Revenge?"

"No. I've cross-referenced every job I worked on, pulled every name that could possibly have reason to come after me. And eliminated every one of them. I think it's tied to Eve's death."

Peter was silent for a moment. "You're not just being paranoid?"

"No. Someone tells me my ex-wife was murdered, and shortly after that, someone tries to kill me. I've got to presume the two things are somehow connected."

"I think you should come in and we'll sort this out together."

"The email also said I was in danger and so were my family."

"Jesus, Noah. Do you have someone watching the children?"

"The senator offered me the use of the company security. I have two people watching them at their grandparents—it's easier to monitor than in the city."

"You've spoken to Michaela about this?"

"A few days ago. That's another thing—could you let her know what's going on? I need to contact Tom and want him to be prepared."

"Of course. I think you're right to trust her." He was silent for a moment. "I know you feel like you've ruled it out, but have you considered that maybe Eve was killed to get you to resign, make you vulnerable?"

Of course he'd considered it. He'd considered everything. "Why, though?"

"Because you were damned good at your job. Project Arachnid was starting to make a real difference, and that was mainly because of you."

"I was just one of a team."

"Don't start with the false modesty now. You have an uncanny ability to understand the reasoning behind the terrorist mind. To work out what they will do next and stop them. There were probably plenty of people who were very happy when you left the project."

"Or just one."

Peter sighed. "Are you still holding onto your theory that there's someone at the center of it all?"

"I've seen nothing to change my mind. If Eve was killed to get me out of Arachnid, then it worked. I'm out. Why come after me now?"

"You're still in the same line of work. You predicted the German attack."

Noah scowled. "Too late to do any good."

"All the same, the alerts went out. It's not impossible that someone traced it back to you. So what do you plan to do?"

"I'm going to look into Eve's death, go back to where it happened, see if I can't find out something new. But to do that, I need to be able to move freely. I need the police off my back. And I need to know the children are safe and that they know I'm okay."

Peter was silent for a while. "I'll see what I can do."

"Thank you. Can you call me back on this number when you have some news?"

After they hung up, he tossed the phone on the cabinet by the bed and sat back, staring at the wall opposite. It would take a while; he had to be patient—never one of his strong points. He couldn't decide on his next move until he knew whether the police were actively looking for him. In the meantime, he needed a shower, and more food would be good.

When he came out of the bathroom half an hour later, a towel wrapped around his hips, Star was sitting on the bed, typing into a laptop. She looked up as he came in, one eyebrow raised as her gaze drifted over him. Did she like what she saw?

Noah had never had any problem getting women.

He'd had a couple of short-term relationships since his divorce, but his job had made breaking them off easy. Undercover work and relationships did not mix. And that suited him fine. He had no intention of ever attempting a relationship again. Look how well the last one had turned out.

But some women found danger a turn on. Was Star one of them?

He'd be a liar if he told himself he wasn't curious. She was different than any woman he had ever known. A combination of naivety and confidence. Plus, she'd saved his life. Obviously, she had an ulterior motive—she needed his help—but all the same that meant something. Tied them together.

"You need some clothes," was all she said.

She was right. All he had were his running shorts and a blood-stained T-shirt.

"I'll go pick you some up from your apartment," Star said. "You can't go near the place yourself, the police will likely be watching it, but they won't notice me. I've been thinking, you're also going to need your passport. Plus I'm nearly broke, so if we're going to follow Eve, then we'll need money and a lot of it." She looked at him. "I take it you have money?"

"I have some cash in the safe at the apartment. And credit cards, though probably not a good idea to use them at the moment." There was some other stuff she could pick up as well. Things from his old life that might come in useful. The reports of Eve's accident were in the safe, too.

Star was right. It was unlikely anyone would notice her entering the apartment building. And as he wasn't a suspect, just wanted for questioning, there was a good chance they wouldn't have searched the apartment yet. "I'll make a list, give you the codes to get into the safe. But if you get there and it looks too risky, then you walk away. We'll get the stuff some other way."

He thought about suggesting she change clothes. She had a pretty distinctive look and would stick out in anyone's memory, but he suspected she didn't have anything less conspicuous to wear, so he'd be wasting his energy. And likely pissing her off.

She left half an hour later. Noah went back to bed, dropped the towel, and slid between the sheets. He still felt weak, and his shoulder was killing him. Star had left some painkillers on the cabinet by the bed, and he took a couple, swallowed them with a mouthful of water, then started going over options in his head.

Peter called an hour later. "You're clean," he

said. "I told them you were involved in a job for us. They're no longer looking for you, but they still want to talk to you at some point. And I suggest you do that as soon as possible."

"Thanks, Peter. I don't suppose you could get me a copy of the police report?" Maybe there would be some information on the identities of the men in the black SUV. They hadn't been carrying any ID, but maybe there had been a fingerprint match or DNA.

"I'll see what I can do, but there's only so many favors I can call in."

"Do what you can. And the kids?"

"I spoke with Harper, told her you'd been called away suddenly. Luckily, they hadn't seen the news report about you, but she did want to know if it was something dangerous. I told her you didn't do the dangerous stuff anymore. Not sure she believed me—that girl has your suspicious nature. They'll be okay, Noah."

"I owe you."

"You do. So what are your plans?"

"I'm not sure yet. Still deciding."

"You know, if you want, I can send the team over for back up. There's still a chance that this is somehow tied in with your work with Project Arachnid. It's a justifiable response."

"Thanks, but I want to poke around and see what I can find, and the team can't help with that.

They'll just alert whoever is after us."

"Us?"

Shit. He didn't want to mention Star just now. "I meant me and the children. The last email said we were all in danger."

"Well, let me know if you change your mind. And I talked to Michaela. She's contacting your assistant—you'll have any help you need."

"Thank you."

"Well, stay safe and keep in touch. And let me know what's going on."

"Of course." Though he wasn't sure how true that was. He didn't want to drag Peter into any danger, though his uncle could look after himself.

"I'll talk to you later."

He ended the call.

CHAPTER TWELVE

Noah was looking up flights on the laptop when Star came back.

She dropped the bag on the bed. "I thought you were in the army," she said. "So what's with the four passports? Are you some sort of super-secret special agent?"

"I did some undercover work."

"And you kept them as souvenirs."

"Something like that."

He opened the bag. Looked like she'd found everything. Clothes, toiletries, the cash from the safe, credit cards—which he could use now the police were off his back—and the report on Eve's accident. Plus bullets. For the gun he'd lost in the cemetery. Not that a gun would be much help if they were going out of the country. It would never get through airport security. And the passports and other paperwork to support his aliases.

He took the bag into the bathroom and dressed in jeans and a T-shirt, boots. He felt almost human and ready to go.

When he came out, Star was seated at the table, going through his notes. She glanced up, but he couldn't tell what she was thinking. He'd never met a woman so hard to read. He took the seat opposite, pulled the laptop toward him, and checked his email. There was one from Peter, and he opened it. The message read: *You owe me.* Attached was the police report of the murders. That was fast work.

He read through the report, but there was nothing new. There was no fingerprint match in the database for either of the two dead men, and the results were not in yet for the DNA. They'd both been killed by a single gunshot—probably with a silenced weapon—to the head at close quarters. Which suggested that there had been more than one shooter. They could hardly have expected the second victim to just sit in his seat and wait his turn. And there had been no sign of a struggle. That would tie in with what he remembered. There had definitely been more than one person after him that night.

So he'd had at least four people following him—five if you counted Star—and he had no clue who any of them were or what they wanted. He had to assume that the two murdered men were working for someone. So while they had been eliminated, it didn't mean the threat was gone.

As he went to close the laptop, an email popped up. Professor Coffell. At last. He read it quickly. It was the information he'd asked for, a list of names of the team with Eve in Mongolia.

The Russian, Yuri Vasiliev, and Tarkhan Ganbaatar were there, but also John Chen, a translator, and Zachary Painter, a journalist doing a piece on Eve's search for the tomb.

"Have you heard of a Zachary Painter or a John Chen?" he asked Star.

She shook her head.

He opened an email to Tom and asked him to dig up anything he could on the two men then sat back and rubbed a hand over his head.

There was still no response from either the Russian or the Mongolian Eve had been working with. "Did you have any contact with the other members of the team?"

"No. Everything went through Eve. I didn't want contact with anyone else."

He blew out his breath. "I never realized archeology was so cloak and dagger. I thought it was digging around in the dirt looking for old bones. What the hell could be so important that someone would go to all this bother?"

They certainly wouldn't find out holed up in this place. And if he stayed in one place for too long, there was always the chance that whoever had already tried to kill him once would try again.

"I think I should head to Russia. We know the last place she was seen alive from the police report. I can talk to the investigators. See if I can't track down her last moves. Find out if she went

anywhere that night after she called you and tried
to call me."

"I've never been to Russia."

"I have." A few years back. It had been
freezing. He remembered that most about the
country. Moscow in January was fucking *cold*.

He studied her a moment. Three people were
already dead that he knew of, and he was having
bad feelings about the Russian and the
Mongolian. No one just dropped out of sight these
days. "Maybe you should stay in London."

"No way. I'm coming. This is my search just as
much as yours. I can be useful."

He wasn't sure whether she was right or not.
But likely she was in as much danger if she stayed
here as if she came with him.

If anyone was looking for him, they'd be
monitoring the airlines, which meant he and Star
weren't going under their own names. He was
covered, but he needed to get another identity for
her, and quickly.

"You need a passport," he said.

"I have a passport."

"You need *another* passport."

He'd make a few calls to a few old contacts in
the intelligence community. Someone would know
where he could get a passport fast.

CHAPTER THIRTEEN

Noah paid the driver while Star dragged the bags out of the back of the taxi.

In the end, they'd had to take a flight to Moscow and then change over to a second flight to Irkutsk, the city where Eve had spent the night before she died. Situated in Eastern Siberia, it was a city of approximately 600,000 people, not that far from the border to Mongolia. Which made sense if that was where Eve had come from and was heading back to.

He took his bag and winced as pain shot through his shoulder then blanked the expression from his face as he caught Star watching him.

She just shook her head, grabbed the bag from him, and slung it over her shoulder with her own. "Go."

He frowned but headed up the steps and into the hotel. According to the accident report, this was where Eve had stayed the night before she died.

It was a small boutique hotel away from the city center in an old building—the sort of place she'd always loved, with plenty of character and an old-worldy feel.

The receptionist looked up as they approached and gave them a professional smile. "Can I help you?"

"I have a reservation, two rooms. Noah Jackson."

He completed the paperwork, and the receptionist handed him two key cards.

"Could you tell me if you remember this woman?" He showed her a photograph of Eve. "She stayed here just over a month ago."

"Can I ask why?" Her English was perfect but with a strong accent.

"She was my sister," Noah said. That was the story they had come up with since they were booked into the hotel under their alias identities. "I was supposed to have come on the trip with her, but I couldn't make it at the last moment. She died in a plane crash while leaving the city, and I'm just trying to get some…closure, I guess. A sense of what she was doing before she died."

"I'm sorry for your loss. I don't remember your sister. Can you give me a name and I'll check the dates?"

"Eve Blakeley."

"Of course." Her fingers flashed over the keyboard. "Yes, here she is. I was on leave those days. Sofia, who was on duty then, will be taking over for me in the morning. She may remember something."

"Thank you." He thought for a moment. "Do you provide safety deposit boxes?"

"No, but we allow guests to deposit valuables in the safe if they require."

"Can you tell me if Eve left anything in the safe when she stayed here?"

The woman appeared unsure then frowned. "It's against policy to share that information."

"Please. It's important."

She finally gave a small nod. "I'll check, but if there is anything, we'll need the proper authority to release it."

"That's fine. I'm sure we can get it." He had no clue what the proper authority was in Russia, but they could worry about that if there was actually anything here.

"Just a moment."

He waited, trying to curb his impatience as the woman worked at the computer keyboard. She came back a moment later. "There was nothing logged in."

Damn. "Thank you for checking."

Noah followed Star to the elevator, and they rode to the fourth floor. As they stopped outside a door, he handed her one of the key cards.

"I'll come and look at your shoulder," she said.

"You don't need to."

"Yes, I do. The last thing I want is for you

collapsing on us again."

He shrugged but moved to the next door along, slid the card in the lock, and stepped aside so she could enter the room. She dropped the bags on the floor and waved him to the bed. "Sit down."

"Are you always this bossy?"

"I can be bossier. Sit down and take your shirt off."

He shrugged out of his jacket then pulled his T-shirt over his head and tossed it on a nearby chair. The bandage was clean, so the wound hadn't reopened. As he sank down onto the bed, she stepped closer and unwound the bandage. His shoulder looked good, no redness or swelling.

He stood up. "All right if I take a shower before you bandage me back up?"

"Go ahead."

He stood under the hot water for long minutes. Afterward, he contemplated putting on some clothes, but he wasn't going anywhere else tonight. And Star had no doubt seen him naked while she was looking after him. So he just wrapped one of the white towels around his hips. She was sitting on the bed, a glass of something in her hand—she must have found the mini-bar—her gaze wandering over him. He sat down beside her, took the drink from her hand, and swallowed the contents in one go. Vodka and tonic.

"Hey!" She scowled but jumped to her feet and

got the medical kit. After cleaning the area with an antiseptic wipe, she wrapped a clean bandage around his shoulder.

"Thank you," he said, flexing his arm. "You're good at this."

"Amazing what you can learn from the internet. Do you want something to eat?"

"No. I just want to crash."

"Okay. I'll leave you to it, then." She picked up her bag from the floor. "I guess I'll see you in the morning."

"Sleep well, Star."

She hesitated. "Yeah. You, too."

As the door closed behind her, he sagged back against the mattress and closed his eyes. He wasn't completely recovered from the blood loss, and it had been a long day. He was asleep in seconds.

CHAPTER FOURTEEN

Noah tapped on the door.

No response.

He'd woken up feeling much better, his head clear, his shoulder aching but no flash of pain as he moved. He was on the mend. Now he wanted to get out there and find some answers.

Was she even in there?

The realization hit hard and fast—there was a good chance that Eve had been snatched from her hotel room. In this very hotel. He and Star were booked under their aliases, so it was unlikely anyone would know they were here. All the same, maybe they weren't taking their personal safety seriously enough. They needed to be more careful.

He knocked on the door, harder this time. A muffled sound came from inside, then footsteps heading to the door, the scrape of a chair being moved, something being knocked over. He tensed, but then the door opened.

She had clearly just woken and was blinking up at him, dressed in a black sleeveless T-shirt that reached to mid-thigh and what looked like nothing else, the long length of her legs bare. He was sure he could see her nipples through the thin material. Judging by his body's reaction, he was definitely feeling better. Forcing his gaze upward to her face, he grinned. "Good morning."

"My God, you look chirpy," she muttered.

"You don't."

She scowled but stepped aside and waved him in.

"You're not a morning person, then?" He stepped into the room then stopped. "What the hell happened in here?"

Her brows drew together. "Nothing."

It looked like her bag had exploded. The clothes she had worn last night were strewn on the floor outside the bathroom. One of the upright wooden chairs was on its side by the door. He turned to her and raised a brow.

She shrugged. "I didn't want anyone to come and kidnap and torture me," she said, then her eyes widened. "Sorry, that was a little insensitive. Eve was your wife, and I'm sure you don't want to think about her being..." She trailed off. "Anyway, I was lying in bed last night and suddenly it occurred to me that—"

"There was a good chance she was taken from here."

"Yeah." She ran a hand through her hair. "Sit down for a minute, and I'll go get dressed and we can get some breakfast. I need coffee." She headed for the bathroom, gathering up her discarded clothes as she went, dragging her bag with her.

He sank down onto the edge of the unmade bed. There was a map of the city on the bedside table — presumably she'd picked it up from the lobby last night. She'd written some notes on the back.

Translators

Taxi companies

Hotels

She'd circled three places: the hotel, the city center, and one more that looked to be close to their current location.

The bathroom door opened, and Star emerged, dressed in her usual black and ready to go. He stood up as she grabbed a small bag from the table and handed her the map. "You've been working," he said.

"I wasn't ready to sleep last night. I had a look around the area."

"Do you think it's wise wandering around on your own in the middle of the night?"

Annoyance flashed across her face but was quickly gone. "Probably not," she admitted. "In hindsight, maybe we should be a little more careful. But that only crossed my mind when I was lying in bed afterward."

"Where did you go?"

"I'll tell you over breakfast." She headed out the door, and he followed. "Let's go down to reception first and see if they can organize us a translator."

A different woman was at the reception desk, a tall blonde. Noah repeated the story about Eve's death, and they ascertained that yes, she remembered Eve when she'd booked into the hotel.

"How about when she checked out?" he asked.

"Her business colleague paid her bill the next morning."

Noah cast a sideways glance at Star. It would corroborate the idea that she had actually been taken from the hotel. "How do you know he was her business colleague?"

"Because that's what he told me."

"Do you have a name?"

"No. He paid in cash, so there's no credit card receipt. I remember—there are not many people pay in cash these days."

No, only people who didn't want you to know who they were. "So you never saw my sister leave?"

"No. I'm sorry."

He forced a smile. It was only what he'd been expecting. "Thank you for your help. One more thing—can you organize a translator for us?"

"For the day?"

He wasn't sure. They'd know more later. "Definitely the day. Starting as soon as possible. Maybe longer."

"No problem. I'll contact the company straight away."

The restaurant was on the first floor. They were the only people in there at the moment, though it was still early. They sat at a table by the window, and he ordered coffee for both of them.

"So tell me," he said.

"I went to the post office. It's only a ten minutes' walk away. I thought maybe—if Eve was feeling so worried—she might have stashed the image someplace safe after she picked it up, but there was nowhere between there and here that I could see."

"You had a busy night."

"Well, someone has to do something. Half the team was asleep. Anyway, I realized she might have taken it to one of the other hotels, probably one of the big names she would recognize— people like the familiar, especially when they're scared. Except they're all a good half hour walk away, so I was thinking she probably took a taxi. We need to talk to the taxi companies and see if anyone remembers her. Likely they won't speak English, so we need some help there."

"Translator, taxis, hotels," he said.

"Exactly."

He was impressed.

Their food came, and they ate in silence. Ordered more coffee. Outside, the sky was a clear blue, everything seemed peaceful, but he couldn't shift the sense of unease.

He really wanted a gun but didn't think the hotel would be able to provide one of those. Maybe the translator might know of somewhere. If not, he'd contact Tom. Clayton Industries likely had connections in the city.

And maybe from now on, he and Star should share a room. He didn't like to think of her as vulnerable. That's not how she came across. She was tough, but tough wouldn't do much good if the other person was armed. "No more going off on your own," he said, putting his cup down.

"Okay," she replied, and he frowned.

"That was easy."

"I'd sort of forgotten for a minute why we're actually here. Someone killed Eve. And they've already tried to kill me once. And a few days ago, someone almost killed you. And last night…"

"Last night…?"

"I just kept getting this feeling that someone was watching me. I brushed it off as paranoia, then I thought of Eve doing the same and then…"

He pushed back his chair. "Come on, let's go see what we can find out. Put an end to this and we can go home."

But he realized that, in a weird sort of way, he was enjoying himself. He'd been shut down since Eve's death, just coping with the children and all the changes in his life. Now he felt alive again.

Their plan was to try the local taxi companies first and see if anyone remembered picking up Eve that night. If they came up blank, then they would go around the big hotels and see if she had rented a safety deposit box. Presumably, that would mean she would have had to rent a room as well; they were unlikely to rent the boxes to anyone off the street.

They got lucky with the second taxi company they talked to. One of the drivers remembered Eve.

Stefan, their translator, was a young man who looked to be in his early twenties. He was a student of languages at Moscow University but was working during the vacation. He was a tall, good-looking boy who'd taken a liking to Star, which was inexplicably irritating. He also seemed too clean-cut to have gun-selling contacts, which was a pity.

"He says he remembers her because she was pretty and not Russian," Stefan translated.

"Where did he drop her off?"

He listened while the question was asked and answered. "He isn't allowed to give out that information."

Noah pulled some money out of his pocket, the bribe Stefan had suggested would be needed. And apparently, dollars, rather than rubles, were always appreciated.

The money was handed over, and the driver spoke some more. Noah picked up the name Marriott in the jumble of words. Looked like they had a hotel.

"You were right," he said to Star. They were sitting in the back of a taxi, Stefan in the front next to the driver who had driven Eve to the Marriott that night. They were chatting in Russian, and he let the words flow over him.

"We still don't know if she left anything," Star said.

"We will soon."

The taxi dropped them off in front of the hotel. It was a big modern building right in the city center. It looked like any other Marriott anywhere in the world. He could understand how Eve might find the anonymity comforting.

He handed over his dollars, this time straight away, and Star asked about Eve. Stefan wasn't needed—the young man at the reception desk spoke perfect English. Noah wouldn't have thought this was a big tourist destination, but after speaking to the staff at two hotels, obviously they were used to dealing with foreigners.

As he tapped into the computer system, a frown formed between his eyebrows. "Yes, there was an Eve Blakeley booked in here that night. There's a flag next to her name."

"What does that mean?"

He tapped some more. "The bill wasn't paid, and there's a note from the cleaning staff that it looked like the room wasn't slept in—they would have been asked because of the unpaid bill."

"My sister was killed in an accident the following day," Noah said. "That would explain the unpaid bill."

The man's eyes widened. "Oh. I am so sorry for your loss, sir."

"Don't be. And I'll clear the bill myself. Right now, I'm trying to find out if my sister rented a safe deposit box here, and if so, what happened to the contents."

"Let me check for you, sir."

As the man disappeared through a door behind the desk, Noah waited, curbing his impatience. He had an idea the man was checking with someone, probably the hotel manager, as to what he should do in the circumstances—he suspected it was hardly a common occurrence. Finally, the man came back, accompanied by another, older man in a dark suit. "It appears your sister did have a box with us, and the contents were not collected. But I'm afraid that without the proper authorization, we can't release those contents to you."

"And what is the proper authorization?"

"Identification and a copy of your sister's death certificate will be sufficient."

Crap.

He would have to get Eve's solicitor to fax a copy of the death certificate to him at the hotel. He considered trying another bribe then decided against it—the man was giving off the wrong vibes, and it shouldn't be hard to get a copy of the certificate. "Thank you. You've been very helpful. I'll be back as soon as I have the documents."

"We could come back later and break into the place," Star suggested as they headed for the exit.

He wasn't sure whether she was serious or not, and for a moment, he considered the idea. But it was no easy job to get into a safe deposit box, hence the word "safe." Plus they had no clue which box was Eve's, and they'd have to open them all. It was probably easier to get the necessary paperwork.

"Let's go get lunch and make some calls. Get things moving."

Stefan was hovering on the steps to the hotel, waiting for them to come out. Noah headed over. "We don't need you for a few hours. We'll pay you for the full day, of course. And we'll need you tomorrow as well if that works?" That should hopefully give them time to get a copy of the death certificate.

"No problem," Stefan replied.

"Okay, meet us back at the hotel, say, four o'clock?"

"I'll be there."

As he turned to go, Noah called him back. He stepped closer. "Do you know of anyone who can sell me a pistol?"

Stefan pursed his lips. "I might."

"Well, decide and let me know when you come back."

Stefan nodded and walked away, hands shoved in his pockets. He could go to the authorities, but why would he? And besides, he had no proof of anything. It was a calculated risk, and the odds were in their favor. And Noah would feel safer with a weapon.

They had lunch in a small restaurant in the center of town, sitting on the terrace under the shade of an umbrella. Noah had never been one for vacations, but he imagined this was what it was like. Well, with a few minor differences, such as no one wanting him dead.

He made his phone call, and the solicitor promised to fax a copy of the death certificate to the hotel. There was nothing else they could do right now until they got into the box and found whatever Eve had hidden there. So they might as well relax and enjoy the sunshine.

Tomorrow morning, they planned to rent a car and visit the site of the plane crash. There would likely be little to see, but he still wanted to go. Then afterward, he hoped to talk to the detective who had investigated the accident. He'd already requested an interview.

Star was drinking cold white wine. He was sticking to water. He wanted his wits about him — so far he hadn't picked up anyone following them, but he needed to stay alert. She swirled the wine in her glass, took a sip, and licked her lips, then peered at him from beneath her lashes. Heat flashed through him, settling low down in his belly. Inconvenient. Or did it have to be?

For a moment, he wondered whether she was doing it on purpose. But he figured if she wanted him, she would come right out and tell him. She didn't seem one for subterfuge. Which meant her actions were natural. A subconscious urge to draw him closer?

It had been a long time for him. His life wasn't conducive to relationships, even if he had wanted one. Plus, the last three months in the States had been spent undercover, and since then, he'd hardly felt inclined.

Now, his mind and body turned to sex.

It wasn't as though they were actually working together, so there were no rules constraining his behavior. All the same, it would complicate some things. And make others easier. He'd already decided they were sharing a room from now on, and he wasn't sure how she would take to that idea. While she had presumably slept in the same room as him in London, he'd been injured back then. She'd no doubt seen him as a patient and not a man.

Now he was pretty sure she saw him as a man.

"Where did you grow up?" he asked, suddenly curious about her. He knew next to nothing about her background.

"In London. Actually, not far from your apartment. My mom was a doctor, half-Japanese, and my dad was a software developer. He was where I got my computer nerdiness from."

"What happened to them?"

"They were in a car accident when I was nineteen. A drunk driver coming the other way. They were both killed instantly."

"I'm sorry."

"So was I. They didn't deserve that. They were good people. What about you?"

For a moment, he wasn't sure what she was asking. Then he had the urge to ask why she wanted to know. Which was stupid. This was what people did—they asked about each other. "I grew up in Chicago. My dad was a lawyer, and my mom stayed at home and looked after us."

"Us? You have brothers and sisters."

He really didn't want to talk about this, but without being rude or telling an outright lie, he wasn't sure what else he could do. "I had a brother, Ben. He was a couple of years younger than me.

He was born with a congenital heart defect, and he died when I was ten. The doctors had told my parents he could die at any time, so we were lucky to have the time we had with him."

Her hand crept out and rested over his on the table. She squeezed. "I'm sorry."

"So was I." He echoed her words. "He didn't deserve it. He was the best."

"It must have been hard on your parents."

"It nearly broke my mother. He'd been her favorite. She was a church goer, and I think all along, despite what the doctors told her, she believed that there would somehow be a miracle and God would save him."

It should have been you.

The words echoed in his head. He'd never forgotten them.

"They still live in Chicago. We're not close." That was an understatement. He hadn't spoken to his mother in…a long time. The truth was he had never forgiven her for those words. She'd fallen apart after Ben had died, taken to drinking. She'd been drunk when she said them. Didn't they say that the truth came out when you were drunk? He couldn't blame her for thinking them. Ben had been so *good*. He had taken after their mother, blonde and delicate. Noah looked like his dad, dark and big. But he could blame her, and did, for speaking her thoughts out loud, and once said, they couldn't be taken back. He'd been a mess at the time, ten years old, and he'd just lost the brother he loved. He'd needed his Mom, and she'd rejected him in the worst way possible.

"She told me she wished it was me who had died. Not Ben."

Her eyes widened. "Bloody hell, she did not say that."

She'd regretted the words, he knew that, because she'd told him, numerous times, but it didn't help. Time to change the subject. "I have a younger brother and sister, though. Both born after Ben died. But the age difference is big, and we were never close."

"Are you close to anyone?"

Eve had probably told her that he was a complete commitment-phobe. And he supposed it was true. Maybe because his mom had let him down so badly, or maybe he'd just been born that way. Probably a little of both. Nature then nurture. "I'm close to my Uncle Peter. I went a little crazy after Ben died. Misbehaved a lot. My parents didn't know how to cope with me, and Peter came along and sort of took me off their hands. He got me into the military school he'd been to, and I loved it. He's a general now, though he'd just joined the army back then."

"Is that why you joined the army?"

"I guess so. I always wanted to be a superhero

and fight the bad guys. It was the closest I could get."

He couldn't believe he was telling her all of this crap. He hadn't even told Eve about what his mom had said.

"And you get to shoot things and blow shit up."

"Not anymore."

Her eyes widened in mock alarm. "God, what are you going to do to let off steam?"

He looked at her speculatively. Was she flirting? Again, he wouldn't have put her down as a flirty type. He guessed she was just changing the subject, and he liked her all the more for it. "I'll think about that and let you know when I have an answer."

The waiter brought their food. And they ate in silence.

Afterward, they walked back to their own hotel. It took half an hour but was pleasant in the sunshine. She had long legs, and her stride easily matched his as they walked together. He glanced at her sideways, and she turned her head and caught him looking.

"Are you trying to decide whether or not it's a good idea to sleep with me?" she asked in a conversational tone.

He snorted. "Actually, I'd already decided that we're going to sleep together. It's whether we do anything else together that's still up for debate."

"You know, I'm guessing I'm not exactly your usual type."

"It's been so long, I don't remember what my type is anymore."

She smiled at that. "Really? So this is just a proximity thing brought on through sheer frustration."

"Maybe. Time will no doubt tell."

CHAPTER FIFTEEN

It was near eleven that night, and they were outside a nightclub in downtown Irkutsk not far from the Marriott. Stefan had informed them that he knew someone who knew someone who could get him a gun. They would meet them here at eleven and hand over one thousand American dollars. It sounded like a lot to Noah, but then he was hardly in a position to bargain.

The line wound down the street, disappearing into the alley off to the left. Stefan led them straight to the front and spoke quietly to the huge bouncer who had a shaved head and a lot of ink. He would have fit right in with the Brothers of Jesus. After a brief glance at Noah, then Star, he waved them through and into some sort of reception area. To the right was a set of double doors through which he could hear the thump of dance music, and directly opposite them was a second, smaller door.

"We have to wait here," Stefan said.

He didn't look happy—a tic twitched in his cheek, and his gaze kept darting to the door to the street as though he wanted to make a run for it.

A minute later, the door opposite opened, and a man appeared. Small, middle-aged, and wearing a suit, he looked more like an accountant than a gangster. "Mr. Buryakov will see you now. You have the money?"

"I do," Noah said.

"Good."

Obviously the man spoke English, so Noah turned to Stefan. "You can go if you like. We'll see you in the morning as arranged."

Stefan's shoulders sagged. Probably relieved he didn't have to go any further.

The man led them through the door and down a narrow corridor before ushering them into an office. A second man sat in a large leather chair behind a desk. He was big, but solid with muscle rather than fat. Blond hair in a ponytail and dressed in a black T-shirt.

"Mr. Buryakov?" Noah asked.

He nodded then waved them to the seats opposite. "Vodka?" Without waiting for an answer, he poured out three glasses, lifted one, and tossed the contents back in one go. He raised an eyebrow, and Noah picked up his own glass and swallowed, the neat vodka burning his throat.

"So you want to buy a gun?"

Noah nodded.

"You have my money?"

"I do."

"Let me see."

Noah placed the envelope on the desk between

them.

Buryakov flicked through the contents then grinned at Noah. "Of course, I could just take the money, shoot you with the gun, and have some fun with your pretty girlfriend."

"I'm not his girlfriend," Star said, taking a gulp of vodka without even a wince. "I'm his bodyguard."

He laughed. "Would you like to come and work for me?"

"No."

He laughed again then reached into the same drawer and pulled out a holster and a pistol. "I'll throw in the holster for free because your girlfriend amuses me."

The pistol was a 9mm Makarov, a Russian-made gun Noah had never used before. It was clean and loaded. Noah pulled out the magazine, checked the chamber was empty, then pulled the trigger a couple of times. It felt smooth. He returned the magazine. "More bullets?"

Buryakov handed him a box, and Noah shoved it in his pocket then stood up and slipped off his jacket. He fastened the holster around his waist with the gun in the small of his back. With his jacket over the top, it was unlikely to be noticed unless someone was looking for it.

"Please feel free to enjoy my club."

"Thanks," Noah said drily. He wasn't a club

person.

The corridor was empty as they left the office.

Star paused as they passed the double doors leading to the nightclub. She glanced up at him. "I'm too wired to sleep." She nodded to the doors. "You want to dance?"

Hell no. "I don't dance."

"I should have guessed that." She studied him, her head cocked to one side. "You want to buy me a drink, then? Something other than warm vodka? I could murder for a cold beer right now."

Why not? There was nothing else they could do for the night, and a cold beer would be good. He gestured toward the door, and she grinned.

The music was loud, though not painfully so, and the dance floor was full of gyrating bodies, the air rank with perfume and sweat. They found a table in the corner of the room as far away from the dance floor as they could get. A waitress appeared immediately, and he ordered a couple of beers.

They drank without talking, but it was a comfortable silence. Noah leaned back and let some of the tension drain from him. They'd made some progress. Tomorrow, they would visit the accident site and talk to the detective who had headed up the investigation, but for now they could relax.

He watched her drink, the flick of her pointed

tongue over her lips, the smooth line of her throat. Finally, when their glasses were empty, he stood up, slid his hand into hers, and pulled her to her feet. Cupping her face in his palm, his thumb stroked the tattoo on her neck. Then he lowered his head and kissed her, slowly. She tasted of vodka and beer.

After a moment, she pulled away and studied him in the dim light, her expression blank. "Let's go."

He nodded, and she led the way out of the building. As they stepped out onto the street, his phone rang. He glanced at the caller ID.

"I've got to take this," he said.

Star gave a quick nod and stepped away. He had the idea she was regretting the kiss and was trying to distance herself physically and mentally. She was probably right.

He lifted the phone. "Tom? What do you have for me?"

"Background checks on the two names you gave me."

"Go ahead."

"I'll send you the reports, but briefly: John Chen was a translator employed by the company funding your ex-wife's research. He seems legitimate, and I couldn't find anything to suggest he was other than that."

One down. He'd been hoping for something

more. Something that might help him work out what was going on. "And the other?"

"The other is far more interesting. Zachary Painter was a journalist supposedly doing an article on your ex-wife's last expedition. But Painter was a pseudonym for a Zachary Martin."

"That name sounds familiar."

"It would. You worked with him for a while a couple of years ago. He's MI6. Or *was* MI6."

He remembered Zach Martin now. And his partner. Zach had seemed like a good guy. He'd had many of the same beliefs as Noah—that there was some sort of central figure who was orchestrating things, weaving a web, putting things and people in place. But in place for what?

"Was?"

"At the time he was in Mongolia, he was taking a leave of absence. Involuntary. He was relieved of duty when he returned to the U.K. His people apparently believe he was passing on information to terrorist groups and that he was directly responsible for his own partner's death—when she started suspecting him—in a suicide bomb attack in Paris just over four months ago."

Noah frowned. When they'd worked together, there had been no indication that Zach had been anything other than a dedicated agent. When had he gone over to the dark side? Or had he always been there and was just a good actor?

"What's his connection to Eve?"

"I'm still looking into that. It might be he has links with the terrorists involved in her kidnapping twelve years ago. Maybe she somehow became a threat and they wanted her taken out. I'll have more information soon."

"You know where he is now?"

"He dropped out of sight. However, we have reason to believe that he was in Russia at the time of Eve's death."

Jesus. Could it be that simple? Something to do with the kidnapping and nothing to do with him at all? Then who had tried to kill him? Who had been following him back in London? And who had killed *them*?

"Thanks, Tom. You've been very helpful. Let me know if you find out anything else."

"Of course. Senator Clayton has instructed me to help you in any way I can."

Noah ended the call and slipped the phone back in his pocket.

The more he learned, the less he understood.

CHAPTER SIXTEEN

Noah wasn't sure what he was expecting to achieve out of this trip to the wreckage.

The plane had gone down, crashed, burned. He'd seen the picture. What would they be able to tell from seeing it?

Before they'd left the hotel that morning, he'd checked in with the children via video chat. He'd told them he was visiting the place their mother died. For closure. He wasn't sure Harper believed him. She'd asked him if everything was all right. She was worried; he could see it in her eyes. What the hell could he say?

Nothing was right.

But maybe the visit would trigger some ideas as to what had happened. Often the smallest of clues could lead to a breakthrough, and Christ, he could do with one of those.

After they'd gotten back to the hotel last night, he'd made a few calls, managed to talk to a contact in MI6, and confirmed the information Tom had given him regarding Zachary Martin. Apparently, it was true—he'd gone rogue and disappeared.

The report had come in from Tom including a list of possible contacts, but it was small. The man had no close family, was divorced. He'd call the ex-wife anyway but maybe not in the middle of the night.

He'd dropped a line to Tom and asked him for a list of all the cases Zach Martin had been working on from the time prior to Eve's kidnapping, twelve years ago, to his disappearance. Maybe there was a connection there.

Tom hadn't even balked.

It was a scary thought that a private company could acquire information on a government agency, but he was beginning to believe there were few limits to the extent of Clayton Industry's reach.

They'd rented a car to make the journey to the crash site half an hour from the city. Stefan was driving, Noah sat next to him in the front, while Star was behind him in the back.

Last night, they'd both pulled back after the kiss.

The kiss hadn't been one of his best ideas. He needed to keep focused. So while they'd slept in the same room last night, sleeping was all they had done, and by unspoken mutual consent, the kiss had not been repeated.

The copy of Eve's death certificate had arrived, and they planned to return to the Marriott that evening when they returned from the trip. Would they find what they were looking for? And if the image was there—he'd use it to draw out Eve's killers.

If that was even what they'd been after.

The roads had quieted as soon as they left the city—at least they could be sure no one was following—and they made good time. They were driving over flat open plains, but in the distance, shrouded in haze, he could see the mountains where the plane had gone down ten minutes into the flight. Stefan had already arranged for a local guide, the same person who had gone in and discovered the plane crash.

A battered gray car was waiting by the side of the road as they pulled up. A big man in jeans and a checkered flannel shirt leaned against the vehicle, a rucksack and coil of rope at his feet. He was young, maybe in his mid-twenties, with overlong black hair and dark eyes, almost black, beneath thick brows. He straightened as Stefan got out of the car, and they spoke in Russian.

Star had climbed out of the back, and Noah went to stand beside her as the two men approached.

"This is Dimitri," Stefan said. "He's going to take us to the site of the crash. And he says sorry for your loss."

Noah nodded and held out his hand. They shook. "Thank you."

Star held out hers next, and it was enveloped in Dimitri's really big palm. "Привет," she murmured, and Noah's eyes narrowed on her. Was she flirting? He'd already decided she wasn't the flirty type, but maybe she was pissed at him for the kiss.

The Russian grinned and spoke something in fast Russian.

She glanced at Stefan one eyebrow raised.

"He says you speak Russian."

"Obviously not. Just greetings and stuff." She shrugged. "I picked up a phrase book from the hotel on the way out."

They had to walk for the last couple of miles, and the day was warm. He let the others go ahead and walked at the back, his gaze drifting to Star's ass. As though sensing his focus, she glanced over her shoulder and smirked. He grinned back, his mood lifting slightly. Maybe the fresh air and the countryside? It was beautiful and the sky overhead a deep cloudless blue.

The walk took thirty minutes, the last mile up a steep incline. Dimitri halted at the top and spoke to Stefan.

"The plane is in the ravine," Stefan told them. "We can't actually see it from here, but we can climb down. It's an easy climb."

Noah peered down where he was pointing. The land fell away steeply, and somewhere not far below, he could hear water running.

Dimitri was already tying one end of the rope

to a sturdy tree trunk and throwing the other over the edge.

"You okay with this?" Noah asked, glancing at Star.

"Of course. I learned to rappel when I was in college."

The drop was only about fifty feet, and she went first, lowering herself hand over hand into the ravine. Stefan went next, then Dimitri, and finally Noah. Pain shot through his shoulder as he lowered himself. *Shit.* He'd almost forgotten about the bullet wound. He shifted his weight to the other arm and hoped he hadn't reopened the wound. Star was assessing him through narrowed eyes as he reached the bottom.

"I'm fine," he said.

"You're such a tough guy." She didn't sound as though it was a compliment.

Dimitri led the way through the heavy growth. The sound of running water was louder here, and they were heading toward it. Finally they came to a narrow, fast-flowing stream. The water looked deep, but Dimitri jumped it, and so they followed. They rounded a last bend in the gorge, and there it was.

The skeleton of the plane was clearly visible amongst the blackened and burned vegetation. The plane lay on its back, one wing broken off, the front nose snapped. Maybe it had hit the ground

nose first then catapulted over onto its back.
Exploded in a fireball. They would have had full
tanks of fuel at that point and no chance of
survival. At least it would have been over quickly.
Likely Eve would have been killed on impact.

Why the hell had she been on that goddamn
plane? The kidnapping had left her terrified of
closed spaces—among other things. What the hell
was she doing in a small plane? She was heading
back to Ulaanbaatar, which wasn't that far. Why
didn't she use the train? Though if she'd been
taken from the hotel, then likely she'd had no
choice. Maybe she'd been dead before she even
got on the plane and this was all a set up to hide
the fact that she'd been murdered.

He moved toward the wreck, leaving the others
behind. The plane was bigger than he'd expected.
About twenty feet long. It was hard to visualize
what it would have looked like. The color was
burned away, now black. He ran his hand along
the metal, warm from the sun.

"How many people were on the plane?" Star
asked, coming up behind him.

"Just Eve and the pilot," Noah said. "So at least
no one else died. She would have hated that."

"Do you know anything about the pilot?" she
asked.

"His name was on the accident report. I ran a
background check on him, but there was nothing

unexpected. Likely he was just collateral damage. Poor bastard."

"I wonder how they did it."

"The investigation found no evidence of any sort of explosive device. Maybe they sabotaged the engine, but the fire destroyed any chance of confirming that."

He doubted they would ever know for sure.

Noah walked around the perimeter, his hands trailing along the side of the plane. He came back to stand beside her. "There's nothing to learn here," he said, his good mood broken. "Let's go."

She looked as though she wanted to say something but then just nodded.

"Why wasn't the plane taken for investigation?" Noah asked as they headed back, and Stefan translated the question.

Dimitri shrugged then spoke.

"He says only the black box was taken," Stefan said. "The rest was considered too much effort and expense. Except the bodies, of course. They were airlifted out and taken to the morgue in Irkutsk."

With nothing left to ask, Noah followed the group back to the vehicle in silence.

He waited until Star seated herself in the back and then got in beside her. "Well, that was a waste of time," he muttered as the car pulled away.

"What did you expect to find?"

He shrugged. "I don't know. I just felt I had to

at least see the place she died. I thought it might help me…understand."

What was clear was that Eve's murder had been meticulously planned. And he still had no idea as to why anyone would want her dead.

"None of this makes any fucking sense," he said.

Star laid a hand on his thigh and squeezed. "It does. We're just not seeing it yet. We will."

He placed his hand over hers; he liked the feel of her touching him but suspected she would withdraw any moment. Then he rested his head back against the seat and closed his eyes. He hadn't slept well. He wasn't used to sharing a bed, not to mention he'd had a raging hard-on all night. He was trying not to think about that.

"Let's go over what we know again."

Noah ran through what was in his head. "Eve was working on something related to the search for the Spirit Banner and tomb of Genghis Khan," he said. "She must have gotten some new information, and it was important enough that she overcame her PTSD to fly out to Mongolia."

"How bad was the PTSD?" Star asked. "While I never met her in person, she always seemed very…together."

"She suffered from acute claustrophobia and hydrophobia, and she was pretty bad. She'd gotten good at hiding it, but she had triggers. They had her for three weeks, but at least she survived. Two of the captives died under torture. Eve was tougher than she thought."

"And she married you."

"Yeah, everyone makes mistakes. I think she married me because she thought I'd make her feel safe. Then she divorced me because the opposite happened. She couldn't cope with the pressures of being a soldier's wife. She told me she had enough fears of her own without adding mine to the mix."

He'd never regret the marriage. They'd had three beautiful children. He'd never expected to have children, and he couldn't believe how much he loved them. He just didn't know how to show it. How to connect with them.

"So she flew out to Mongolia on the twenty-eighth of May and met with her team: a Russian archaeologist who appears to have vanished, a Mongolian scholar who also seems to have dropped off the face of the planet, a translator who apparently is just what he seems but again is nowhere to be found, and a rogue MI6 agent. We don't know how long she was in Mongolia," he continued. "And we haven't yet been able to track her movements after she arrived in the country—"

"I'm pretty sure she was heading to the Khentii Mountains."

"You are?"

"That was where the spear was located. Or at

least where Eve had me looking. But I don't know whether she found it or even if she got there. When she turned up in Russia, I assumed she was having trouble with the Mongolian government—they're pretty strict on who they let into the area."

"Okay. We'll check that. I have someone searching the hotels—we hadn't picked anything up, but maybe she wasn't registered under her own name. One of the others could have checked them all in." He made a mental note to get Tom to check out the other names on the team. "Fourteen days later, she tries to call me because she was worried about something. The following day, she turns up dead in Russia." He sighed and scrubbed a hand over his head. "Any of this making any sense?"

"Nope."

His brain hurt. "According to her old professor, she'd been working on this Genghis Khan stuff for years and had never been to Mongolia. What changed?" He shifted in the seat so he could look into her face. She was chewing on her lower lip, seemingly thinking hard. "Are you sure she never said anything to you?"

She shrugged. "Not that I remember. We've been over this before."

"Then go over it again. We're missing something."

She closed her eyes for a moment. "I'm sorry,

but we didn't have that sort of relationship. We talked a lot, but about work. She was so passionate about her research. While I knew she didn't do field work, I always thought it was because of the children. That she didn't want to leave them. She never mentioned the kidnapping." She gave him a hopeful look. "You know, maybe she got better. Decided to move on with her life. Twelve years is a long time."

Yeah, but it didn't feel right. "Harper told me Eve had been worse in the week or so before she left for Mongolia. That she wasn't sleeping, and when she did, she usually woke up screaming."

"So, not better then. Maybe someone made her an offer she couldn't refuse."

"Who? And why couldn't she refuse? Money didn't interest her."

"Maybe someone threatened her or the children."

He'd already considered that, but he just couldn't get the facts to click into any sort of pattern that made sense. "So you sent the image to a PO box in Irkutsk. It has to be tied in somehow. So we assume they killed her for the image. Did she not tell you what you were looking for?"

"Not the details, just that it would help her get a step closer."

"But you don't know what it was?"

"No."

"Eve's old professor told me there was a legend about a talisman that Genghis Khan carried into battle. Maybe that's what she was looking for."

Her eyes narrowed as she considered his question. "Perhaps." She tugged on the earring. "They came for me after Eve's death, so presumably they didn't get what they wanted from Eve — the image I sent her. They took my stuff to see if they could recover it."

"And I'm guessing they couldn't."

"No. I deleted everything after I sent the image to Eve."

"Was that normal?"

She shrugged. "Sometimes. It depends on where and how I get the information."

Probably illegally.

So maybe Eve had hidden her copy. Maybe she'd sensed something, someone following her, gotten nervous, and hidden the image in the safe deposit box at the Marriott. If that was the case, and if he was able to retrieve it, then he needed to use it. Get the word out that he'd found it and set himself up as bait. Draw whoever had killed Eve out into the open.

At that moment, they pulled up outside the police station in Irkutsk.

They climbed out of the vehicle and followed Stefan up the stone steps and through the double doors into a reception area. A uniformed officer sat behind a glass panel, and Stefan approached and spoke in rapid Russian. He listened to the reply then turned to Noah. "We have an appointment with the lead investigator, Rurik Pozniak. He will see you in his office. We just need to wait for someone to escort us."

He'd had to arrange the meeting under his own name. It was a calculated risk. Hopefully, it wouldn't blow his cover and alert anyone to his whereabouts.

Maybe he should have left the pistol in the car. Would they be searched? It burned into the small of his back. But in the end, a second uniformed officer led them through the station, paused in front of a wooden door, knocked, and nodded for them to enter.

Investigator Pozniak sat in a chair, his feet resting on the wooden desk in front of him. He wore a shiny blue suit and had black hair, a mustache, and shrewd—and not very friendly—gray eyes. They narrowed on Noah as he watched them approach, lines forming between his brows.

He didn't rise as they halted in front of the desk, but he slowly lowered his feet and sat up straighter. Stefan spoke in rapid Russian, but the man looked beyond him.

"I speak English, Major Blakeley."

"Good. Then can you tell me what happened to

my wife?"

He shrugged. "Not more than you already know. It was all in the report. Your wife's death was an accident. The pilot called in with engine trouble shortly after takeoff. He was supposed to turn around and head back to the airport but crashed before he had the chance. Both the pilot and your wife were killed outright. I'm sorry."

He didn't sound particularly sorry. "And the bodies were brought back to the morgue here. Is that normal?"

"Of course." He frowned. "I'm not sure what you are looking for, Major, but I assure you, everything was done by the proper procedures." He stood up and shoved his hands in his pockets. "Just go home."

Noah had a feeling he wasn't going to get anything else from the investigator. He just didn't know why. Maybe the man didn't like foreigners. Could he be hiding something? If Eve had been murdered, then it had been covered up extremely well. Maybe Investigator Pozniak had been bribed to write the report he had written. Noah had an idea that he might find himself thrown in a cell if he suggested such a thing. All the same, he couldn't help the assessing stare he gave the other man, and he allowed some of his thoughts to show. They stared at each other for a minute, and a small smile curled the other man's lips.

"Is there something you would like to share with us, Major Blakeley? Some reason why you consider there might be more to this case? If so, I can arrange for your stay here while we…talk."

"That won't be necessary. Thank you for your time."

He turned and walked away, feeling a prickle down his spine, expecting to be stopped at any moment.

"That went well," Star muttered as the door closed behind them and they stood on the steps outside the police station. "I thought he was going to throw our asses into jail."

"I believe he was considering it."

"You think he knows more?"

"There's a good chance. But he won't talk."

Another dead end.

CHAPTER SEVENTEEN

They dropped Stefan at the train station since they were heading to the Marriott and wouldn't need a translator. They'd already spoken to the manager; he was waiting for them and would open the safety deposit box as soon as they handed over the relevant paperwork.

It was late afternoon by the time they parked the car and entered the hotel. He rubbed at his shoulder. The bullet wound ached. The climbing hadn't helped.

"Are you okay?" Star asked.

"I think I might have opened up the wound again."

"I'll take a look when we get back to the hotel. You want to leave this until later?"

"Hell, no. Maybe we'll get lucky and we'll find a diary with exactly what happened."

"Did she keep a diary?"

"One of her therapists had her do it for a while. I don't think she kept it up for long."

The manager came out of the back office as they approached the reception desk. He shook hands with Noah and then with Star. "Come through, please."

They followed him into the office then through

another door into a room behind with a bank of safe deposit boxes along the wall opposite. Noah pulled the paperwork out of his pocket and handed it to the manager. After a quick glance, he opened a box in the middle row and took out an envelope. "That's all there is. I hope it's what you're looking for."

"Thank you." Part of him wanted to open it now and find out if it contained any answers. Another part wanted to put it off. The envelope was A4 size, padded, and had clearly already been opened. Noah shoved it in his pocket and glanced at Star. "Let's get out of here."

They were silent on the way back. Star drove, no doubt to give his shoulder a rest, but she kept casting him sideway glances. When they got back to their hotel, they still didn't speak until the door closed behind them.

He leaned back against it, hands in his pockets. Now he was here, he was reluctant to look. If the envelope contained nothing of use, then he had to decide where to go next.

"Come on, Noah."

He blew out his breath then pulled the envelope out of his pocket, stared at it for a moment, then reached inside.

It contained a single sheet of paper.

On the back was scribbled: *Is this what you're looking for? Star xoxo.* He turned it over. It showed a black and white image, not a photo exactly, more a contrast of light and dark. It just seemed like a blurred mess to him. He handed it to Star.

"Your image?" he asked.

She nodded. "I used an ultra-high definition satellite imaging technique that allows us to see beneath the ground. The images are taken from satellites, and then the computer gathers all the information and makes this."

"But what does it show?"

She laid the image on the bed and sat down. Noah came to stand over her shoulder as she studied it, tracing her finger over the patterns. "There it is," she murmured, and he could hear the wonder in her voice, which struck him as odd since this wasn't the first time she had seen it. Her finger traced a white outline just off center, small maybe a centimeter across. "See, it's hexagonal. At this scale, it looks like it's maybe two feet across. And some sort of dense material. Stone or rock, maybe just really hard wood. The Talisman."

As he concentrated on the image, he could sort of make out what she was referring to, though it took a hell of a lot of imagination.

Then again, what had he expected? A picture of a grave with an angel over it and a big fucking sign saying, "Genghis Khan lies here"?

"You have to know what you're looking for,"

she continued, "and what you're looking *at*, but believe me, this is what Eve was after."

"Where is it?"

She pointed to a set of numbers in the corner. "Those are the GPS coordinates. They give the exact location." She slipped the image back in the envelope.

"So we can go there?"

"If that's what you think we should do."

She didn't sound so sure. Hell, neither was he. The more he found out, the less he understood what was going on.

He stood, staring at the envelope, then he turned to look at her and caught an expression on her face. She was playing it cool, but underneath there was a gleam of excitement that she clearly didn't want to share.

She stood up and stretched. "It's been a long day. Why don't you go shower? I'll order some room service, and then I'll take a look at your shoulder. We'll sleep on it, and in the morning, we'll decide what to do next."

He looked at her, considered pushing the matter—finding out exactly what she was thinking. Instead, he shrugged out of his jacket and examined his shoulder. There was no sign of blood, so hopefully, he'd just pulled it during the climb. He unbuckled the holster and dropped the gun on the bed then ran a hand through his hair, over his scalp, around the back of his neck, trying to ease the tension. He waved a hand at the envelope where it lay on the table between them. "Is it what you expected to find?"

"Well, yeah. I sent it. But I thought maybe it had gone up in flames in the plane crash and the information had died with Eve. That we would never be able to reconstruct the coordinates and it was lost forever."

Her words sounded reasonable, but he sensed that she was hiding something from him. Maybe she'd open up to him later. "That's good, then. I'll go shower."

In the bathroom, he stepped under the warm water and closed his eyes. What was his next move?

He didn't have a lot of choices. The only strategy they had was to put the word out that he had the image and see who followed the bait. He'd start making calls and sending emails in the morning. He was guessing somewhere, someone had a flag on his name and would pick up the chatter.

He also needed to decide whether to get some back up. Right now, his gut was telling him to stay out of the loop, do things alone, but that had always been his natural inclination.

He switched off the water, dried himself, and pulled on his jeans. As he came out of the bathroom, she scrambled to her feet, her gaze running over him with more than medical interest. Or was that wishful thinking? He had an overwhelming urge to lose himself in her, just for tonight, to forget…

"Sit down," she said, nodding to the edge of the bed.

He sat on the dark red coverlet, and she stepped up close to him, so he could breathe in the warm scent of her. She unwound the damp bandage, dropped it in the trash.

"Okay?" he asked, twisting his head to take a look. While one of the stitches had broken, the wound was still closed, and he didn't think it would need another.

"You'll live."

"Yeah, but for how long?"

"Hopefully long enough," she said, wrapping a clean bandage around the wound.

He rolled his shoulders when she was done, aware of her gaze on him. He could see the rise and fall of her breasts under her T-shirt, her breathing fast. Reaching out, she trailed a finger across his chest, and a shudder ran through him.

Without thinking, his arm snaked around her waist, and he pulled her close, pressing his forehead against her belly. For a second, she relaxed, the tension seeping from her, and her hand moved to his head, her fingers running over his hair.

She pulled away. "I have to go shower. I smell."

He breathed in deeply. "You smell good to me."

"Huh." She stepped back as a knock sounded on the door. "That will be room service. Make yourself useful and get my dinner." She turned away then glanced over her shoulder as she opened the bathroom door, a smile of…promise on her face. Then the door closed behind her.

He could hear the shower running as he set out the food on the table. He thought about joining her, but he was hungry. And from the amount of food she had ordered, he was guessing so was she.

Good thing they had all night.

He switched off the main light so the room was lit by the rosy glow from a lamp. Very atmospheric. There seemed to be no pulling away tonight.

The door opened, and she stood there, dressed in one of the hotel's fluffy white robes and no doubt naked underneath. The muscles in his belly tightened at the thought. He waved her to the table, and she sat down opposite him, a smile curving her lips. Her face was free of makeup, her skin golden.

"Very domesticated," she murmured. He raised his glass as she sat, and she picked up her own. "What are we drinking to?"

He thought for a moment, and a wave of

sadness washed through him. "To Eve. Who solved the unsolvable but never quite made it to the end. That would have pissed her off."

She raised her glass. "To Eve."

"Now, no more work for tonight. Eat."

The food was delicious and the wine cold and sharp. He watched her eat, the movement of her lips, her throat as she swallowed. Afterward, she put down her knife and fork, swallowed the last of her wine, and stood up. Holding his gaze, she tugged open the robe and dropped it to the floor, and heat flared through his body.

She held out her hand. He took it, and she led him to the bed, where he did his utmost to clear both their minds of all that had happened and all that might happen tomorrow.

CHAPTER EIGHTEEN

Harper lay in the darkness listening to the creaks of the old house as it settled around her.

She wasn't a little kid. She knew that something bad had happened.

Otherwise her dad wouldn't have left them. Not so soon after her mom had died. She glanced toward the door. Even after all these weeks, she still expected her mom to come walking in.

Bad things happened to adults.

She wanted to go look for her dad, but she had to stay and take care of Lucy and Daniel. They were so little, and they didn't understand.

And there were strangers in the house. Her gran had tried to tell her that they were the new groundsmen. But since when did groundsmen have guns? She'd seen one of them. And since when did they sleep in the house? No, they were bodyguards for her and Luce and Dan. Because they were in danger. Her mom was dead and her dad was gone, and she had to stay strong and protect her sister and brother.

They were sharing a room down the hall. Maybe she should go join them. Check they were safe. She could share Luce's bed for tonight.

She didn't want to be alone.

There, she'd admitted it.

But that was different than being afraid.

She was just about to slip out of bed when something tapped against the window. A scrape and then a *click*, and she froze in place, a strange fluttering in her belly.

Someone was there.

Or maybe it was just a bird.

The scrape came again.

For a moment, the curtains parted, and moonlight slid through the gap. A shadowy figure formed between the window and the bed, and a small squeak escaped her throat. A scream for help filled her head but wouldn't come out, trapped inside. She lay turned to stone—she'd heard the phrase but hadn't understood it before now. A small whimper leaked from her mouth, and she squeezed her eyes tight shut.

Then the shadow was upon her and she could move at last. She shot upright in the bed, flailing, her eyes flying open. Too late. Hard hands held her down, fingers gripping into the bare skin of her arms. Then something was over her face, sharp and smelly. She tried not to breathe, but her lungs were burning, and at last she took a huge gulp of air and her nostrils filled and her head swooned.

As she was going under, her last thought was if she would see her mom again.

CHAPTER NINETEEN

Noah rolled onto his back and lay with his eyes closed. His shoulder ached, but otherwise he felt good. Like he'd just had a night of great sex.

Which he'd had.

It was what he'd needed. What they'd both needed, from her response; she'd been as wound up as him. He reached out a hand and patted the mattress, but the bed was empty, and he reluctantly opened his eyes.

It was tomorrow. Time to make some difficult decisions.

"Star?"

No answer.

He dragged himself up, leaned his back against the padded headboard, and listened. There was no sound from anywhere in the room. Maybe she'd gone to get coffee and she'd be back in a few minutes, but he had a strange twisting in his gut.

He flung off the sheet and climbed out of bed. His jeans were on the floor, and he dragged them on then sank back down onto the mattress. He felt almost hungover, a dull ache in the back of his skull. Too much sex. He pressed his fingers to his forehead, trying to get his brain to work.

Had she mentioned going anywhere? He didn't

think so. Not that they'd talked much last night.

He pushed himself up and went into the bathroom, splashed cold water onto his face, then came back and finished dressing—he needed to be ready for whatever came next, and clothes seemed like a good idea. No doubt Star would be back soon bearing whatever passed as a Starbucks in Russia.

He picked up his phone and hit her number. He heard a ringing and went into the bedroom and found Star's cell phone on the table. As he ended the call, it went silent.

He crossed the room to the door, opened it, and peered down the corridor.

Empty.

He went back, searched for a note. Nothing. And something occurred to him. They'd left the envelope with the image on the table, and now it was gone. Had she moved it? Maybe she'd been unable to sleep and had spent the time studying the image.

Somehow, he couldn't convince himself of that. And there was that twist in his gut again.

The hotel phone rang, and some of the tension eased from him. But when he picked it up, it wasn't Star on the other side, but Stacey, Eve's mother.

"She's gone. Harper is gone. They've taken Harper."

For a minute, the words were just a jumble of nothing as his brain refused to allow them to make sense. He shook his head. "Tell me what happened."

"In the night. They broke in through the window. Took her out the same way."

"Lucy and Daniel?"

"They're fine. They didn't wake up. Only Harper."

"What about the guards? Concentrate, Stacey. This is important."

"There was one on duty overnight. We found him outside. He was unconscious and Harper is *gone*."

"Did you call the police?"

"No. They left a note. They said they would kill her if I talked to anyone but you. They gave me this number and told me to tell you. And that if you don't do what they say, then they'll kill her."

His phone beeped then, and he glanced down. A text message.

Talk to no one or she comes back to you in pieces. We'll be in touch.

Jesus.

"Get her back, Noah. You have to get her back. This is down to you. The life you lead. This is your fault. Get Harper back!"

He took a deep breath. "I will. I'll contact you when I hear anything."

He ended the call. He had to think. Concentrate. Instead, he sat with his head in his hands. They had his little girl. Harper pretended to be so brave, but she must be terrified—if she was even alive. He couldn't think like that. *Wouldn't* think like that.

Was this tied in with Star's disappearance? Had someone come in the night and snatched her, too? Or maybe someone had gotten to her. Offered her something in exchange for the image. Her life, maybe. Or the life of someone she loved. Or money. While he would have sworn that she wasn't the mercenary type, how well did he really know her?

Hell, for all he knew, she could have been involved in Harper's kidnapping.

He rubbed at the base of his skull where the ache still throbbed.

Had she drugged him? He remembered now. She'd gotten up in the early hours of the morning, brought him a glass of water. He'd been thirsty after working hard for most of the night, and he'd gulped it down and fallen asleep.

While she'd snuck out, stealing the image.

He had no clue where to go next. Until he heard from the people who had Harper, he had no idea what to do. He would go crazy with the waiting. He stared at his phone, willing it to ring.

Instead, there was a thumping on the door, and

he almost jumped. For a moment, he stared at it, dread turning his stomach molten. He pushed himself up and crossed the room, peered through the peephole, and frowned. Three men stood outside. Two in uniform — the local police — and the third in a shiny blue suit. Investigator Rorik Pozniak. What the hell?

One of the uniforms banged again, and Noah looked around him. He had no choice except to let them in. Maybe the investigator had some more information on Eve.

As he opened the door and stepped back, one of the uniforms grabbed him by his injured shoulder, turned him around, and slammed him into the wall. Acting on instinct, Noah went limp until the man's hold loosened then he tore himself free, whirled around, and kicked the man in the gut. He went down with a guttural choke of pain as the second uniform lunged for Noah. He kicked him in the thigh then punched him in the throat so he went over backward.

In the ensuing silence, he heard a sharp *click*.

He went still then turned slowly. Pozniak was standing just inside the door, legs braced, a pistol in his outstretched arm, aiming for Noah's chest. He eyed it up. Could he take him? Before he got a bullet off?

"Stand down," Pozniak growled, his finger tightening on the trigger. Noah had no doubt he would pull it.

He stepped back, put his hands in the air, and forced his breathing to slow. The adrenaline was still spiking in his bloodstream, and he needed to bring himself down. Pozniak looked pissed enough to shoot him just for fun.

"Just what I needed this morning," he muttered. "A goddamn lethal weapon. What was that? Fucking karate?"

Noah didn't answer; he was trying to get his head around this. He'd probably overreacted, but his emotions and instincts had already been on high alert, and he'd snapped. It had never happened before, but he had been provoked. "Why the strong arm stuff? If you wanted to talk to me, couldn't you have just...talked to me?"

Pozniak pursed his lips. He glanced at his men. One was still prone on the floor, the one he had punched in the throat. The other was dragging himself to his feet, shaking his head. He took in Noah with his hands raised and sank down on the bed behind him.

Pozniak reached for his belt and tossed Noah a set of cuffs. "Cuff yourself."

He didn't want to cuff himself.

"Do it!"

He snapped the cuffs onto his right wrist then his left. "What now? Are you going to tell me what this is about?"

"I got a call earlier this morning, informing me that you were planning a terrorist attack on Russian soil. That you were armed and dangerous. We decided to act first, secure you, and then talk." He cast a look of disgust at his men. "Obviously, that didn't go down as planned."

"A call from whom?"

"I have no clue." He holstered the gun but kept a wary eye on Noah. "You." He pointed a finger at the man slumped on the bed then spoke in rapid Russian, none of which Noah understood.

"I'm no fucking terrorist and you know it," he said.

"I know nothing of the kind. Perhaps you could explain why you are booked into this hotel under a name that is not your own."

Shit.

The uniform called out, and Noah knew what he must have found. His gun where he'd dropped it when he stripped off last night. Pozniak approached him, the holster and gun hanging from one finger. "You have a license for this? In any name?"

Noah remained silent, and Pozniak snorted. "I'll take that as a no. I'm going to read you your rights now, which you won't understand as they're in Russian. I'm sure you'll get the general gist."

Noah didn't even attempt to listen, just let the words flow over him. He had to get out of this. He had to find his daughter. This couldn't be happening.

Who the hell had made that anonymous call?

Star's face flashed up in his mind.

Goddamn it.

Whether she'd done it personally or paid someone else didn't matter. The latter was more likely, as her Russian wasn't good.

She'd given herself a little time to get away.

And probably killed his daughter in the process.

CHAPTER TWENTY

Noah shoved his hands through the bars, and the uniform unlocked the cuffs and disappeared from sight. He rubbed at his wrists and tried to ignore the pain in his belly. Pozniak's men had gotten in a few punches in the back of the car on the way to the station. Payback. Pozniak had ignored them. The bastard.

"Why are you doing this?" Noah asked.

Pozniak pursed his lips and studied Noah through the bars of the cell. "Maybe we just don't like know-it-all bastards sticking their noses into our business."

"My business as well. She was my wife."

"Ex-wife, I believe. Or maybe I disliked you inferring that I would take bribes. That is what you were inferring, is it not, major?"

Maybe he *should* offer the man money. Except he didn't have any. It was all back in his hotel room.

He thought about telling Pozniak about Harper. But for all he knew, this could be some sort of test. Pozniak could be in their pay, whoever *they* were. They were testing him to see if he would follow instructions.

Christ, he didn't know what the hell to do.

Always before it had been *his* life on the line. He could cope with that. Hell, it had made him feel alive. Now he could sense the panic clawing at his gut, mingling with the pain of the beating.

What if the kidnappers tried to contact him and he wasn't there? Would they hurt Harper? "You have to let me out of here."

"Actually, I don't. You've obviously made enemies. Pissed someone off. Someone other than me. Now you take the consequences."

"Let me make a phone call."

"Perhaps later."

He grabbed the bars. "There's something I need to do. Something important and I can't do it from here. Look, contact General Blakeley. He'll vouch for me." He could feel the anger rising, a red mist in his brain. "Just call him. You don't need to do this."

"I'll think about it." He smiled. "Might take me a day or two, though."

And he was gone. The outer door clicked shut, leaving Noah alone. For a second, his hands tightened on the bars, then he released them with a choked cry.

He backed up then slid down the wall to sit with his legs stretched out in front of him. Wrapping his arm around his stomach, he closed his eyes.

All he could see was Harper.

Two fucking days.

Noah gritted his teeth and resisted punching the wall. Or yelling. Except he knew from experience it would do no good. He figured they'd put him somewhere out of earshot.

Pozniak, that bastard, had been true to his word. While Noah had been fed three times a day, the officers had not said a word. He probably wouldn't have understood them if they had.

Shit, he needed to get out of here. He needed to find out what was going on. What had happened to Harper.

He paced the short distance back and forth across the cell. Everything was wound up tight. He was an explosion waiting to happen, and he'd never felt so powerless in his life.

He sank down onto the cot bed, head in his hands, tried to see a way forward. The truth was, while he was in here, he could do nothing.

Except think.

About Harper. About Star.

Where the fuck was Star? For the first day, he'd lived with the hope that she would somehow appear. That she really had just been off on some errand when he'd been arrested.

That hope had died a death by the second day.

She had gone.

What had happened to her? Had she gotten scared and run? Maybe she'd been taken by someone. Someone who had snuck in, taken Star, stolen the envelope…and left him untouched and sleeping peacefully in his bed? Yeah, that didn't gel.

Maybe she'd been using him the whole time, and the meeting, saving his life, had all been part of some elaborate plan to get him to lead her to the image in the safety deposit box. Could she have been working with the enemy all along? Been in their pay? Except she'd *had* the image. She was the one who sent it to Eve in the first place. And someone had tried to kill her, too.

Noah groaned and pressed his fingers to his forehead, swallowed the growl of frustration rising in his throat. He couldn't think about Star now. If he could get to the bottom of this thing with Eve, it would all come out in the end.

Eve was hunting for the tomb of Genghis Khan. Someone had given her the incentive to move out of her comfort zone and go to Mongolia. With Star's help, she had found the location of the tomb but had died without actually visiting the site.

Why had she gotten on that plane to Mongolia the next day without the image? Had she memorized the coordinates? Maybe she hadn't wanted any physical evidence. Maybe it was her way of ensuring they kept her alive. If so, it hadn't worked.

A door clanged, and he glanced up. He didn't think it was mealtime, and he jumped to his feet, crossed to the front of the cell, and peered out. Pozniak strolled along the corridor, and he wasn't alone. Noah closed his eyes for a moment as relief flooded his system.

He stepped back as the door opened.

His uncle was dressed in civilian clothes, and Noah had never been so pleased to see anyone in his entire life. He stood in the open doorway and looked Noah up and down. "You need a shave. You look like shit."

"Yeah, thanks to this asshole." He nodded to where Pozniak stood off to the side. The other man just laughed.

Bastard.

"Let's get you out of here," Peter said.

"I can go?" He addressed the question to Pozniak.

He shrugged. "I have been assured that a terrible mistake has been made and keeping you longer could trigger an international incident."

"And you don't have anything on me," he guessed.

"I have an unlicensed gun taken from your hotel room and a false passport."

"Can I have them back?"

"No."

Peter shook his head. "Do we need to do any paperwork?"

"No, he's cleared to go. Just get him out of here and preferably out of the country."

"Good. Here are your things." He handed Noah a bag. It contained his watch—it was just after seven in the morning—and little else. Most of his stuff had been left in the hotel room.

He followed the two men down the corridor, his mind whirling with what to do next. He wanted to talk to Peter, but he'd been told not to talk to anyone, and he didn't want the conversation to be observed. While he doubted anyone would be watching the police station, maybe they would have spies at the hotel. He just didn't know what he was dealing with.

As they came out onto the street, he took a breath of fresh air then looked around him. Was anyone watching? He could see nothing out of place, but then on a busy street, it would be hard to tell.

"Can we go somewhere to talk?" he said.

"Of course. I'm at the Marriott," Peter said. "We can walk there. I'm amazingly interested to discover how you got yourself thrown into a Russian jail. I taught you better than that."

There were numerous answers he could have given. Probably the most accurate was that he'd slept with a woman he had no right to sleep with and let his guard down and paid the price. Though maybe sleeping with her was irrelevant and it would have gone down the same either way. Maybe the sex—which had been amazingly good—was his consolation prize for being a complete fucking dickhead.

So instead, he shoved his hands in his pockets and set off.

They walked the ten minutes to the Marriott in silence. As they crossed the reception area, he spoke again. "Can we talk in the bar?" He'd rather not go to Peter's room. Rooms could be bugged, but it was unlikely anyone would bug the public areas.

Peter cast him a thoughtful glance then nodded. "Though looking like that, they might refuse to serve you."

The bar was quiet, and they found a corner booth. Noah ordered a coffee and a sandwich. His stomach was in knots, but he needed to eat. Then he sat back, closed his eyes, and allowed the tension to drain from him. He had to think clearly, and his anger was clouding his mind. He waited until the waiter had brought their drinks, and then he opened his eyes. He picked up his coffee, took a sip, and forced the words out. "Someone took Harper."

Peter's eyes widened. "What?"

"Three nights ago. Stacey called me the following morning. They knocked out the guard on duty and took her from her room."

"Why? Have you heard anything?"

"Just a text saying not to talk to anyone and they'd be in touch. That was just before the police arrived." He hoped his phone was still in his hotel room. He needed to get back there, find out what they wanted in exchange for his daughter. Then he had to work out how he could get it.

"You can't talk about this to anyone," Noah continued. "They can't know I told you." He hadn't made the decision lightly, but he trusted Peter. And if something happened to Noah, then he needed someone who would go after Harper.

"Of course not." His uncle seemed shaken by the news, but then he was fond of Harper. "I can't believe this. What the hell was Eve involved in?"

"I don't know." Though he was starting to have a few ideas. Something occurred to him. "Did Pozniak contact you?"

"Who?"

"The Russian investigator who arrested me. Is that how you knew where I was?"

"No. I was trying to get hold of you. I uncovered some information that I thought you should know about. When I couldn't get you, I dug a little deeper and eventually found you. Not where I was expecting to. You want to share why you were arrested?"

"I might have pissed Pozniak off. And that was your teaching. You told me to push until I got answers. He was the lead investigator on Eve's accident. I may have hinted he took bribes, and I guess it pissed him off a little. When he got the chance for payback, he took it." Which reminded him — who had made the anonymous call to the police? He was guessing Star, but was there any way to find out? "So what did you discover?"

"I think I was wrong and there's a good chance that Eve's death was no accident."

Well, that wasn't news. "Go on."

"A week before she was killed, Eve was at a hospital in Ulaanbaatar."

"Why? Was she injured?"

"She was admitted on the first of June with a bullet wound to the right side."

"Bullet wound? Someone shot her?" He struggled to wrap his brain around the idea.

"It would seem that way."

Why was he so surprised? Someone had murdered her only a few days later. Was it the same people? Had they finished the job? "Police reports?"

"There were none. It would seem there was some…government interference. The police were asked not to pursue the investigation. A matter of national security, apparently. According to the records, she was in the hospital until the seventh of June when she was booked on a flight to London. She never made the flight."

"Instead she turned up dead in Russia."

"Maybe Russia was incidental. Maybe she just needed to get out of Mongolia and this was where she ended up. I had a look at the transport links. You can take a train from Ulaanbaatar to Irkutsk."

That would have appealed to her. Maybe she had just wanted somewhere to lay low while she worked with Star. Then she headed back to Mongolia once she had the information she needed.

"Did you find what you were looking for here?" Peter asked. "What *were* you looking for, anyway? What did you expect to find?"

Noah sipped his coffee while he thought about how to answer. How much to say and how much to keep back. "I was working with a woman called Sara Riley—also known as Star." Peter's eyes flickered at that. He knew something. Noah kept going. "Star is a space archaeologist who worked with Eve. She sent her an image the day before Eve died. A couple of days later, there was an attempt on her life, and she went into hiding. She saved my life, and we decided to work together. Star was scared. She couldn't go back until she worked out who was trying to kill her and why. I needed to know why Eve was dead. We had a common cause."

"Where is she now?"

"She disappeared just before I was arrested."

Peter reached into his pocket and pulled out his phone. He flicked through the images then showed a picture to Noah. A woman with blonde hair and ring in the side of her nose. She was also dead and on a slab in a morgue somewhere. Her head was turned slightly from the camera, and he could make out a tattoo on the side of her neck. A star. He'd never seen her before in his life.

Something churned in his stomach. He had an idea he wasn't going to like what came next. "Who is she?" he asked.

"Her name is Elizabeth Parker, also known as Star in the world of space archaeology, where apparently she's quite famous. Sound familiar?"

"What happened to her?"

"She was found dead on June the eighth. In a warehouse close to where she lived in London. The autopsy showed she died of a heart attack, likely induced by torture. The bones in her right hand had all been broken. Her apartment was burned out, her computer equipment stolen." He looked into Noah's face and raised a brow. "So whoever you've been with for the last few days, it wasn't 'Star.'"

He'd been played. And he was guessing by an

expert.

He stared at the dead woman then remembered the moment he'd seen the tattoo on Star's neck, and everything had seemed so obvious. Like taking candy from a fucking baby. He hadn't even questioned who she was.

Not even after she'd disappeared.

He tried to think back over their interactions. Was there anything he should have picked up on? Everything she had done and said had seemed so...believable. Right from the moment they'd met.

"Well?" Peter prompted.

"She saved my life." Another reason he hadn't questioned whose side she was on. Because she had saved him—which meant she was on his side. Maybe that had been a set up and she had orchestrated those murders. Maybe even killed the men in the SUV that night. Could the woman he knew be that ruthless? Except of course the woman he'd known was nothing but a construct. She'd been undercover, playing a part. And she was fucking good.

The parallels between the two of them were unbelievable.

Who the hell was she?

Could she have been responsible for Harper's kidnapping? Not personally, but could she be working for the same people? Maybe she'd even suggested that it might work. Might give him the incentive he needed. He'd talked to her about his children. She knew how he felt.

His anger was rising again, threatening to cloud his brain. And he needed clarity here. He slowed his breathing, waiting for the thud of his heart to calm. He couldn't afford the self-indulgence of anger right now. Later.

"I think you should back away from this, Noah. You're too close. Let your old team take over. We'll get Harper back for you."

He actually considered it. His team were the best. He'd worked with them for two years, and they were good. But his daughter's life was at stake. He was the only one who could save her. This was down to him. "I can't risk it."

"You have two more children."

Jesus. "Can you get them to safety?"

"Of course. We'll take them into protective custody."

They would be so scared. He was a complete failure as a father. He'd let them all down, but then, so had Eve. What had she allowed herself to get involved in? If he uncovered that, then hopefully, it would lead him to Harper. He needed to get back to the hotel, find out if the kidnappers had been in contact with him. What they wanted. Decide whether there was a way he could give it to them. He had an idea it was tied in with the image they'd found in the safety deposit box. In which case he was shit out of luck, because the image had gone, along with Star, whoever the fuck she was.

Which meant he'd have to find her.

He didn't even have a picture. If he'd had, he could have gotten Peter to run it through the facial recognition software and he might have come up lucky. Maybe there was something from the airport. "Could you check airport security surveillance when we left the U.K.? See if you can get a picture of my Star."

"Of course, send me the flight details."

"I will."

What a crappy mess. He stood up. "I have to go. You'll check in on the children?"

"Of course. But I wish you would rethink this."

"I can't."

CHAPTER TWENTY-ONE

He thought about getting a taxi, but in the end, he walked. He needed to clear his head.

Who the hell was she?

Had anything she said been the truth? It seemed unlikely.

He was almost back at his hotel when he became aware he was being followed. The tail was obvious, and he was pretty sure they weren't trying to hide. He didn't want to turn around and look in case he frightened them away. Right now, he was fresh out of leads and he'd talk to anyone.

He walked on until he came to a pedestrianized alley that ran between two blocks of buildings. Taking a sharp right, he took cover in a deep doorway a few feet from the street.

Soft footsteps approached. He waited, his gut tingling, his senses alert.

As the man drew level, his pace slowed. Noah stepped out.

He recognized his stalker instantly.

Zachary Martin. Rogue MI6 agent.

He'd been with Eve in Mongolia and was reported to have been in Russia the night she was murdered.

Noah whirled around, kicking the other man in

the chest, sending Martin crashing to the ground. Martin was fast, though, and he rolled to his feet, holding his hands up in surrender, but Noah was unarmed and couldn't take the chance his opponent would pull a gun on him at the first opportunity.

Besides, this was what he needed. What he'd wanted since he'd woken up and found Star gone and his life had turned to complete shit. He lashed out with his fist and caught Martin on the chin, the force of the blow sending him backward.

His eyes narrowed on Noah, then he swiveled and caught him in the ribs with a solid kick that sent him stumbling. Noah righted himself and swiped the other man's legs from under him. Grabbing his shirt, they both went down together, rolling on the ground. For a moment, Noah was on top, and he got in a good punch to the other man's face. Then somehow their positions were swapped and Noah was on his back, staring at the strip of blue sky between the tall buildings. An arm was wedged across his throat, cutting off his breathing, black spots dancing before his eyes. Pushing with all his strength, he ignored the sharp pain shooting through his shoulder. He managed to get his knees up between them, shoved hard, and tore the man's grip free, throwing off his weight and rolling to his feet in one smooth move.

He lunged forward then stopped.

His opponent lay on his back on the ground, a gun in his outstretched hand, aimed straight up at Noah's chest. Noah growled and took a step closer.

"Don't."

He gritted his teeth but held himself still.

"Do you remember me?" the man asked.

He nodded. "Did you kill my wife?"

"Ex-wife. And no. I didn't kill Eve."

Did he believe him? He had no clue. That was a pretty familiar feeling these days. "Do you know who did?"

"Maybe."

Noah forced his tense muscles to relax. "What do you want with me?"

"To talk. I think we're on the same side here."

"Which side is that?"

He grinned. "The side of the bloody righteous. And as a sign of good faith…" He lowered the gun then turned it in his hand and offered it grip first to Noah.

Noah looked at it for a moment then took it, shoved it down the back of his pants, and held out his hand. Zach grasped it, and Noah pulled him to his feet.

"Thanks," Zach said. "Did you know you're bleeding?"

Noah glanced down at his shoulder. He could make out the dark stain of blood against the dirty blue of his T-shirt. Looked like something had torn. He shrugged. "I'll live."

"Yes, but for how long?"

There was that question again. "Why were you following me?"

"I told you—we need to talk."

"So talk."

"Not here. I need a drink. There's a bar close by."

Part of him wanted to ignore the man—he needed to get back to the hotel, find out if Harper's kidnappers had contacted him—but he couldn't afford to ignore any potential source of information right now. At the same time, he wasn't sure that his room wouldn't be watched or bugged or both. So he nodded. "Lead the way."

The bar was directly opposite the hotel, and either it opened early or hadn't closed for the night. He followed Zach inside. Zach waved him to a table by the window and then headed to the bar. He came back a minute later with a couple of bottles of beer and handed one to Noah.

He didn't sit straight away. Instead, he went to stand by the window and stare out at the hotel across the road. He turned to Noah. "Eve called me from this bar—probably this exact spot—the night she was killed."

Shock coursed through him. He'd been about to take a mouthful of beer; now he put the bottle down. "Why?"

"She thought her life was in danger. Someone was waiting for her outside the hotel, and she believed they wanted to kill her."

"Why would she think that?"

"Because they'd already tried once before. And failed. She presumed they were back to finish the job."

Noah thought back to what Peter had said. Eve had been treated for a bullet wound at a hospital in Mongolia. "Was he the one who shot her?"

Zach smiled. "No. That was somebody else. Popular woman, your ex-wife. I liked her, you know. I liked her a lot. It took guts to come out here and do what she did."

"You know about the PTSD?"

"I know."

"So what changed? Why did she come?"

Zach ran a hand through his hair, a look of... regret flashing across his face. "Because I asked her to."

"Tell me."

Zach sank down onto the seat opposite him and took a gulp of beer. Giving himself time to think? Time to lie?

"About four months ago, my partner and I were caught up in a terrorist attack in Paris."

"I remember it," Noah said. He'd seen the reports. "A suicide bomber."

"Yes. My partner was injured—fatally, it turned

out. The only lead I had was a payment made out of an account in the Cayman Islands to the daughter of the suicide bomber. Then nothing until about a month ago, when I traced another payment from the same account to a U.K. bank. To a Dr. Eve Blakeley."

"What the hell?"

"Yeah, my thoughts exactly. While Eve at first seemed an unlikely terrorist, when you looked deeper, perhaps not so unlikely. There was the kidnapping, but there was also you."

Yes, she had more ties than most.

"I went to see her," Zach continued. "It turned out the money was a payment from a group who funded her research, the Mongolian Historical Society. They wanted her to lead an expedition to Mongolia to hunt for the Spirit Banner of Genghis Khan." Zach must have seen something in his face, because he shrugged. "Yeah, I know. I was the same. What the hell could that have to do with terrorism?"

"And she agreed to go?"

"No. She told me she didn't do field work. I persuaded her otherwise, and believe me, I regret it. Look, my partner had been dying a slow death for three months, and Eve was my only lead."

"The partner you supposedly killed?"

"Is that what you were told? Well, it's a lie. Though maybe I was responsible for her death."

He considered Noah for a moment. "Remember that thing we talked about? The global conspiracy?"

"I do."

"The day after my partner and I had gone to my boss with what I believed to be a pretty convincing argument, we were caught up in the Paris attack. It was a deliberate attempt to take us out."

"So MI6 is infiltrated."

"Every-fucking-where is infiltrated."

That was a whole other conversation, and right now, he wanted to understand what had happened with Eve. "So what went down in Mongolia? And why?"

Zach pursed his lips and then took a gulp of beer, obviously not entirely happy with what he was about to say next. "I think you need to suspend disbelief a little for the next part and just hear me out. I didn't believe it when I first heard, yet it makes a strange sort of sense."

Christ, nothing would surprise him with this. It was all fucking crazy. "Just get on with it."

"Okay, so Genghis Khan died around eight hundred years ago. And on his deathbed, he apparently made some sort of prophecy that one day someone would come along and complete his destiny of a unified global empire. And that day would only arrive when his soul was reunited with the Talisman."

"The Talisman?" From what Star—or whoever she was—said, that was the object buried with Khan, but he wanted to hear confirmation.

"I was putting off that bit because that's when things get really iffy. The Talisman is this artifact that Khan carried on campaigns with him. It had some sort of magical shit and guaranteed that he'd win every battle. It's buried with him."

"So whoever finds the tomb finds this Talisman and becomes the ruler of the whole world." This was just confirming what Don had told him, and Noah didn't like it any more the second time around. He emptied his beer and got up. He needed more to drink. "Another?"

"Yeah. It has that effect."

At the bar, he held up his beer and then two fingers and took the bottles back to the table. He wasn't sure what to make of Zach's story. While it was definitely far-fetched, it also corresponded with a lot of what he had learned so far. So he'd keep an open mind. For now. Did he trust the other man? Not entirely. He stared out the window like Zach had, imagining Eve standing in this exact same spot. And hours later, she was dead.

He slid back into his seat. "So Eve was looking for a magical talisman."

"You're getting hung up on the magic thing.

Don't you see? The magic part doesn't have to be real. It just needs enough people to believe. Bloody hell, most terrorist attacks are motivated by religious beliefs, some of them crazy as shit. Yet people believe them."

"Never underestimate the power of human stupidity."

Zach raised his beer. "Yeah, to that. But Tarkhan—he's the scholar working with Eve—believed it was true. That there's a secret organization, the Descendants of Genghis Khan, and they've been around for every one of those eight hundred years, spreading out across the world, infiltrating organizations and governments, putting things in place for the day when they take over." He cast Noah a look. "Does that sound familiar?"

It was exactly what they had talked about when they'd met two years ago. The theory he had discussed so many times with Peter.

That wasn't what he was struggling with, though. He'd always considered that if they found his spider, it would be something new, something born out of the aftermath of 9/11. Maybe even with an ultimate goal of stabilizing a world that was teetering on the edge of chaos.

Not some ancient organization searching for a magic talisman.

He scrubbed a hand through his hair. "So you

believe this is the group Eve was working for?"
Unknowingly, he imagined. Eve would never have
willingly worked for terrorists.

"I believe so. When I looked into it, the
Historical Society was nothing but an empty shell
set up to fund Eve's research. There was no trail to
follow."

Of course it was a shell. The reasons why
people did things often made no sense to
outsiders. As with most extreme groups who used
terror to get their message across, their reasons
and beliefs looked like nonsense to those brought
up to a contrary belief. Posing as a historical
society would eliminate any questioning.

But even if Noah suspended disbelief and told
himself yes, this group existed and they believed in
magical Genghis Khan artifacts—strongly enough
that they paid or coerced his ex-wife into hunting
for this spirit banner and tomb—it still made no
sense. "If she was working for them, why shoot
her?"

"Well, that's where it gets interesting. When
Genghis Khan died, he was buried in secret, like
really secret. And then everyone who was involved
and who knew the location was killed. They went
to incredible lengths to hide the location. One of
those lengths was a tribe of people—fifty families
at the start—who were to guard the area."

"Wait? There's an area?"

"It's known as the Great Taboo, and until recently, no one was allowed to visit. These families guard the place. They're called the Darkhats, and their one function is to ensure the tomb is never found."

"So *they* shot Eve."

"When she got close to finding the Spirit Banner, yes. One of their members, Yuri Vasiliev—"

"The Russian archaeologist working with Eve?"

"That's the one. He shot her."

He'd kill the bastard. Or would if he knew where the hell he was. "What happened to him?"

Zach grinned. "Eve stabbed him with the banner. He's dead. Hidden depths."

Noah couldn't help but smile at that. "She found the Spirit Banner?"

"She did. Then it was taken from her, and she was pissed."

"Who took it?"

"A John Chen."

"The *translator*?" Christ, was no one who they seemed? Didn't Eve have more sense than to go off into the fucking wilderness with a group of people she obviously knew nothing about?

"We believe he worked for the Descendants. He tried to kill her, but she stayed his hand. Told him she had information that would lead to the tomb. That kept her alive long enough for me to turn up and save the day."

Great. "Where the fuck were you while she was being shot?"

"That's another story, and it can wait."

Not for fucking long, but he didn't want to risk pissing Zach off before he'd gotten all the relevant information. "So what happened next?"

"Eve was in hospital. She was supposed to fly back to the U.K. Instead, she vanished."

Noah gritted his teeth. "Why the hell didn't you stay with her? Make sure she got back? You shouldn't have left her!"

"I know. But I didn't have a choice. I was about to be arrested by the Mongolian police, who weren't too happy about the number of dead bodies piling up. I was also pretty much under arrest by my own people, who took me back to London for debriefing. I did what I could. Got her some protection."

"For all the good it did."

"Yeah. I'm sorry. I believe the Descendants got to her, threatened her, or more likely threatened your children, and made her finish the search for the tomb."

"So you think the Darkhats killed her? To stop her from finding it?"

"I don't know. Except it was John Chen she saw that night."

A Descendant, then. Had they somehow found out that she had received the final image from Star — the *real* Star — and decided they didn't need her anymore? Sent this guy in to kill her and pick up the image? If that was the case, he had killed Eve but obviously failed to recover the image, and someone, somewhere must be pissed off. Unless they had gotten a copy off the real Star — she had been tortured, after all — and that's why they didn't need Eve. His Star had said that there were no copies, that she'd destroyed all the records once she had sent the original to Eve. But that could be a total fabrication. How could he believe anything she had said?

His head hurt.

"Before we go any farther," Noah said, "let me ask you something. Do you believe this stuff?"

"I don't believe in magic. The rest — yes, I believe it. I didn't want to at first. It seemed too far-fetched. But the more I thought about it, the more I realized that it fits. If I presume the terrorist attack in Paris was a response to my taking my theory to the next level, then there's a direct link to Eve's research. They were funded by the same source. I can't think of any other explanation. This central group orchestrated Paris to get me out of the picture, and they funded Eve's search for the tomb."

It did fit. And Noah had often found that the

most obvious answer, however unbelievable, was the right one. "Which means this group is out there and they've been out there for centuries, putting the pieces in place. And once they're in place, and they find the banner and the tomb, in their minds, they can and will take over the world."

"They already have the banner."

Shit. If the fake Star was working for them, they were close to finding the tomb. He needed to tell Zach about Star, but that was information he wasn't willing to part with just yet. Not until he was sure he could trust the man. For now, he had to get back to the hotel and find out if there had been any contact from Harper's kidnappers. What they wanted and how he could give it to them. He stood up. "I have to go."

"Just one more thing. I think this is happening soon. I've been following the patterns. I was heading to Germany before I came here. You heard about the attack?"

"The poisoned water supply?" He frowned. "You were there? Coincidence?"

"No. I told you I'd been following the patterns—same as you, I expect. I guessed the next attack would be in Germany, but I was too late to do any good, and no one would listen to me. I think the attack was to force the Germans to attend the—"

"The Global Terrorism Summit," Noah finished for him.

Zach smiled. "So you have been following. Yes, Germany was the only important nation not attending. They are now. And I think the big move is happening at the summit. I think they're planning something. Maybe taking out all the world leaders. They'll have people ready to replace them, and they'll be in control of the world's biggest nations."

That was it. That was the last puzzle piece. "Christ, that's less than a week away." It made perfect sense. He needed to contact Peter. Warn him. And he needed to get to the hotel.

Save Harper.

His head was spinning.

"Who is at the center of it all?"

"I don't know. I'd planned on following the banner, but it didn't happen that way. I lost it. But the answer is in Mongolia. In the Great Taboo."

Noah agreed. But right now, he had calls to make. "I have to go."

"I'm coming with you."

"No, you're not. The hotel might be watched, and I'd rather we weren't seen together. I'll meet you back here in thirty minutes."

CHAPTER TWENTY-TWO

The receptionist gave him a strange look as she handed over a new key card. Had she been on duty when Noah had been hauled off in handcuffs two days ago? He hadn't been paying that much attention.

He took the stairs two at a time. Now that he was alone, a sense of urgency filled him.

A woman with a cart was entering the room Star—no, Sara...or was that name a lie, too?—had used. Noah went and peered in through the open door, but all trace of Star was gone. Clearly she had packed up when she left two days ago.

Where was she now?

He went back to his own room, stood inside the door, and scanned the area. At first sight, it was exactly as he had left it. He did a second sweep, and his gaze snagged on a piece of paper on the coffee table. The hotel stationery. He picked it up; a single line was printed across the page. "Look in the fridge."

His gaze flashed to the small fridge under the TV.

His heart started a slow thud, and his skin prickled. He crossed the room slowly and stood for a moment staring down. Finally, he reached out and opened the door. A narrow black box, about six inches in length lay on the top shelf.

He didn't want to pick it up. Didn't want to look inside. And he had to force his hand to move forward. The box was light. Maybe it was empty. His breathing sounded harsh, loud in his ears, as he fumbled with the lid. It fell to the floor, and he stared at the contents.

A pale severed finger lay on a bed of red velvet.

For a moment, his mind went mercifully blank then filled with a rage he'd never encountered before. Someone would die for this. His vision clouded, and he had to force himself to examine the finger.

Small. Just the size of an eleven-year-old girl. The nail was short, unpainted. It had been severed cleanly just below the knuckle. Really, there was nothing to show that the finger belonged to Harper. How sad was it that he didn't even recognize his own daughter's finger?

He bent down and picked up the lid, covered the box, and stood, taking deep breaths. At that moment, across the room, his phone beeped. It was on the table beside the bed where he had left it two days ago, and he moved toward it, each step slow and deliberate as he wrapped himself in a cloak of control.

It was a text message.

You have five days to find the lost tomb.
After that, your daughter dies. Tell no one
or we'll send her back a piece at a time.

A video was attached, and he forced himself to press the play button and watch to the end, to listen to his daughter's screams. It was the least he could do. This was his fault. He'd failed to keep her safe, and now she was paying the price.

He swayed, light-headed, then sank down onto the mattress and lowered his head to his knees, gritting his teeth against the scream that welled up in his throat.

He'd seen worse things before, and always he'd managed to stay detached.

But this was Harper.

They'd cut off her fucking finger.

For a brief moment, he allowed the anger to wash over him, a red burning rage that filled his mind. Then he straightened, slowed his breathing, forced the anger down, and his mind cleared. He could do this. He had to. Right now, she was still alive, and he needed to keep her that way.

The Descendants were the ones who had her; he was sure of it. Who else would want him to find the tomb? Were they watching the hotel? Had someone seen him arrive and sent the text? Or maybe one of the hotel workers had been paid to make a call when he returned.

He read the rest of the messages on his phone. They were all from Peter, asking him to call. He didn't want to talk to Peter right now, but he needed to warn him about the summit, in case something happened to him—someone needed to know. He hit reply and sent a text message.

You need to check out the Global Terrorism Summit. Something big is going down there. Maximum security required.

He stripped off his clothes as he headed to the bathroom. The bandage on his shoulder was dark with blood, and a sharp pain jabbed him if he raised his arm. There wasn't a lot he could do now, but Star's first aid kit still sat on the table. He would take that, and Zach could check it out later.

He had to find Star and the image, and that would take him to the tomb. Except he had no clue where to start. So he was heading for the Great Taboo, because the tomb was somewhere in that area. He had five days to find it.

Or Harper died.

After dressing quickly, he shoved his things into his bag, including the box with the finger. He tucked Zach's pistol down the back of his pants, and he was ready to go.

The reception area was empty as he stepped out of the stairwell, except for the receptionist seated behind the counter. He walked toward her, dropped his bag on the floor, and drew the pistol in one fluid move. Her eyes widened, but she didn't move.

He pointed the gun at her face. "Did you just make a call about me?"

Her eyes were glued to the gun. Then they flicked over his shoulder toward the door, looking for a means of escape.

"Whatever they paid you, it's not worth dying over."

She gave a jerky nod.

"Did you see them?"

She cleared her throat. "No. They called."

"Write down the number for me."

She did, with a shaking hand. He glanced at the number, but it told him nothing, and then shoved the paper in his pocket and the gun back in his waistband. He picked up his bag and turned and walked away.

He realized as he pushed through the door that he hadn't paid the bill. He didn't turn back.

He had five days.

CHAPTER TWENTY-THREE

Zach watched him go. He had a feeling that Noah was holding something back. That he didn't entirely trust him. Could he blame the man?

All the same, they needed to work together on this, because he couldn't do it alone. And right now, Noah was his only option. Plus, while Zach had been cut off from the intelligence community, Noah still had connections.

After his failed trip to Germany, he'd come here because he'd used up all his other leads and had nowhere left to go. This was where Eve had died. Maybe he could backtrack somehow. Find John Chen. Kill the bastard, but only after torturing him to find out who he worked for.

While he'd found no trace of John, he had seen another face he recognized at the hotel where Eve had spent her last nights. Noah Blakeley. They'd worked a case together a couple of years ago and found they had a lot in common. But while Zach's bosses had written him off as a crazy guy with unsubstantiated conspiracy theories, Noah had been listened to. Perhaps having a bloody uncle who was also a general had something to do with that. He'd gotten to head up a special project focused on finding patterns in terrorist attacks.

Predicting where new attacks might happen.

Noah had been with a woman when Zach had spotted him, as different from Eve as it was possible to get. He didn't know her. He'd taken a picture and sent it off to an old buddy who still owed him a favor, but the results had come back negative—she didn't have a file. He'd watched them and seen the woman leave the hotel the next morning with a bag and Noah arrested a few hours later. Zach had been loitering ever since waiting for his new partner to get out of jail.

His phone rang. He glanced at the caller ID, but it wasn't a number his phone recognized. He accepted the call.

"Zach?"

The voice was familiar, and he exhaled. At fucking last. "Tarkhan. I've been trying to get hold of you for days."

"I was out of contact for a while. I've been laying low. But I might have some information for you. Someone you can talk to."

He'd asked Tarkhan to put him in contact with the Darkhats. They had a common enemy, after all. If they had been responsible for Eve's death, then they would pay, but only after they had helped him destroy the Descendants.

Tarkhan claimed he didn't know any Darkhats, that they were nothing more than a story people whispered in the shadows. Zach hadn't believed him.

"Where?" he asked.

"Meet me at the spot where you saved my life."

Very cryptic, though he knew the place. During Eve's search for the Spirit Banner, Tarkhan had taken a fall when his horse was shot dead from under him by a pursuing helicopter. He'd broken a leg, and Zach had gone back for him, got to him just before a vehicle had arrived to finish the job.

"I'll have company," he said.

"Who?"

"Noah Blakeley."

"Eve's husband?"

"*Ex*-husband, and he wants to know why Eve died. I believe he's a good man."

"Okay. Text me when you have a time."

He got another beer and sat back in his seat, angling the chair so he could watch out the window. Around twenty minutes later, Noah emerged from the hotel. He'd clearly showered and changed, and a bag was slung over his shoulder. There was a pinched expression on his face. Clearly something had happened since they'd parted.

He stood as Noah pushed through the door.

"Let's go," the man said. "You have a car?"

"Yes."

"Then you're driving."

Zach had left the car parked a few streets away,

and he led the way out the side door of the bar, along an alley, then onto the street. Beside him, Noah was silent, lost in his thoughts, his lips a tight line, a tic jumping in his cheek.

"What happened?" Zach asked.

"Nothing."

He thought about pushing it, but the other man seemed to be on the point of explosion. Maybe best give him time to calm down. As he stopped by a blue SUV, he hit the unlock button, and the car beeped. "I heard from Tarkhan," he said as they climbed in. "He arranged a meeting with some people who might be able to help."

"Who?"

"Darkhats, I believe."

"They're the ones who shot Eve, right?"

"Yes, but ultimately, they want the same thing we do. To stop the Descendants. And right now we don't have a lot of allies. As long as we're not trying to find the tomb, they should have no problem with us."

Noah cast him a glance he couldn't quite decipher. "Where?"

"The Great Taboo. Close to where Eve found the Banner." He turned on the engine and pulled out into the traffic before speaking again. "Who was the woman you were with?" he asked.

"The woman?"

"Pretty, dark haired—ring through her nose."

He glanced at Noah, saw his lips tighten. "I have no clue."

"Come on. I've told you everything I know. Give me a little something here."

"I told you, I don't know who she is. She told me her name was Star—"

"The space archaeologist Eve worked with?"

"So I was led to believe. However, the real Star was found dead shortly after Eve died. She'd been tortured. So I don't know who *my* Star was."

Zach had never met the woman, but Eve had liked her. The list of people who had died because of this was growing, but it was nothing to what would come afterward. "Have you any idea why she was killed?"

Another look, then Noah shrugged. "She was helping Eve to find the location of the tomb. I believe they found it. Star—the real Star—sent Eve an image showing the location, which she picked up the night she died. I'm guessing that's why they came after her. They meant to kill Eve—they didn't need her anymore—and take the image, which would lead them to the tomb."

"So they have everything they need?"

"No. They didn't find the image that night. Eve didn't have it on her when she was taken. My guess was they killed her prematurely, realized the image wasn't there. Then they took the real Star, trying to get a copy, but there were no copies. So they have to find the original. Or maybe they already have."

"Go on."

"We found it. In a safe deposit box in the Marriott hotel, where Eve went after she called you."

"So where the hell is it? You do still have it?"

Noah scowled. "The morning after we found the image, I woke up and Star was gone and the image with her. Shortly after, the police turned up, and I was arrested. Apparently, they received an 'anonymous phone call' that I was armed and dangerous and planning a terrorist attack."

"You think this woman made the call."

"Maybe."

"And you think she's working for the Descendants?"

"Maybe."

"Jesus," Zach growled. "Say something other than maybe."

They pulled up at a red light, and he cast Noah a sideways glance. He was frowning, then he gave a shrug. "We find the image, then we find the tomb, and no doubt we'll find our spider. He or she is coming for that talisman."

"You really think they'll come in person?" Zach wasn't convinced. They'd been so secretive up to now.

"Yes. It's too important. Too symbolic. They

won't be able to resist."

"What if they already have the image?"

"It doesn't matter."

"Yes, it does," Zach said. "We might never find them. You don't know this place. It's wild and vast, and people have been hunting for this tomb for years and never found it. If they have the location, they'll be in and gone with the Talisman while we're still stumbling around looking for them."

"Well, we'd better find the location then, or we're all fucked."

CHAPTER TWENTY-FOUR

Noah rested his head back and tried to make sense of it all.

When Zach had explained the Descendants and the Darkhats, Noah's initial reaction was that Star must have been working with the Descendants. That she'd latched onto him in the hope that he would lead them to wherever Eve had stashed the image.

Except Star had taken the image over two days ago now, and he had just received the text about Harper. Why would they be asking him to find the tomb if they already had the location?

Maybe whoever she was, she was working alone and had her own agenda.

Or was she with the Darkhats?

If so, there was one thing he didn't understand: he was still alive. These were ruthless people. While he was pretty sure the Descendants had killed Eve, the Darkhats had tried first. So why had Star left him in the land of the living? He'd been drugged. It would have been so easy to finish him off. Why hadn't she? Maybe she found it hard to sleep with a man and kill him the next day.

And then there was Harper.

Noah had decided back at the hotel that he

wasn't going to tell Zach about her. Not yet, anyway. He didn't know the man well enough to trust him with his daughter's life, and it was likely that he would not see Harper's safety as a priority here. Zach had already admitted that he was directly responsible for Eve's death. He'd used her when it must have been blatantly obvious that she was far from ready to be thrown into the middle of something like this.

But she had been Zach's only lead, and so he'd sent her out here — or at the least strongly encouraged her to come. And she'd died. He clearly felt guilty about that, but that didn't mean he wouldn't do something similar again. The man was driven. He would no doubt consider Harper to be collateral damage. Much like he'd seen Eve.

"You trust this Tarkhan?" he asked.

"As much as I trust anyone. And I told you — I saved his life. He owes me. Mongolians like to pay their debts; I've learned that much."

The truth was they needed back up. This organization — the Descendants — clearly had immense resources. They couldn't go up against them alone. And right now, he would take any help he could get. He just wouldn't trust the bastards.

"Okay, so we go to the meeting and see what they have to say. But you don't tell them I found the image. If they're as paranoid as you think, I won't last long once they know that."

"Okay."

"Tell me what you know about Tarkhan." He needed to understand who and what he was dealing with. He also needed something to take his mind off other things.

They'd chopped off her goddamned finger. She was eleven years old. What sort of monster could do such a thing? And they wanted to take over the world. What sort of world would they have with people like that in charge? He couldn't let his mind wander to what Harper must be going through. The best-case scenario was that they were keeping her drugged.

He wanted to kill someone so badly in that moment that his whole body tensed.

"Hey, are you okay?" Zach asked.

"I'm fine," he lied. He was as far from fine as he'd ever been. He had an eighteen-hour drive to try and come up with a plan. Though until he met these people, he wasn't sure what his next move would be. "Tarkhan?" he prompted.

"He's a historian who has spent most of his life studying Genghis Khan," Zach said. "Mainly working on analysis of various translations of something known as *The Secret History of the Mongols*. A sort of memoir of Khan. His parents were also historians. They taught at the university in Ulaanbaatar. But any study of Genghis Khan was frowned upon under the Soviet regime — they didn't want him to become a rallying point for the Mongolian people — so his parents were sent to a labor camp when Tarkhan was still a child. He grew up mainly with his grandparents. His father died in the camps. Tarkhan defied the regime, continued his studies in secret, or as it turned out, not so secret, as he also ended up in a labor camp. He spent twenty years there. Was released when the Soviet regime collapsed. He's one of the most respected scholars in the country. And he's been working with Eve for around six years."

From when she returned to the U.K. after their separation. She'd gotten a position in Cambridge almost straight away through a recommendation from her old professor.

"Though they'd never met before Eve's trip to Mongolia, they had talked a lot."

"And how does he tie in with these Darkhats?"

"I'm not sure. When he first told me about them, he made out that they were little more than a legend. That no one really knew whether they existed or not. However, I'm not sure that's the case. I think he knows they exist and has contacts within the organization, and he's sympathetic to their beliefs. It was Tarkhan I called the night Eve died. I thought he might have been able to get someone to her quicker than I could. Obviously not."

"Could he have turned on Eve? Maybe he didn't want her finding the tomb any more than his Darkhat friends."

"I don't believe so. He was genuinely fond of her. Besides, at that point, we didn't know she had the answer. Why kill her, then?"

"Maybe they didn't know where she was before."

"Are you saying I handed her to them?"

"It's a possibility."

Zach was quiet while he thought it through. "Perhaps," he conceded. "But I don't think so. I think John Chen killed Eve. She liked him. John Chen, I mean. Your ex-wife had atrocious taste in men."

"Yeah. Did she like you?"

"I think so." He sighed. "She was happy, you know."

Noah frowned. "You mean when she was shot or when she was killed?"

"When I met her in England, she was like…a shadow. Scared of everything. Closed off."

Noah had known that; he just hadn't been able to reach her. Hell, if he had, or even if he'd tried harder, then they might have stayed together. She might be alive. "Go on."

"When she came out here, it was like she was waking up. As if she'd been in a nightmare and she was only just escaping. She changed in front of our eyes. In the end, she faced up to her fears, and she was so fucking brave. She killed a man with a goddamn spear."

"And now she's dead."

A wave of exhaustion rolled over him. He hadn't slept too well in his prison cell. Too much on his mind, frustration, anger…fear. He wasn't really used to fear. Usually in times of conflict, his mind went crystal clear—he actually functioned better. This was different. Fear was like a live thing crawling inside him. Clawing to get out. Clouding his mind.

He rested his head back against the cool leather of the seat and closed his eyes. He cleared his thoughts, forcing out the anger and the images and the fear, leaving his mind blank. And finally, lulled by the motion of the car, he fell into a light sleep.

He woke briefly as they crossed the border into Mongolia. No one stopped them or questioned them, and they were through the border control in minutes. He took over to give Zach a chance to rest.

They swapped back a couple hours later. Noah managed to fall asleep again but woke at the sound of Zach's voice. He kept his eyes closed and listened.

"We'll be there around mid-day tomorrow," Zach said and then ended the call.

The car slowed, and Noah peered out of the window. They were pulling up in front of what he guessed was the Mongolian equivalent of a motel.

"We're stopping?" he asked, sitting up straight and running a hand over his eyes. The sun hadn't yet risen. The lights from the hotel reception lit up the parking area, but all around was darkness.

"For a couple hours."

"Why?" He didn't want to stop. He was on a schedule here.

"We can't take the car into the Great Taboo," Zach said as he turned off the engine. "The roads are non-existent. Last time, we used horses." A shudder ran through him. "Not happening again. I've organized an ATV. We'll pick it up where the tarmac ends."

"We can't go now?"

"The ATV won't be there until morning. I couldn't organize it sooner. Besides, it's not a good idea to drive off road in the dark. We'd likely crash."

It made sense, but he didn't like it.

CHAPTER TWENTY-FIVE

Noah shifted on the hard seat; his hands gripped the edges as they crashed over another bump in the non-existent road.

The ATV was an open-sided vehicle with a canopy of dark brown canvas across the roll bars to form a roof, which at least shaded them from the sun.

Zach was driving again. Noah's shoulder was aching like a bitch. Last night when they'd gotten to their room, Zach had cleaned it up as best he could. Another of the stitches had torn, but the rest had held, and he didn't think it needed more—just a tight bandage to hold it together. And probably him resting for a few days, which wasn't going to happen. Zach had done the bandaging and then insisted on giving him an antibiotic shot just in case.

He'd talked to Peter. Lucy and Daniel had been moved to a safe house, and he'd spoken to Eve's parents and told them it was just a precaution.

Noah hadn't mentioned Zach. He was wanted by his own people, and Peter might have felt compelled to hand him over. Right now, Noah's need was greater.

The first couple of hours had been driving on tarmac. Then the road had come to an end, and they swapped the car for an ATV. Now, they were driving along a dirt track over rolling hills. A mountain range loomed ahead of them, beneath a deep blue sky. They hadn't seen another vehicle for over an hour. He didn't think he had ever been anywhere so remote. They did see the occasional bird of prey hanging high overhead, and once a group of wild, feral-looking ponies galloped along beside them for a few miles. Otherwise, the place was vast and empty.

They came to a stream, and Zach drove straight through it, water splashing over the sides, then up the other bank without slowing.

"Hey," Noah said, clutching tighter onto the roll bar. "You do know where you're going, right?"

"Same route as last time. I have a photographic memory for routes. We were on ponies then, so it took a lot longer. Eve looked great on a pony. I fell off."

Noah smiled picturing the scene. While he'd never ridden with Eve, he knew she had as a child, and all their children had taken lessons. He'd learned to ride in Afghanistan by necessity. He'd been undercover with one of the mountain tribes for a while. He'd liked it—until his horse had been shot from under him by a sniper.

After another hour, Zach slowed the vehicle

and waved a hand out of the window. "This is where we camped for the night. We'll stop for a minute. Have something to eat. Drink…whatever else. We're close now, and we have an hour before we're due to meet Tarkhan."

Noah got out, rolling his shoulders to ease the tension. It was nearly noon, and the sun was high overhead and hot on his skin. Only weeks earlier, Eve had stood in this very place, and a few days after that, she'd been dead. A wave of sadness washed through him. He'd been too busy in the days and weeks following her death to mourn her. Also maybe a little bitter. She'd left him because of the inherent danger in his job, but then she'd somehow managed to get mixed up in something just as dangerous, got herself killed, and fucked up his life. It had been a selfish thought, and he was ashamed for even thinking it.

He went back to the vehicle and got the small black box from his bag. Zach was nowhere to be seen, and Noah walked away from the ATV into the shadow of the trees. At the base of a tall birch tree, he dug a hole and buried his daughter's finger.

Her mother had been close by. It would have to do.

He stood for a moment but couldn't think of anything to say, then he shook his head and headed back. He pulled a bottle of water from the cooler in the back of the ATV and perched on a rock. He was trying not to think about Harper. Why hadn't he done more to keep her safe?

Maybe he was wasting time. He should contact her kidnapper. Lie. Tell them he had the location and would give it to them in exchange for his daughter. Somehow, he would make it work.

And would it really make a difference if they got this talisman or not?

The thing that held him back was that he didn't trust them not to kill Harper anyway. These were ruthless people. They'd killed Eve, and she had evidently been working for them. There had been no real reason for her death. So he had to work out a plan that would guarantee Harper's safety, and right now he was scrambling to find an answer. Maybe after this meeting, he would have a clearer picture, would be able to see a way forward.

One thing he did know—if any more harm came to Harper, he would dedicate his life to hunting down her kidnappers and ensuring they suffered the same fate.

Zach cleared his throat, and Noah glanced up. The other man stood a couple of feet away and was watching Noah, a small frown between his eyes. "Is there something you're not telling me?"

Noah swallowed the last of the water and stood up. "Why do you ask?"

Zach snorted. "Just a guess. For a moment there, you looked like you wanted to kill someone. Like it was personal."

"It is personal. They murdered my wife."

"Ex-wife."

Why the hell did he keep emphasizing that? Just what had his relationship been with Eve? "They killed my *ex*-wife. And they had a damned good try at killing me."

Zach studied him for a minute longer. "I think there's more. You still don't trust me. I can't say I blame you totally, but we're in this together." When Noah didn't reply, he frowned. "Well, if you feel the need to share, I'm here. Let's go. It's nearly time."

Noah climbed back into the passenger seat of the ATV and braced himself against the inevitable bumps and jolts. They were driving through a narrow valley between two steep rises, the sky a deep blue strip above their heads.

Zach slowed the vehicle. "The attack happened not long after we set off that morning," he said. "A helicopter came from behind and started shooting. The horses were out of control. Tarkhan's was shot from under him, and he went down."

Noah could picture it, the helicopter overhead, the horses panicking, nowhere to go but straight on. He searched the area and saw what must be the carcass of Tarkhan's horse. It had been picked clean, only the bones left. Vultures or dogs. Did they have wolves here? He wouldn't be surprised.

"Tarkhan broke a leg but managed to drag himself to cover over there." Zach waved a hand to the left where an area of huge boulders would provide a place to hide. He increased their speed and drove for another few minutes then pointed to what looked like a gap in the wall of the canyon, protected by a rocky overhang. "The rest of us took cover in there, but it's a dead end. And it was only a matter of time before they picked us off. Or landed and came after us on foot. We had two pistols between us—not enough to fight off well-armed men." He pulled the ATV to a halt and switched off the engine.

"Two pistols? You and John Chen?"

"Actually, Yuri had one as well, but he wasn't letting on back then."

Noah followed him out of the vehicle. About fifty yards away, he could see the burned-out wreckage of a helicopter. Choppers could be vulnerable, all the same, taking one down with a handgun was pretty impressive. "How did you bring it down?"

Zach scanned the area then pointed to a ledge about twenty meters' climb up the side of the canyon. "I positioned myself there, and John distracted them from the ground. I took out the pilot."

"Good work."

"Yeah. After that, Eve, John, and Yuri went off after the spear. I went back for Tarkhan. I was going to have to stretcher him out—we had one horse between us, and he was in no state to walk or ride. Then we heard a vehicle approaching. I provided a distraction, and we managed to take it and go after Eve."

"A busy day." He thought for a moment. "So you know who they were?"

"Not really. At the time, I thought they were on the same side as the helicopter. Since then, I've changed my mind. I think they were on different sides. I think the helicopters belonged to the Darkhats—the same side as Yuri. They wanted to stop Eve from finding the spear. The guys in the land vehicle were John Chen's lot. They were there as back-up but also to get John and the spear out once they had found it."

Noah went still as a shiver ran down his spine. They weren't alone.

Zach opened his mouth, but Noah gave a small shake of his head. A rider appeared at the top of the canyon, silhouetted against the blue sky. Then another and another, until there was a line of them staring down. "Looks like Tarkhan brought a few of his friends along. What do you want to do?"

Zach's eyes narrowed. "I think we should get the fuck out of here."

They walked slowly backward until they hit the ATV. Noah squinted upward, but he was looking into the sun and couldn't make out any details of the riders. Were they armed?

They both climbed in, the skin of his shoulders prickling in anticipation of a bullet. Zach started up the engine. They pulled away, and Zach turned the vehicle around so they were facing the way they had come. Then he hit the gas, and they shot forward. Noah gripped the bars of the cage to stop from being thrown around.

He glanced back over his shoulder as riders appeared around a bend in the canyon, galloping flat out toward them. He heard the crack of a rifle. Drawing the pistol, he turned in his seat. He aimed, shot, and one of the riders fell, but there were too many and he was soon out of ammunition.

"In front of us," Zach said, and he turned back. A horse galloped toward them, the rider leaning to the side, a rifle in his hand. The loud crack of a shot and the ATV lurched to the right.

Then they were rolling, and Noah was thrown around inside the cage. His shoulder slammed into the bars, and pain flashed through him. Then the vehicle hit the canyon wall and came to an abrupt halt. His head crashed against the roof of the cage, and everything went black.

When he opened his eyes, he was upside down. He blinked to clear his vision and could make out a sea of legs surrounding the vehicle.

Beside him, Zach groaned.

The door was wrenched open from the outside, and a hand reached inside, grasped his arm, and pulled him out. He grabbed the edge of the vehicle for support as his legs threatened to give way under him. He swayed then took stock. He didn't think he was badly hurt, though blood trickled down his forehead from a cut on his scalp and he was sure the wound in his shoulder had opened up again.

He glanced across as Zach was pulled from the vehicle and caught his gaze. Zach shrugged. At least he looked in one piece, but how long would that last?

They were surrounded by armed men.

Mongolians, from the dark hair and eyes, their clothing a mixture of denim and leather. Behind them, he could hear the stamping and snorting of horses.

Without warning, someone kicked him from the side. His legs were swept out from under him, and he crashed to the hard ground, landing on his damaged shoulder. Pain lanced through him, and he swore under his breath then rolled onto his back.

His hands were wrenched in front of him, metal cuffs snapped onto his wrists, and he was yanked to his feet again. Across from him, Zach didn't seem to be getting the same treatment. He was talking with a tall man who appeared to be their leader, their voices too low for Noah to pick up what they were saying. They both glanced his way, and Zach caught his gaze and gave another shrug.

"Tarkhan has vouched for me. I have safe passage. You, they're not sure about. Apparently, they suspect you may be working for the Descendants. Plus, you shot one of their men. They're not happy."

He wasn't fucking happy, either. He didn't have time for this. He forced his breathing to slow. This was not a situation where losing his temper would help, but he could feel the waves of panic building inside him. Swallowing, he took a slow deep breath. "So what happens now?"

"I've persuaded them not to kill you on the spot, which was option number one. They're going to take us to their base camp and then decide what to do with you. So spend the time working out how you can convince them you don't work for the Descendants and you haven't been trying to find the tomb of Genghis Khan."

He didn't get a chance to say anything in

reply—his arm was jerked and he was led to where a dark brown horse with a black mane and tail stood, head almost hanging to the ground. It looked up and snorted as they stepped beside it.

The man said something, presumably in Mongolian, he had no clue what. Then he nodded to the horse. Presumably he was to get on.

Noah lifted his cuffed hands to the pommel of the saddle, stuck his foot in the wide stirrup, and pulled himself up. The man tied a rope to his cuffs and lashed it around the pommel holding him in place then took the horse's reins. He crossed to the next horse and leaped into the saddle, and then they were moving. The horse whinnied as the reins were pulled taut, and Noah balanced himself as the horse danced under him. He glanced over his shoulder; Zach was toward the rear of the group, looking awkward and uncomfortable in the saddle. Then the speed picked up, and he tightened his grip on the pommel and closed his knees around the horse's side.

The sun was hot on the back of his neck, and he felt lightheaded, probably from hitting his head. Hopefully he didn't have a concussion. He had to decide how he was going to persuade them he didn't work for someone he hadn't even known existed until a few days ago. Even now he wasn't totally convinced it wasn't all some fabrication. This whole thing was surreal.

Maybe the truth was his best option. At least up to a point.

They rode through a sparse forest, and it was cooler under the canopy, the light dappled. Then they splashed through a shallow stream and up the opposite bank. He'd eventually gotten the feel of his mount and finally relaxed in the saddle, going with the horse's movement.

They'd had files on all the major terrorist groups when he'd worked for Project Arachnid, and he had never come across the Descendants of Genghis Khan. Or anything to do with Genghis Khan, for that matter. Could they be so powerful and yet so well hidden? It didn't seem possible that he'd not even had a whiff of them.

Having said that, it tied in almost perfectly with his own theories. An organization without allegiance to any country or government at the center of it all, using other groups to do their dirty work. Setting things in motion, putting the pieces in place.

And now they were almost ready to make a move. After which he suspected the world would never be the same.

They had to be stopped. There were only days to go before the summit, days to go before Harper would die if he didn't give them what they wanted. And how could he do that when he was handcuffed on the back of a goddamn horse going

God knew where?

The panic was rising again, blurring his mind.

These people had to be the Darkhats. And according to Zach, they'd tried to kill Eve more than once, even if they hadn't succeeded. He supposed he was lucky he was still alive.

Could they be allies? As Zach said, they had a common enemy. If he managed to persuade them he wasn't working for the Descendants and had fuck-all interest in finding anyone's tomb except so far as it might mean life or death for his daughter, maybe he stood a chance at winning them over.

He glanced around and realized that the group had shrunk. Obviously many of the riders had peeled away and disappeared off in another direction. Zach was still at the rear and still on his horse, if only just. He caught Noah's gaze and scowled. Had he led Noah into a trap?

His gut feelings told him no. That Zach could be trusted. Only thing was he wasn't sure he trusted his gut anymore. His gut feelings hadn't done him any good where Star was concerned. He'd never questioned that she was who she'd said she was, and he'd believed every word that she'd spoken. He'd let his guard down, and look how that had ended up. He still had no clue who she really was and who she worked for.

His head hurt, and his shoulder hurt.

They'd been riding around two hours, and he still hadn't decided what his next move should be—not that he had many options—when he caught sight of where they were heading. A camp of sorts, though there were no permanent structures, just a number of the large circular yurts he'd seen dotted around the Mongolian landscape. They rode through the camp and to a corral on the other side. His horse halted. He couldn't dismount because his hands were tied to the pommel, so he waited, trying to push down his impatience, that feeling that time was running out. That they were all teetering closer to the edge of the abyss.

All around him, men dismounted, unsaddled their horses, and released them into the corral, where they shook themselves and got down in the dirt and rolled away the sweat. He looked around for Zach, but he'd disappeared, and nobody seemed to be taking much notice of him. Finally, someone untied the rope that bound him to the saddle, and he swung his leg over and stepped down, trying not to jolt his shoulder, which was on fire. He leaned against the horse for a moment, swaying as a wave of weakness washed over him. His mouth was dry.

At that moment, Zach appeared at his side eying him up. "You look like shit."

"Thanks."

"Here." He handed Noah a bottle of water, and

he took it with his cuffed hands and drank, feeling almost immediately steadier. "Look," Zach said, "there's something you need to know. Something they told me on the way here. I still can't quite believe it."

Noah frowned. "What?"

"Noah?"

At the woman's voice, he turned around, his eyes widening. What the hell?

"*Eve?*"

CHAPTER TWENTY-SIX

Was he hallucinating?

Maybe he'd banged his head harder than he thought when the ATV crashed.

He blinked a couple of times. She'd come to a halt only feet away from him. She looked real. And alive.

In fact, she looked good, if a little pissed, her mouth in a tight line, her eyes narrowed, hands on her hips. She wore a pair of denim shorts and a tank top, her arms and legs brown from the sun.

"You're not dead," he said.

"Really?" She sounded…sarcastic.

He ran a hand through his short hair, trying to get his brain to function a little faster. "Eve, what the hell's happening here?"

She took a step closer to him, within touching distance, then raised her hand and stroked her fingers over his forehead. He winced. Then her gaze dropped to his shoulder, and her eyes narrowed even further. "You're bleeding."

He glanced down; the material of his T-shirt was drenched with blood. He must have torn open the wound pretty badly this time. Right now, he didn't care. Right now, he just wanted to know how his dead wife had suddenly miraculously come to life. Not that he wasn't happy, he just wanted to understand.

Because absolutely nothing made sense.

He took a step toward her, swayed. His head swam. Then the ground was somehow coming to meet him. He put his cuffed hands out to break the fall, but they gave way, his strength gone. And then for the second time that day, everything went black.

When he came around this time, he was lying on his back, staring up at an off-white canvas ceiling. He was on some sort of mattress on the ground. He thought about moving but decided he didn't want to quite yet.

"Couldn't you have looked after him a little better?"

That was Eve's voice, so he hadn't imagined her after all. She was alive. He tried to get his head around that—how he felt. He wasn't sure. Why the hell had she let them all believe that she was dead? Him, maybe he could understand. But the children?

"Hey, I didn't shoot him," Zach said. "And I think your husband—"

"Ex-husband."

"Your *ex*-husband is quite capable of taking care of himself." He looked at Noah, saw he was awake. "He's back with us." He turned his attention to Noah. "You've got to stop this fainting business."

As Noah made to push himself up, Eve placed a hand on his good shoulder and shoved him back down. "Stay there."

He didn't remember her being this bossy. Maybe that's what rising from the dead did for you. She was kneeling at his side, a pair of scissors in her hand. He stayed still; he wasn't sure how safe this was. She cut his T-shirt up the middle and peeled it away from his shoulder then cut through the sodden bandage and did the same with that. He tried to raise his head to look at the wound, and she frowned. "Stay still."

He stared up at the ceiling. Right now, it seemed like good advice. He might never move again. Except he had to, because Harper was relying on him.

Oh God, Harper. He had to tell Eve, though he didn't want to while Zach was in the room. Actually, he didn't want to at all. He was going to break her heart. First, he wanted to know what the hell was going on. Were they all prisoners? Though at least the cuffs were gone.

He searched her face. She looked good. Always before there had been a hint of fear, a darkness behind her eyes as though she had seen bad things and expected them to happen again. Now her expression was clear, the lines between her brows smoothed away. "You look good for a dead woman."

"I'm sorry." She must have taken his words as an accusation, and he supposed they were.

He tried to shake his head, but pain flashed through him. He sank back down to the ground. "What happened?"

"The crazy fucking Darkhats happened." She took a deep breath and visibly calmed herself. "Just let me clean this up, then we'll talk." She pressed a warm damp cloth to the wound in his shoulder, and he held himself very still. A waft of antiseptic filled the air, and sweat broke out on his forehead. She pressed harder, and he hissed. Finally, she took the cloth away and examined the wound. "You need a doctor."

Zach came and hunkered down beside him, studied his shoulder. "No. The bleeding has already stopped. He could maybe do with another stitch in there. I can do it." He stood up and rummaged through what Noah presumed was a medical kit. He came back with a syringe. Without saying anything, or asking permission, he crouched down again and jabbed the needle into Noah's arm, just below the wound. He pressed the plunger, pulled it out, and jabbed him again on the other side. It was over before Noah could protest. Not that he wanted to. Almost immediately, the pain receded, a lovely numbness taking its place. "Local anesthetic," Zach said. "Give it a minute to work, and I'll sew you up."

Noah turned his head so he could see Eve. "Talk," he said.

She pursed her lips then sat back on her heels and ran a hand through her hair. "Zach told you I called him that night?" He nodded. "I was scared. I believed John Chen had come back to finish the job. After I called Zach, I went to the Marriott, got a room, and waited for someone to come and rescue me." She snorted, casting Zach an accusatory glance, before shifting her gaze to Noah to give him more of the same. "I called you. You weren't there. But then what's changed?"

He considered pointing out that she was actually the one who had left him. Plus he was in the States and would have been able to do little to help her in some out-of-the-way town in Russia, but he decided to keep his mouth shut. In some ways, she was right—he had never been there for her, always off on some job of his own.

"I tried to stay awake but must have dozed off, because I woke in the night, and someone was in my room. I felt a jab on my arm and after that, nothing. The next time I woke up, I was in a goddamn yurt."

He'd never known Eve to swear so much. She had definitely changed. And actually, it was for the better. He needed her to be strong because he was going to have to tell her about Harper; it wasn't something he could keep from her.

"I had no clue what was going on. They wouldn't tell me anything."

"You were a prisoner?"

"Yes, and I was going crazy not knowing what was happening. I didn't even know who they were, which side they were on. And I didn't know you all thought I was dead until Tarkhan turned up a week later, by which time I was going seriously crazy. He told me that when Zach had called him for help, he hadn't known what to do. He was in Mongolia; no way could he reach me in time. Besides, he was still on crutches from his broken leg and hardly in a position to help. So he'd reached out to someone he trusted. Tarkhan has been around a long time. He knows lots of people. He'd been in a labor camp with some man who was high up in the Darkhat hierarchy under the Soviet regime. They're good friends. The Darkhats already had people in Russia—following John Chen, actually. He'd been flagged when he came into the country, and they'd been watching for him since he ran off with my spear." She paused for breath, and Zach leaned closer and pressed a finger to Noah's shoulder. He felt nothing. Bliss.

"Just let me do this," Zach said.

Eve nodded and got to her feet, paced the

room, peered out the flap that covered the opening of the yurt, then came back to stand over him, foot tapping on the ground. He glanced at his shoulder, where Zach was threading a needle through his skin, drawing the edges of the wound together. He felt nothing. Finally, Zach snipped off the suture with a pair of scissors. "Done."

"Go on," he said to Eve, pulling himself into a sitting position. He was fed up with lying down.

She sank onto the floor and sat cross-legged, facing him. "Once Tarkhan came, things were better. While I was still a prisoner, they let me wander around the camp. Tarkhan eventually told me that they'd faked my death. I begged to call you and the children, to let you know I was alive, but they wouldn't allow me any contact. I was still considered pretty high on their enemy list. They'd saved me because of Tarkhan. I suspect, if it hadn't been for him, they would have put a bullet in my head before John even had a chance. Especially if they'd known I'd found the location of the tomb."

"They don't know you found it?"

"It wasn't something I wanted to tell them. I didn't know how far Tarkhan's friendship would stretch. They might have shot me anyway." She frowned. "How did you know I had the location?"

"We found it in the safe deposit box at the Marriott."

She glanced between him and Zach, who was

rummaging again in the medical kit, presumably looking for a bandage. "The two of you? You've been working together?"

"No. I was working with someone else. A woman claiming to be Star—"

"Star?" She jumped on the name, a smile breaking out on her face. "She's okay? I was worried that someone might have gone after her."

He should have kept quiet. "Star is dead. Her body was found not long after we got the notification of your death. She'd been tortured. They believe she died of a heart attack under interrogation."

Eve blinked. "She once told me she had a weak heart. It's one of the reasons she took up what she did. It was something she could do with little physical exertion." She was silent for a moment. "Bastards. Do they know who did it?"

"No."

She frowned. "But you said Star helped you."

"I thought it was Star. She had a tattoo of a star on her neck and claimed to be her. She told me she'd worked with you. She had a lot of information. I never doubted her."

"So she was probably someone working for Star's killers?"

"I don't know. Maybe." That didn't make a lot of sense, though, because if she was, then why were they still trying to get him to find the tomb when Sara could have given them the location herself? Why were they threatening to kill his daughter if he didn't do as they asked? All he could think was maybe Sara had gone out on her own, planning to sell the information to the highest bidder.

"There's something else," he said. "But finish your story first." He wasn't sure how much he would get out of her once he had told her about Harper, and he needed to know all the facts.

Eve shrugged. "There's not a lot else. I've been here ever since. People come and go, but I think this is a permanent base camp. Well, as permanent as they get. They like to follow the old ways, or so Tarkhan tells me. Anyway, he left a week ago then arrived back last night and informed me that you and Zach were on your way. And that's it."

"Do you know what happened to John Chen?" Zach asked.

"Not for sure." She bit her lip. "I think they took him. Tortured him to find out where the spear was. I don't think John would have talked, so I'm guessing he's dead now. These people are ruthless. So what happens now?"

Zach came over with the bandage, and Noah pushed himself to his feet then raised his arm to allow him to wind the bandage around the wound. He rolled his shoulders but felt nothing; the area was still numb.

"Our biggest problem is the summit," Zach said. "It's connected to what's going on here."

"What's the summit?" Eve asked.

"A meeting of all the top leaders to discuss a global response to terrorism. It's taking place in Russia in four days' time, and we believe they're going to do something big—probably take out all the world leaders."

"Who is?"

Zach and Noah exchanged a glance. "The Descendants."

They were in agreement there. But the summit wasn't Noah's priority—Harper was. Even so, while he had no clue what the Descendants were planning, like Zach, he was guessing it would be big, and it couldn't be allowed to go ahead.

"I sent a message to Peter," he said. "He should have flagged an alert by now. Hopefully they'll stop it or at least up the security, but there's no guarantee they'll take the warning seriously without evidence to back it up. We need to get them something, and fast." *After* he had found Harper. He wouldn't do anything overt until his daughter was safe.

He wandered over to the doorway and peered out. There was no guard, but armed men and women were milling around the area. Likely, he'd get some attention if he stepped outside. The camp was quite large from what he could see, maybe between twenty or thirty yurts, and the corral had held around a hundred horses. There had been guards at the perimeter.

He had no doubt that they would shoot him if he attempted to leave.

He glanced back at where Eve stood talking to Zach. There was a closeness to them, and as he watched, she reached out and touched him on the arm. It was a curiously intimate gesture. Just how close had these two gotten? He shook off the thought, because really, it should be none of his business.

"Eve."

She must have heard something in his voice, because she glanced up then came toward him. "What is it?"

He looked at Zach, but he figured it was safe to talk in front of the other man. He had an idea Eve would tell him anyway. Just how the hell was he supposed to word this? "It's Harper," he said. "Someone took her."

For a moment, the words didn't seem to sink in, and she blinked a couple of times. "I don't understand."

"She was taken from your parents' house four nights ago."

"Why? Who took her? Is she all right? Oh my God."

"I was arrested almost immediately after I

found out and had no contact for two days." He swallowed. "When I got back to the hotel, they'd left me her finger."

She made a small noise and swayed. Noah reached for her, but Zach beat him to it, wrapping an arm around her shoulder and holding her against him.

"What do they want?" Zach asked.

"They want me to find the tomb. And I have a week to do it. Less now."

Zach frowned. "Why would they think *you* could find it when everyone else failed?"

"Maybe because I was tracking Eve. I assume they know she had the location before she died — or they think she died. Maybe they got that much from the real Star."

"The Descendants?"

He nodded. Eve still hadn't spoken, her face pressed into Zach's chest, but now she raised her head. Her eyes were dry, haunted, and her skin was pale. "I should never have left them. I should never have gone after the spear. If only I hadn't come here. She must be so scared. And hurt." She pulled free and took a step toward him. "Are you sure? That the finger was hers?"

"There was a video." He took her hand. "At least it proved she's alive and we'll get her back."

"How?" She turned away and wrapped her arms around her middle, paced the length of the yurt then came back to stand in front of them, biting down hard on her lower lip. Then something flared in her eyes. "What about Lucy and Daniel?"

"They're fine. Peter has them in a safe house, his own people watching them."

"We've got to get out of here, and then we give them what they want. If they want the tomb in exchange for Harper, then give them the goddamn tomb. What does it matter?"

He took a deep breath. "I don't have the location."

"But you said you got into the safety deposit box. You said you had it."

"Sara took it. The fake Star. The morning after we found it, she disappeared. I assume she made the phone call to the local police and got me arrested." He studied Eve. "Can you remember the location? Could you reconstruct the image?"

She shook her head. "No. I didn't have much time to study it. I was so rattled that night, I just put it in the safe deposit box."

He pressed a finger between his eyes, trying to get his brain to see a way through this. One thing was for sure—they had to get out of here. Then he had to find Sara, and he had no clue how to do that. He could feel the panic rising inside him, swirling in his mind, choking him, Harper's scream echoing in his head. He shut it down. "Is Tarkhan still here?" he asked Eve.

"I think so."

"Then let's go talk to him. I think we need to tell him the Descendants are planning something at the summit. It sounds like our best chance of getting their cooperation. At least we can get an idea of who these people are. Whether we can expect any help from them."

He watched as Eve visibly pulled herself together. She was a different woman than the one who had left him. Somehow she had conquered her fears. While she was clearly devastated by the news, she was functioning. She gave a quick nod.

He was naked from the waist up, but his T-shirt was clearly unwearable. And his bag was nowhere in sight. There wasn't a lot he could do about it. Eve led the way out, then Zach. As Noah made to exit the tent, a man stepped in front of him, a rifle in his hands. He gestured with it back into the tent.

Eve turned back, a frown on her face. She said something in what he guessed was Mongolian, but the man just shrugged.

"You're not to leave the yurt," she said. "We'll find Tarkhan and talk to him."

He clenched his teeth but gave a curt nod then glanced at Zach. "Make this work."

CHAPTER TWENTY-SEVEN

No.

The word was screamed over and over in Eve's mind. Panic clawed at her stomach, fear threatening to crawl out of her throat.

She'd lived with PTSD for twelve years, and for most of that time, panic and fear were close companions. She thought she'd conquered her fears, but obviously they were just waiting in the background for something to bring them front and center of her life again.

Oh God. Harper.

She couldn't get her head around it. Her brain refused to process the information. Her vision blurred, and she stumbled, felt Zach take hold of her arm and steady her.

"I'm sorry," Zach said. "If I'd left you alone, not bullied you into the trip, then none of this would have happened."

Eve ignored the comment, mainly because he was right. It was irrelevant now. She *had* come on the trip, and it had happened. And now, some depraved monster who cut the fingers of innocent children had her beautiful daughter. She held her lips tight together to stop the whimper falling out. She couldn't bear to think about it. Harper scared and alone, in pain.

Unconsciously, she rubbed her hands together, tugging at her fingers. How much would it hurt? To lose a finger. Which finger was it? She almost turned around to go ask Noah. As though it mattered. She forced herself to walk on.

"They likely have her sedated," Zach said from beside her.

She stopped again and turned to face him. "You don't know that."

"And you don't know she isn't." He rested a hand on her arm, squeezed. "Look, Eve, you have to get past this. And it won't help imagining what your daughter is going through. Imagining the worst. Just focus on finding a way through. Of getting her back."

She searched his face. She'd thought they were growing close before all this had happened. When they'd been traveling together. However, she also knew how highly motivated he was. "Do you even care? Or is this just a way to get to your terrorist?"

"I care."

"Harper comes first," she said fiercely. "She's the number one priority. We get her back, and then we find them and we stop them."

"Of course."

She studied his face, unable to read anything from his expression. "You cross me on this, and I'll rip your jugular out."

A faint smile flashed across his face then was gone, and he gave a nod of acknowledgment. "What do we tell Tarkhan?"

She bit her lip. While she was fond of the scholar, she was no longer sure how far she trusted him. "We don't tell him about Harper. And we don't tell him that I had the location and that Noah found it."

"That doesn't leave a lot we can tell him."

"We need to get him to persuade them to let us go—they need to think we're no threat. Especially Noah. That we'll just go home and give up. And also see what he can find out about this woman Noah was with. Whether they know who she really is. Anything that will help us find her." Because if they found the fake Star, they would find the location of the tomb, and that would give them the means to get Harper back.

She stopped in front of the yurt she knew Tarkhan was using. "Hello," she called out.

Footsteps headed toward the door, then it opened from inside. Tarkhan gestured for them to enter.

Unlike the Yurt they'd put Noah in, this one was actually furnished. There was a small desk covered in papers, a chair with a stool in front of it, and a cot bed. He waved them to the cot bed, and she sank down onto it, gripped her hands in her lap. Zach sat beside her.

Tarkhan was still using crutches, and he'd aged in the last weeks. He was in his eighties, though she would never have known that; he'd appeared decades younger. Now his years were catching up with him. He hobbled across to the chair and sat down, rested his leg on the stool, and leaned the crutches against the desk.

"How's your husband?" he asked. "I heard he was injured."

"Ex-husband. And he'll be okay. Though they have him locked up, and he's not happy about it."

"I'm sorry, but you can understand why."

"Noah is no threat. He has zero interest in finding the tomb."

"Then why is he here?"

Zach replied, "Because someone told him Eve had been murdered and his family was in danger. He was just trying to find out why so he could keep them safe."

"You trust him?"

"Yes. He's a good man, and he's no longer in the military. Now that he's found Eve, his interest in this is over. Let him go, and he'll return to his old life."

And so would she. She was just not sure how to achieve that right now. She needed to think up a story as to why she was suddenly resurrected from the dead. She wanted to get Harper safe, and then she wanted her life back, and that was going to take some explaining. Probably some sort of amnesia was her best bet. She'd been wandering around not knowing who she was for the last few weeks.

"So why did you want the meeting with the Darkhats? You came a long way. How do you think they can help you?"

"I think the Descendants are planning their next move."

"Go on."

"They're plotting a coup on a worldwide scale. In a few days' time, the Descendants will be in charge, and after that, nothing will stop them."

"They'll be out in the open," Tarkhan said. "At least there will be an enemy we can fight."

"Not necessarily," Zach said. "I think they plan to simultaneously take out all the major world leaders. There's a summit taking place next week, and all the influential nations will be represented. I believe they have their own people in place to slide into those positions, but they may be no more than puppets. We need the person or persons pulling the strings."

"You're sure of this?"

"I've been tracking these people for years. I'm sure."

Tarkhan shook his head. "I don't think it will make a difference. But we can ask."

"There's one other thing," Zach added. "Noah

was traveling with a woman he knew as Star. She was supposedly the space archaeologist Eve worked with, but the real Star was killed shortly after Eve's staged death. We thought she might be with the Descendants."

"What does she look like?" Tarkhan asked.

"About five ten, black hair, slim, pale skin, brown eyes—could well be Mongolian. And a tattoo on her throat of a star—presumably that was added as part of her cover."

He pursed his lips. Eve could almost see him thinking. Did he recognize the woman? Eve had no clue where his loyalties lay. Was he a member of the Darkhats or merely a sympathizer?

She'd thought they were friends. Now she just didn't know anything. It made no difference; she had to try. This woman was their only hope of getting Harper back. Eve stepped forward and rested her hand on his arm. "Please. We need to find her, Tarkhan. Can you ask them?"

He blew out his breath then pushed himself to his feet and picked up his crutches. "Come with me. We'll go and talk to the leaders."

"Thank you."

"Don't thank me yet. They'll likely tell you nothing."

CHAPTER TWENTY-EIGHT

Noah lay on the floor of the tent, gazing up at the vaulted ceiling. As tents went, it was elaborate. He concentrated on the details to take his mind off the fact that every bit of him throbbed with pain. Whatever Zach had given him to numb his shoulder was wearing off, and it hurt like a bitch. There was a dull pounding in the base of his skull and a sharper pain on the side of his forehead, where he'd hit his head in the crash. Just about every inch of his body was bruised.

He wished he could close his eyes, shut it all out, yet as soon as he did, he saw an image of Harper. He kept remembering back to the night she had caught him with his gun and asked if they were in danger. And he'd said no. What must she be thinking now? That he was a goddamn liar.

Christ, he had to get her back. Had to find a way. Someone must know who Star was. *His* Star. He'd sent Peter the information about their flight. He needed to chase him up—see if he had found any pictures from the airport security. Get a description to every contact he had. Every organization that had a database. Peter would do it. He loved Harper. He'd also get him to send any pictures to Tom; he could run them through the

Clayton Industries systems. He didn't have to reveal why he needed the information. He'd already told too many people about Harper—he couldn't risk it getting out.

At least Harper would have a mother to go home to if he managed to get her back—no, he *would* get her back. Failure wasn't an option.

He was still trying to get his head around the fact that Eve was alive. He'd been too shocked when he'd first seen her to be happy. Now a smile tugged his lips. She'd looked good. Well, right until he'd told her about Harper, then she had collapsed in on herself.

Did she blame him? Probably.

He hadn't realized just how…weighed down she'd been by the fear that had been her constant companion. He'd known many people with PTSD over the years. Some found it harder to shake than others. Eve had carried hers around like a heavy burden.

And he'd been unwilling to compromise on his job, not even to help mitigate her fears. He'd been doing something he saw as important. More important than his family.

Now he just wished that things could have been different.

That somewhere along the way, they could have made different choices and not ended up here. Ironic that the very quality that had drawn her to him was the same thing that had forced a wedge between them.

He could return to his old life if they ever got out of this situation alive. His children would have their mother back, who was way better at caring for them than Noah had ever been. Except for when she was traipsing across the world looking for goddamn spears. He realized there was still a residual anger lingering in his brain. She should never have come here. Certainly not after she had discovered there could well be a terrorist tie in.

He forced the anger down, because it wasn't her fault. It was his. If he had been there for her, then maybe he could have talked her out of it. Or found her some reliable back up. Or...

What was the point?

He was going around and around in ever-decreasing circles and getting nowhere. He could only hope that this hadn't been a wasted trip and they would get something useful from these Darkhats.

He'd learned to sleep when he got the chance, and there was nothing he could do right now except wait, so he closed his eyes and didn't try to banish the images. Just let them fill his mind. He slowed his breathing and finally slept.

He woke to a commotion and raised voices outside the tent.

• • •

Sara dismounted and stood for a moment leaning against her horse, exhaustion aching in every bone of her body. She felt like she hadn't stopped moving in days, which she hadn't. But there were things she'd needed to do, to put in place, just in case everything went to shit.

She'd gone against a direct order, and that would have consequences.

She'd been born close to this place. On the banks of the river Onon. She could trace her ancestry back to the first of the Darkhats. She'd had no choice in life. This was what she was destined to do.

While she'd grown up in the U.K., fostered from the age of five, she'd lived in the camp before. They all did rotations here, guarding the Great Taboo. So they didn't forget what their purpose was. And she loved those times, loved this place with the wide blue sky and the mountains. She wasn't a religious person, but when she was here, she always felt that maybe there was something more. A purpose to everything. Most of the time, she just couldn't see what it was.

Plus here, things were so simple. In the outside world, she was often faced with decisions she didn't want to make. Orders she didn't want to follow. Lately, she'd been feeling more and more that she didn't agree with the way her people worked. They were too ruthless. And what of their cause? Did it really matter if the tomb of Genghis Khan was found? Was it really worth all the people who had died to protect the secret?

Her stomach rumbled. It was already late afternoon, and she hadn't eaten since breakfast. But she needed to report in. She was supposed to have been back here two days ago.

The place was busier than usual, and she frowned. "What's going on?" she asked as a man she recognized stepped up and took her horse's reins.

"Foreigners in the camp. Americans and English."

She'd been about to turn away but now she stopped. "American? Who? Do you have a name?"

"Blakeley."

What the hell?

He was supposed to be back in England. Safe. Why hadn't the Russians just gotten rid of him and sent him home?

The last time she had seen Noah, he'd been sleeping deeply. Probably due to the drug she'd added to his water. They'd spent the night making love, and it had been so good. At the same time, at the back of her mind, was the communication she'd just received. She'd reported in that they were hunting for an image that had been sent to Eve Blakeley the night she died. Her people hadn't known about the image. She'd only suspected its existence when Noah had first mentioned that his anonymous emails had said that Eve had information. And it changed everything.

"Where is he?"

The man waved a hand at a yurt in the center of the camp. There was an armed guard on the door. Christ, Noah was here. She felt a strange fluttering in her chest and ignored it. Now was not the time. Probably never would be the time for her and Noah. Likely, he was going to hate her for what he perceived to be her betrayal. Yet how could she betray someone to whom she owed no loyalty?

She nodded to her horse. "Look after her." Then she strode away toward the yurt, her feet slowing without conscious thought as she neared the waiting guard. What was Noah doing here? How had he even found the place? And what did he hope to achieve? Was he still hunting for the people who had killed his ex-wife? Maybe he had found them. While she didn't know for sure—she hadn't been part of the operation back then—there was a good chance that her people had either killed Eve Blakeley or arranged for her to meet an accident. Another reason for Noah to hate her. Still, she couldn't put this off. She had to talk to him. Find out what he had told them. She had a feeling she was well and truly fucked, but she still needed to find out just how much shit she was going to have to crawl out from under.

She halted in front of the guard. "Stand down. I need to talk to the prisoner." Everyone in the camp knew who she was, and she outranked him. He nodded and stepped aside.

Still, she hesitated then took a deep breath, tucked her hair behind her ear, and pushed open the door. The yurt was empty of furniture, the only contents a big angry man. Menace rolled off him in waves. Then, as she watched, he pulled himself under control.

He stood at the far side of the tent, watching the door, his face totally void of expression as he took her in. He was wearing pants but was naked from the waist up, a white bandage around his shoulder. A cut on his head. He looked bruised and battered, and she had to fight the urge to run to him, wrap her arms around him. It would probably hurt like hell, and she doubted he would appreciate the gesture.

Taking a step closer, she thought about what to say. Although she had so much that needed to be said, the words wouldn't seem to come. "Hello."

An expression of disbelief flashed across his face, and he shook his head. "Who are you?

Because I know for a fact that you're not Star."

Well, at least he was to the point. Her hand went up automatically to the tattoo at her throat. She'd gotten it done especially for the role. There was no point in lying to him now. He had obviously found out that the real Star was dead. "My name is Sarangarel. Sara."

"And you're one of these Darkhats."

She nodded. "I was born into the group."

"And I'm guessing your job was to make sure I didn't find the tomb."

Again, she nodded. "At first, I was just monitoring you. Later, when it became clear you were looking into Eve's death, I was ordered to make contact, find out what you knew. I have a background in computers, so I was the best choice for taking over the role of your space archaeologist."

"You saved my life."

She bit her lip. Should she tell him the truth? She had an idea lies wouldn't help now. "Not really. It was my people who killed the men following you — I think they were likely bodyguards protecting you." They'd spotted her — she hadn't really had a choice but to silence them. "I needed you to trust me, and that seemed a good way."

"You had your people *shoot* me?"

He seemed outraged at the idea, and she bit

back a smile. There was nothing funny here. "It worked. You trusted me."

"Christ, I never doubted you were who you said you were." He ran a hand through his short hair, a gesture she recognized as frustration. Then his expression cleared. "Where is the image?"

She hadn't expected him to be so open. Did he not know what would happen if the people here even had an inkling that he had seen the image? At least the guard spoke no English. All the same, she darted a glance at the tent flap then cast Noah a narrow-eyed look and stepped closer. "They can't know we found the location. They'd kill you and likely me as well."

"You didn't tell your people?"

"I couldn't. I told you—they'd kill you if they knew."

"And you expect me to believe that you would care one way or the other?"

She didn't expect anything, but suddenly she didn't want him to hate her. Her eyes pricked. She was tired; that was all. The last few days had been emotional. A lot of good-byes. "My orders were to kill you if we found anything. No second chance. You had to die. That's how we work. No one can know the location. For eight hundred years, that has been our purpose. To ensure the tomb remains lost."

"Yet I'm still here."

She gave what she hoped was a casual shrug. "Without the image, you would never find the tomb. There was no risk."

"And maybe even you can't fuck a man one minute and put a bullet in him the next."

She didn't bother to answer. What could she say? He was right. She should never have allowed herself to get emotionally entangled. Actually fucking and shooting she could probably have coped with. It was *caring* for Noah and shooting him had been a whole other matter. She wasn't going there—not now.

He moved a little closer, as if now he understood that this conversation was best not overheard. "So where is it? The image? This is important. I need that image."

Why? "I destroyed it."

Something flashed across his face. Disbelief. Fear. He turned away for a moment, his fingers pressing against his skull. "No," he murmured.

A frown tugged at her brows. Why did he care so much? He had no vested interest in finding the tomb. That had never been what this was about for him and one of the reasons she had felt justified in not killing him. He'd wanted to find his wife's murderers and a way to make his children safe.

His shoulders were tense, his hands fisted at his sides. Something was very wrong. Well, something more than the obvious. And she filled the silence with words. "I told my people that there was nothing to find. That the image had never arrived or had been destroyed when Eve was killed. They still wanted me to eliminate you. I told them killing you wasn't necessary." And she was sure she would be punished for that decision. At least Noah was still alive, so they hadn't just killed him out of hand. Why was he here? "I phoned the Russian police. Said you were a suspected terrorist. I thought they would lock you up for a couple of days until they found out who you really were then send you home." When he remained silent, she shifted from foot to foot. "Noah, what is it?"

He turned back. The look in his eyes was a pain so deep she reached out to him then let her hand drop to her side.

"They've taken my daughter," he said.

The words didn't make sense. "Who?"

"At a guess, the Descendants of fucking Genghis Khan. They've taken Harper."

Harper was the older daughter. Sara had seen her at the cemetery that day. She looked like her father.

"They sent me her fucking finger," he continued, "and promised to return her in pieces unless I give them the location of the tomb. I'm nearly out of time, and when I saw you come in just now—I thought—it's over. I can give them what they want. Harper is safe. You took the image that night. You had the fucking image."

She gave a helpless shrug, her mind in turmoil. What to do? What to say? She'd spent so long thinking this through, going over her options—which were almost non-existent—that she couldn't make her mind process this new information. "I'm sorry."

She stared straight ahead, saw the movement of his throat as he swallowed.

"Why?" he asked. "Why destroy it?"

"I had no choice. This is what I've been brought up to believe. Burned into me from the moment I was born. It's our duty to keep the secrets of the tomb. So I destroyed the image to protect you—but also because I had no choice."

"There's always a choice," he growled.

"If they knew the image really existed, then they would kill you and likely me at the same time. It would be seen as a betrayal of everything we hold sacred. And I have a daughter as well. She's six years old, and I would do anything for her. If they even suspect me of lies, I'll never see her again." She forced her brain to go over the facts. "You didn't tell them you found the image?" Of course he hadn't; otherwise he'd be dead.

"No. Eve said that it was best. That they would kill us. She'd already told them the image never arrived. She never saw it."

Shock held her rigid. "Eve?"

"She's alive." He snorted. The sound held no amusement. "You mean they didn't tell you?"

No, they hadn't told her. But then what was new? Secrecy was the way they existed. The way they survived. *Don't tell one person what the next is doing.* And she hated it. Blind obedience had never been her strong point.

A wave of familiar bitterness washed over her. They were expected to do as they were told, kill if necessary, and all on faith. She was no longer sure she even believed the tomb worth protecting. What was it other than a pile of old bones?

She realized Noah was waiting for an answer. She shook her head. "No. They never told me."

"They faked her death."

"Why?" If they'd believed Eve was getting close, then why not just kill her? They had tried before.

"Someone called in a favor."

Who? She didn't know. Her mind was struggling to make sense of everything, to see a way forward through all this. How Noah must be hurting. She could see it in every line of his body. He'd always seemed so sure. Now he looked lost.

She imagined if it was her baby, held by strangers, mutilated, in pain, and her whole mind shied away. She needed to think this through.

Noah was right. She always had choices.

Sometimes they might seem like between bad and worse, but there was always a choice. "How long do you have?" she asked.

"Three days."

"I'm sorry," she said again.

"Yeah, I'm sure you are." He shook his head. "Tell me, would you have done anything different if you'd known about Harper?"

She thought about lying, but in the end, she decided on the truth. "I don't know."

CHAPTER TWENTY-NINE

Eve trudged slowly across the camp, Tarkhan hobbling on his crutches in front of her, talking quietly with Zach. He'd obviously done his best; they'd listened to him.

And then said no.

There had been a whole lot of discussion in Mongolian. She'd picked up some of it. Tarkhan had tried to persuade them to help, but apparently some summit in Russia was beyond their remit. Bring them proof that the Descendants of Genghis Khan were involved and they might help. Until they saw that proof—nothing.

They also claimed to have no information as to who the fake Star really was. Which was not good as it looked like she was their only hope of getting Harper back.

Find the fake Star and they would find the image and the location of the tomb.

And as far as she was concerned, the Descendants could have it. If she'd learned anything in the past few weeks, it was that people were what mattered. Not some ancient burial site.

The guard in front of the yurt stepped aside as they approached. She followed Tarkhan and Zach inside then stopped abruptly. Noah was not alone.

He stood at the opposite end of the tent, a woman close beside him. They clearly knew each other; there was a tension between them, and hope lit up in Eve's heart.

Then she glanced at Noah and went still. Something was very wrong. Stress radiated from his body, and his expression was fixed, his eyes grim.

The woman had turned as they entered. She was tall, much taller than Eve, and very thin. Dressed as were all of the Darkhats, men and women, in dark pants, boots, and a gray shirt, her clothes were dusty and worn as though she had traveled a long way. While she wasn't beautiful, there was something about her, a vitality that shone from her face. She looked as grim as Noah, and…sad. Eve's gaze went to her throat and the tattoo of a star. This was the woman Noah had been working with. The one who had stolen the image. So why was Noah looking so bleak? He stood with his hands shoved in his pockets, shoulders hunched.

Stepping forward, the woman held out her hands to Tarkhan, and a smile curved her lips. She spoke in Mongolian.

Tarkhan took her hands and drew her close for a moment then stepped back. Still holding her hands, he stared into her face and spoke.

She nodded then stepped back and pulled free.

She headed for the door, her steps faltering, and she paused in front of Eve. "I'm sorry."

Eve watched her go. Something was definitely wrong. She wanted to grab the other woman and drag her back. She was their only hope. Why was Noah letting her walk away? He seemed held in place, locked in his thoughts. She turned to Tarkhan. Clearly, he knew the woman well, was fond of her.

"Who is she?" Eve asked.

"Her name is Sarangarel. She's the daughter of Ulagan—leader of the Darkhats. I've known her since she was born, though she grew up in London. She'll be the next leader. If the group survives."

Ulagan was the man Tarkhan had met in the Siberian labor camp. He'd been the clear leader of the group they had just met with. And no doubt the man responsible for deciding they would get no help. Bastard.

"You believe us then?" Zach asked. He sounded bitter and almost as defeated as Noah appeared. He'd put too much hope into this.

"I believe you. But I'm not one of them." Tarkhan sighed, looking every one of his eighty-plus years, his skin pale, face etched with pain. "I'll keep trying. You should go before they change their minds." He moved to her, and she stood still while he kissed her cheek. "Keep safe. I enjoyed working with you."

The deal was they would leave the country as soon as they could and not return. Clearly Tarkhan believed they would do that, but then he didn't know about Harper.

She waited until he had left then crossed to where Noah stood. He hadn't said a word since they'd entered. She reached out, rested a hand on his arm below the bandage; his skin was cool. "What happened? Won't she give you the image. Did you explain?"

Noah finally looked into her eyes. She didn't want to analyze what she was seeing reflected in his gaze—hopelessness, despair. "She destroyed it. We have no way of finding the tomb."

Somehow she'd been expecting him to say that she wouldn't hand the image over. And she'd already decided she'd come back and torture the other woman herself if that's what was needed. Now she forced her mind to process his words, and a scream rose up inside her. Her whole body was shaking, and her vision was going dark at the edges. Noah grabbed her arms and shook her, his fingers tight around her upper arms. He was speaking, but she couldn't hear the words beneath the roar in her ears. He shook her again. One hand released her, and a moment later, she felt the sharp sting of a slap on the cheek. The blow broke through the panic, and the fog in her brain cleared a little. She heard a sobbing and realized it was coming from her, then she was drawn tight against his chest, and she gave in to the tears that had been building since he'd told her about Harper. She cried horrible jagged tears against him, and he held her tight until her nose clogged and she couldn't breathe and she had to lift her head or starve of oxygen.

At least her mind had cleared. She closed her eyes for a minute, sniffed until she could breathe again. She opened her eyes. Noah's grip loosened, but he still kept a hold on her as though he was scared she would lose it again.

And maybe he was right.

She peered inside herself—the panic had receded. She could think again. Though perhaps that wasn't such a good thing. She looked up at Noah, seeing the worry and fear in his eyes.

He'd never been good with tears. And in the early years, she'd cried a lot. He'd initially tried a tentative pat on the shoulders. When that had failed to have an effect, he'd tried distracting her with sex, then later he'd just backed off and let her cry through it. Whatever *it* was.

Maybe he'd grown up some in the years they'd been apart. Or maybe the last few weeks had also taught him a lesson about what mattered in life.

She breathed deeply. She wouldn't give in. Shaking free of Noah's hold, she stepped back and stared into his eyes. "This is not over," she said, each word tightly enunciated. "We will get Harper back." Or they would die trying.

She turned away, pulled a handkerchief from her pocket, wiped her eyes, and blew her nose. She sniffed then glanced at Zach, who was standing to the side. He also looked worried, and she forced a smile. "I'm good," she said. "Crying all done with."

After searching her face, he nodded. "Good. But don't do that again. My nerves can't take it."

"I won't." She was in no way sure that was true, but he was safe for the moment.

Zach had picked up Noah's rucksack on the way over here, and he handed it to Noah. "Get dressed. We're leaving. Before they change their minds."

CHAPTER THIRTY

Noah watched her warily as he hunkered down and dug into his rucksack for a T-shirt. He'd been scared. She'd seemed beyond reason, and he'd never been comfortable with crying.

His mother cried a lot. Growing up, he'd learned to distance himself from it. At first he'd tried to comfort her. Most of the time, she hadn't wanted his comfort. Hadn't wanted him at all. He'd been a poor substitute for Ben, which he'd soon realized and backed off.

The other times had been even worse. The times when his mother had been wracked with guilt and had tried to smother him with love, while crying jagged tears and ranting that she hadn't meant it.

His shoulder spasmed as he pulled the shirt over his head, and he winced. He suspected he had a couple of cracked ribs.

"You okay?" Zach asked.

"Yes."

Eve snorted. "Of course he's not okay. Look at him."

Zach raised an eyebrow then crossed to where the first aid kit sat on the floor. He rummaged inside it and came up with a bottle of pills. He tipped three onto his palm and held them out to Noah. He shook his head—he needed a clear mind.

Eve pursed her lips and studied him, hands on her hips. "If you want to get out of here, you're going to have to ride a horse, and we don't want to be picking you up off the ground every five minutes. Take the bloody painkillers, Noah."

Zach chuckled at Noah's expression.

He'd never seen Eve like this, but at least she wasn't crying. She seemed like a different woman. Maybe the strong woman she should always have been.

He was being an asshole, maybe even thinking he deserved the pain, because if he didn't find a way to save her then Harper would die because of him. And maybe the pain was better than the fear that he would fail his daughter. But he took the pills—because Eve was right—and dry swallowed them.

Eve gave a small nod and turned away as he hefted his rucksack onto his good shoulder and followed them out, staring straight ahead as they walked through the camp. He was aware of people following their progress but ignored them. Just concentrated on putting one foot in front of the other. By the time they reached the corral where the horses were kept, the painkillers had started to kick in. He didn't know what they were, except they were strong. He was almost light-headed.

Four horses were saddled and ready outside the corral. They nickered and stamped as their small group approached. An older man on crutches stood beside them—Tarkhan at a guess—together with a big man, almost as wide as he was tall, with dark brown eyes, a round face, and a goatee beard. He grinned at them.

"This is Jochi, your guide," Tarkhan said. "He'll lead you out of the area. We've arranged for a vehicle to be waiting. Unfortunately, it's late, so you won't make it tonight. You'll have to camp out."

Someone handed him the reins, and he stood for a moment, staring at the stirrup, unsure whether he could actually get on.

"Do you need some help?" It was Tarkhan, his voice gentle.

Noah ignored the offer, gritted his teeth, and lifted his foot into the stirrup. It was another asshole move, and he paid for it when pain flashed through him. He ignored that, too, and heaved himself into the saddle. He landed with a thud, and the horse pranced beneath him in protest. Grabbing hold of the pommel, he held on tight, his fingers white until the horse settled. He looked around. They were all watching him with various levels of concern. "I'm fine," he snapped.

The guide led the way. Eve followed, clearly

comfortable on the horse. Zach nodded to him to go next—he probably wanted to be able to keep an eye on Noah in case he fell off. He nudged the animal, and it moved forward, and he held his breath until his body relaxed into the movement and the pain subsided to a bearable level.

As they rode up the hill out of the camp, he felt a prickle run down his spine, and he turned in the saddle and looked back. His gaze was drawn to the woman standing at the edge of the camp, her hand shading her eyes as she looked into the sun.

Star. Sara. He couldn't see her expression.

It wasn't her fault. She hadn't betrayed him. She had never owed him any loyalty, after all. In a way, she had betrayed her own people and beliefs in allowing him to live.

None of this was Sara's fault. It was all his. And down to him to solve it. All the same, it felt like she had betrayed him, and as she raised a hand in farewell, he couldn't bring himself to respond. Instead, he turned back in the saddle and stared straight ahead.

He was on autopilot as he rode, his gaze fixed on Eve ahead of him where she sat straight in the saddle. Occasionally, she would look back over her shoulder, her lower lip caught between her teeth. He kept his face expressionless.

There were no tracks to follow, yet the guide led them unwaveringly, through gorges with steep narrow sides, over ridges, splashing through shallow streams. The light was dimming as Zach rode up beside him, studying him. "How are you feeling? Do you need more painkillers?"

He shook his head. The painkillers were wearing off, leaving his mind clearer than since before the ATV crash. And the pain was bearable. "I'm fine," he said. "Functional, anyway."

"Good. Just another hour and we'll stop for the night."

By the time they came to a stop in a small clearing, he felt stronger. He sat for a moment taking stock. He could feel the tight pull of the new stitches, but he could move his shoulder without pain. If he pressed a finger to his forehead, there was a bruise, but the headache was gone.

He swung down from the saddle as Eve approached him. Her gaze ran over him, and she pursed her lips but then nodded. "You look better."

"Yeah."

"Why don't you rest while we set up camp?"

He sat on the ground with his back against a tree and watched as they unsaddled the horses and hobbled them on the edge of the clearing. Night had almost fallen, and the stars were coming out, an infinity of pinpricks in the clear sky.

He closed his eyes, trying to empty his mind of the fear that had been his constant companion since he'd learned Harper was gone.

Always before when things got tough, he'd found himself focusing, his senses sharpening, rising to the challenge, relishing the test. He had to rediscover that strength within himself, to find a way to ignore the emotional connection like he always had, but he suspected that would be impossible. He was no longer the same person. Losing first Eve and then Harper had shown him how much he cared.

So he needed to accept that but compartmentalize so he could focus. Maybe he would fail and Harper would die, but it wouldn't be because he had given up. The answer was out there.

Though it was the middle of summer, they were still in the mountains, and now that the sun had gone down, there was a slight chill in the air. Off to the left, he could hear the stamping of the horses. They were restless. Jochi had lit a fire in a circle of rocks in the center of the clearing—he was guessing this was a regular campsite. The others were seated around it, and he could hear the low murmur of voices.

He pushed himself to his feet and crossed the space between them to stare down into the embers, feeling the warmth of the fire against his skin. On the other side of the fire, a bulk of blankets—presumably the guide—lay fast asleep.

Eve and Zach sat side by side, their heads close together as they talked. They both glanced up as he arrived, and Zach raised a half-empty bottle. "Here—a present from Tarkhan."

He took the whiskey and raised it to his lips, relishing the burn as he swallowed.

"There's food if you want it," Eve said, getting to her feet.

His stomach rumbled at the idea. He nodded, and she handed him a pan and a fork. "Mutton stew. They eat it a lot here."

"Thanks." The food was good, and he could feel the strength flowing through his body.

"We've been talking," Eve said as she sat down again. "Trying to decide what to do. There has to be a way to find her."

He paused in his eating and glanced at her, a frown tugging his brows together. They had only three days left to the deadline. Somehow in that time, they had to break through the shroud of secrecy surrounding the Descendants, identify who had taken Harper, find her, and come up with a way to get her out.

He finished the food. He already felt stronger, his mind racing over the possibilities. After placing the empty pan on the ground, he took another slug of whiskey and sat staring into the fire, trying to make the pieces fall into place.

"Some maniac has our daughter," Eve said, grabbing the bottle from him and taking a gulp. "What do you plan to do about it?"

Maybe he should suggest she go slow on the whiskey. He glanced at Zach and found the other man watching him.

Eve jumped to her feet and paced the clearing a couple of times. Then she came back and stood over him. "Please, Noah. You're supposed to be the best at what you do. You understand these people, how their minds work. Think of a way to save our baby. Please."

He forced his brain to focus on the problem, to go over the facts one more time. They had to find some link to the kidnappers if there was any hope of tracing them. So what did they know?

"What we need is a way to get to the Descendants. What about the funding organization? The people who paid for the expedition."

"The account was shut down. There was nothing. A trail through a few dummy corporations and then a dead end. Same with Mr. Tuul, the guy who Eve dealt with when she was hunting the Spear. He was like a ghost. Just vanished."

He'd already sent that information to Tom but wasn't expecting to find out any more than Zach already knew—he'd been thorough. Who else did they know? "How about the guy who was following you in Russia?"

"John Chen?" Eve said, with a shake of her head. "He's a dead end."

"How do you know?"

"When I first came to Mongolia, John saved my life. I got the feeling he was more than a translator. I asked Peter to look into him for me."

"Peter?" Noah felt like he was being slow, but that didn't make sense.

"Yes. I wanted to check Zach out anyway. He said he'd worked with you, so I tried to call. You were obviously undercover at the time, and I got hold of Peter instead. I asked him to check out Zach and also to look into John Chen at the same time. He came back and said that John Chen was exactly who he said he was—a translator employed by the people funding the trip. There were no files on him. He was clean."

Maybe he had an exceptionally good cover. But still, something didn't add up. "Wait a moment. Back up. So Peter knew, before your 'accident,' that you'd been approached by MI6?"

She nodded. "When I called asking about Zach, I told him I'd been interviewed by an agent from MI6 and that he believed the people funding my expedition had possible ties to terrorists."

He wanted to shout that that didn't make

sense. Instead, he kept his mouth firmly closed. If she had told Peter about the MI6 connection, then why hadn't he passed the information on to Noah? Maybe it might be believable that it had slipped his mind after Eve's accident — except nothing slipped Peter's mind. Ever. Every little minutiae of information was examined from every possible angle to search for the slightest meaning and significance.

And even if by some strange accident he had forgotten the call, surely when Noah had told him about the anonymous email stating that Eve had been murdered, he would have remembered. Yet he'd said categorically that he'd looked into her death and there was nothing to suggest it was anything other than an accident.

The great big glaring connection to terrorists... and Peter had not thought it worth mentioning to Noah?

"Noah, what is it?" Eve asked.

Instead of answering, Noah pushed himself to his feet. He needed to move. Something was stirring in his mind, pressing against his thoughts, trying to get out. And part of him didn't want to think this through, take it to the logical conclusion, because if he did that, then his life would change forever. Nothing would be the same.

The facts: Peter knew that Eve was involved with MI6 and yet he had failed to tell Noah.

Peter hadn't wanted Noah to know the connection.

What motive could his uncle have had for not telling him?

His mind flinched away from the answer, and he had to force himself to concentrate. He glanced over to the fire; they were both watching him, Eve chewing on her fingernails. Zach's eyes were narrowed.

Peter hadn't told him that Eve was involved in some shady goings on. Why?

Maybe because he was already aware that Eve's death was no accident.

Except that didn't make sense, either. Because Eve wasn't actually dead. Peter couldn't have known she was murdered…but he could have suspected. Suspected that people he was involved with had also been responsible for Eve's death.

Could it be part of some investigation Peter was working on?

Maybe he was going after the Descendants and didn't want Noah involved? No, that wasn't possible. If there was an investigation into the Descendants, Noah's old team would have been right at the center of it, and he'd never even heard the name until a few days ago.

Taking a deep breath, he forced himself to ask the question. Could his uncle be somehow involved with the Descendants of Genghis Khan?

Noah was pretty sure that his father's family wasn't descended from Genghis Khan, but what did he really know? If they were, then his uncle had kept very quiet about it.

He was grasping at straws.

The reasoning was tenuous. Was he reading things in where they didn't exist? No, he wasn't. Finding connections was what he did. He took the facts, and they formed patterns in his head. And one was forming now.

He thought about the last undercover job that had gone so wrong. Someone had talked. He'd been getting so close to his spider. Too close maybe.

Then his mind went to other jobs, where they had been on the point of making a breakthrough and everything had inextricably fallen apart. He'd suspected a mole within the group but hadn't been able to pinpoint anyone suspicious.

It had never occurred to him to examine Peter. Why would he? Peter was the one man he trusted in the whole world. Above suspicion. He had been there when Noah had needed someone.

A little voice whispered in his head and wouldn't be quieted. What better job for a man involved in a secret terrorist group than overall controller of the country's top anti-terrorism force?

It was genius.

He'd believed all along that the group he'd been hunting all these years had infiltrated everywhere. Zach was sure they had people high up in MI6. Why not Project Arachnid?

His head was going to explode. He clamped his lips on the scream of fury and betrayal rising in his throat.

Halting in front of a huge tree, he slammed his fist hard into the trunk.

No!

The word screamed inside his head.

He allowed himself one moment of total rage, then he closed it down and cleared his mind.

"Christ, Noah. What the hell is wrong?" He turned around. Eve was on her feet and stalking toward him. "As if you needed any more goddamn injuries. Just talk to us."

"Yeah, Noah," Zach said, "talk to us."

His mind was crystal clear now, processing the information, seeing the patterns solidify in his mind. Eve had come to stand in front of him, hands on her hips, glaring.

"Sit down," he said.

She blinked then frowned, and he waved a hand toward the fire. He needed to discover just how deep Peter was in this thing, and he suspected Eve had information—even if she didn't know it—that would help him untangle the mess.

He waited until Eve was seated and then went

and sat down so he could watch her face as she talked.

"Hey, he's back from the dead," Zach said.

Noah ignored the comment. "I think Peter may be connected with the Descendants."

Eve blinked at him a couple of times. He turned his attention to Zach. The other man was frowning, clearly going over the information but not dismissing it out of hand. Of course, he didn't have the personal connection to Peter, and he'd already suspected that the Descendants had infiltrated most organizations.

"What are you going on?" he asked.

"He knew there was a terrorist connection to Eve, and he never told me."

"Protecting you?"

"I don't need protecting. He knows that. After I got the message that Eve's death was no accident, I asked him to look into it. He said there was nothing suspect. No mention of you," he said to Zach.

"Anything else?"

"I'd been suspecting there was a mole in the organization for a while. The last mission was compromised. And others before that. I hadn't been able to flush them out. I never even looked into Peter. It never occurred to me..."

"You're wrong," Eve said, but her voice was shaky, unsure. "You have to be wrong. He would never harm Harper."

"Maybe he didn't know." Noah tried to remember back to when he had told Peter. He'd been shocked; he would swear the emotion was genuine. "The way the organization works, I would guess that only whoever is at the very top knows everything. That's how they would maintain secrecy." He rubbed a hand over the roughness of his jaw. "I thought I knew him so well. He was always there for me. I just can't reconcile that with a man who would condone terrorist attacks."

Then he started thinking back to many of the conversations they'd had about terrorism. How Peter would point out that in some circumstances the end justified the means if the ultimate goal was something good. "How could he be connected to the Descendants? I've never even heard him mention Genghis Khan."

"I have," Eve said.

Noah turned his attention to her. She was chewing on her nails, frown lines between her eyes. "Go on."

"It was shortly after I left you," she said. "I was at a function in London, and Peter was there. He said he wanted to introduce me to someone, that he thought we'd have a lot in common. And he was right."

"And how the hell did Genghis Khan come up?" Zach asked. "It's not something that gets mentioned in general conversation."

"It depends who you're talking to. The senator told me she'd always been fascinated by Khan. That she'd been following the hunt for the tomb. We talked about that and how I would go about finding it."

Noah's mind was still locked on the one word. "Senator?" he asked.

She nodded. "Senator Clayton. She and Peter seemed like good friends. He joined in the conversation. He was very knowledgeable."

Noah's mind was whirling. The senator? It didn't seem possible. But then neither did Peter. And in fact, the more he thought about it, the more it made sense. "You never mentioned this," he said, and he was sure his tone was accusing.

"Why would I? We weren't exactly talking much then. And it didn't seem important. Yet looking back…" Her frown deepened.

"What is it?"

"I was just thinking about the timing. It was just before I got the job at Cambridge and the funding for my research. I'd had an interview at the university, but I didn't think I would get the position. These things are usually filled internally. Then the day after I met Peter and the senator, I got a call saying the position was mine and they'd already had an offer of funding."

"So wait," Zach said. "You're saying you

believe that Senator Clayton was behind your funding?"

"I didn't at the time. To be honest, it never even occurred to me. Now, thinking back, it was such a coincidence. And she certainly has the money." She glanced between the two of them. "What am I missing?"

Zach looked at Noah. "You think the senator is with the Descendants?"

Noah didn't answer immediately. He was putting the pieces in place. Why would Senator Clayton not have mentioned that she had met Eve when they had talked at the cemetery at Eve's funeral? It was the sort of thing you said on those occasions. She was Peter's good friend. He'd known they were acquaintances, but that was all. A woman in a position of power, with the ear of the president. A woman with an information-gathering service that rivaled the American government's.

Had she given him the job so she could keep an eye on him?

Maybe she wanted him to go after Eve's killers. It would have been easy enough to send those emails from inside Clayton Industries' system.

She hadn't killed Eve, though, because Eve wasn't dead.

But maybe she had killed Star.

And she'd employed and coerced Eve into

searching for the spear and the tomb. Then, when she was so close to finding the location, Eve had been killed. It must have driven the senator crazy. So they'd gone after the real Star, looking for the source of the image, but she had died under interrogation and given them nothing. Except that the image had been sent.

Noah had been under surveillance back in London. He was betting by the senator's people.

And then when the senator ran out of options, had been unable to locate the image, as a last resort she had set Noah off. Given him the motivation and the tools to go and follow in Eve's footsteps and maybe find the answers.

All this time, he'd been pretty much telling Tom his every move. And believing every piece of information sent back. They'd fed him what they wanted him to hear—Jesus, they'd played him for a fool.

There was something else. "I asked Tom, my assistant at Clayton, about Zach and John Chen. He'd said John was a nobody, but he actually pointed the finger at Zach as a potential suspect for Eve's murder." Which was a complete misdirection and meant that Tom had known all along what was going on. Noah had been fooled by them all. Tom, the senator, Peter. How had he not seen it? How could he have been so fucking blind?

Zach snorted. "They were probably hoping you would take me out. They've been trying for long enough. Jesus. Senator Clayton? You really think she could be at the center of all this?"

Noah had seen the vastness of Clayton Industries. The power and infrastructure. He could well believe they had the resources to infiltrate terrorist groups and twist the attacks to their own benefit. He remembered back to that face-to-face meeting. He'd thought her beautiful, charismatic, that they had similar goals. Certainly there had been nothing to suggest she was a ruthless megalomaniac with plans to take over the world.

At least they now had somewhere to focus. Someone to go after. They just needed to work out a strategy.

Something else occurred to him. The summit was only three days away. They'd been relying on Peter to put a stop to it or at least ensure that security was increased.

"What I really think is that we're well and truly fucked."

CHAPTER THIRTY-ONE

General Peter Blakeley passed through the various security checks without hardly noticing. He was so used to it now. The security guard led him through into the private quarters and left him alone. As the door clicked shut behind him, he relaxed, allowing his shoulders to slump. He was exhausted. He'd taken a private plane back from Russia, but he hadn't been able to sleep, and his eyes felt gritty.

He crossed to the drinks cabinet and opened it, found the bottle of his favorite scotch, and poured a stiff measure. Closing his eyes, he savored the first sip, feeling the warmth slide down his throat and spread heat in his belly.

He had to be careful, now more than ever. His loyalty couldn't be questioned. Hell, he *was* loyal. He would always be loyal. As he was pouring his second drink, the door to the bedroom opened, and she stood there.

A frisson of excitement shivered over his skin as she walked toward him. Her eyes were half-closed, and she swayed as though to some music only she could hear. She was the most sensuous woman he had ever met, though she usually kept that side of her nature under ruthless control.

He was honored he was the one who got to see it.

She stopped in front of him and smiled. "I missed you."

"I missed you, too."

She took the glass from him, swallowed the contents in one gulp, placed the glass on the table, and took his hand. She led him to the bedroom, with its huge bed, then turned to face him once more. "Take off your clothes," she ordered.

Heat shot through him at her words. All the same, for a moment, he resisted—they needed to talk. Except he wanted this, and talking could wait, and maybe she'd be a little more...receptive to what he had to say afterward.

So he held her gaze as he started to undress.

An hour later, he lay back in the bed, the pillows bunched behind his head. He'd gotten them both drinks, and they sipped the scotch in companionable silence. It wouldn't last long. She hardly ever stopped moving, but for now she seemed relaxed. He figured she'd needed this as much as he had. Maybe more.

It had been good. Hell, it was always good between them. They'd been doing this for over twenty-five years. She'd been nineteen when he'd met her at a political rally. He'd been twenty-one and trying to decide whether to go into the Army or to study law like his brother. He'd gone to a military school and loved it but had still wavered about making the army his life. She'd persuaded him he should. By then, he would have done anything she asked because she was the most charismatic woman he had ever met.

Beside him, she shifted restlessly. He knew the signs; their time was nearly up. Now or never. She spoke before he could get the words out.

"Where is he?"

"Mongolia."

"Good. And have you heard from him?"

"I got a text. He knows or at least suspects about the summit."

She snorted. "Then it's a good thing his mind is on other things right now."

"Why didn't you tell me?" he asked.

He wondered whether she would pretend she didn't understand the question, but he doubted it. She never backed away from anything she did. Always took responsibility for her actions.

"We needed to ensure his cooperation. This was the best way to do it within the time frame we have."

"That's not what I asked. Why didn't you tell me?" Was she doubting his commitment after all he had done? He'd dedicated his whole adult life to her cause. Betrayed everything he was supposed to hold true to and never wavered. Because he believed in her. And believed in the world she planned.

What they had now wasn't working. The world teetered on the edge of chaos, and at any moment, they would all slip into the Abyss. And any hope would be gone.

"You didn't need to know," she replied with finality.

"She's my goddaughter," he snapped. "My niece. I love her." The thought of what the child might be going through right now sliced at his heart. There weren't many people in the world he loved. Harper was one of them. But he wouldn't only lose Harper; he'd lose Noah as well.

He'd never married, had never even come close. The only woman he would have ever considered was beyond him. She'd married once for political reasons and because she had needed an heir. That had never happened, and it had nearly broken her.

He'd long held hopes that Noah would join them. He'd watched his nephew carefully over the years. He'd grown into a good man, exactly the sort of man they needed going forward. While he didn't balk at doing what was necessary, he had a strong moral code.

So far, the time had never been quite right, but he'd told himself that Noah was still young. Now it would never happen. While Noah had a strange affinity for the terrorists of the world, often a sympathy and understanding of why they did what they did, he also saw things in black and white and hated the end results. The murder of innocents. If someone killed his daughter, he would hunt them down whatever the consequences. No compromise.

She shrugged then reached out a hand and rested it on his arm. "I'm sorry, Peter. We're so close now. Time is running out."

"Then at least give the girl into my care. I'll keep her safe, and I won't let Noah know."

"It doesn't work like that. We don't know where she is at this point. The operatives have their orders, and they've cut off contact."

His mouth filled with the sour taste of despair, as though the walls that held up his existence were crumbling around him. He had nowhere to hide and nowhere to belong. He was only functioning because he'd learned to compartmentalize his life. Not let the various disparate parts overlap. "I could have done it," he said. "If you'd asked, I would have taken her and pretended she was kidnapped. She's only a child."

"And would you have done what was necessary?"

He closed his mind as to what that might be. He'd never wavered, and now he had to bite back the urge to beg.

"It's better this way, Peter." She squeezed his arm. "We must find the Talisman before the summit. Noah is going to show us the way."

The fucking Talisman. It was the one thing they had argued about over the years. He couldn't see why some piece of junk buried eight centuries ago mattered. Yet it held almost a mystical allure to her. Some magical talisman that would ensure her success. They didn't need symbols.

He took a deep breath. "What difference will it make if we have it or don't have it? Everything is in place for the summit. Just forget the fucking Talisman. We don't need it."

She removed her hand from his arm and drew back. Her green eyes were cold, and a shiver ran through him.

"Many have rebuked me for allowing you to have so much influence over me. This is why. You will never understand us totally. For you, this is merely some power play on a global scale. But for us, it's the culmination of a prophecy made hundreds of years ago. A prophecy my people have striven and died to bring to fruition. We are not some random group of individuals who have been tossed together. We are the Descendants. My people need to see the physical manifestation of the prophecy."

"Why? You don't believe this thing has magical

properties any more than I do."

She stared ahead for a moment, and he was sure she was going to dismiss him. Then her expression softened. Her long dark red hair hung loose about her shoulders; her green eyes shone with sincerity.

"Let me tell you the story of my birth. I've never told you before, but it's interesting and will help you to understand. I was born on the banks of the River Onon," she said. "In a yurt, just like my ancestors before me. And like Genghis Khan, I was born clutching a blood clot in my hand. This was taken as a symbol by my people. A symbol that I was the one they waited for. From my earliest moments, I remember my father whispering that I was intended for greatness. That one day I would hold the Spirit Banner of my ancestor—the very *soul* of Genghis Khan would be in my hands—and I would carry the Talisman into battle and rule an empire that stretched around the entire globe."

He sat in silence, not moving in case she stopped. She seldom spoke of her past, only of what she would do in the future.

"I had enemies. News spread of my birth. The Darkhats heard the rumors and sought my death. There were three attempts on my life in the early years. For my protection, I was taken in secret from Mongolia when I was five years old and adopted by an American family who belonged to the group. I never saw my father and mother again."

"Are they alive?"

"No, they died for the cause." She twisted a little so she could look him in the eye. "My people wanted the Darkhats to believe I was dead, so I could grow up in safety. One night, they took me away, and they burned the yurt to the ground. My parents were inside."

"They killed them? Their own people?"

"We all have to make sacrifices."

Acid crawled up his throat. He'd thought he was beyond shock.

"It's not the individuals who matter," she spoke softly. "It's the whole. We seek to make a united world."

He cleared his throat. "Of course. Go on."

"There have always been people within the group who dispute my claim. Those who thought they had a higher right or who believed a woman could never take the place of Genghis Khan. Sometimes I've had to be ruthless to prove that I'm a suitable heir. Yet I have never done anything without a reason. While many have died, their deaths have not been in vain. They have always taken us closer to our ultimate goal. Now we are nearly there, but I need the support of *all* my people. I can't afford to have opposing factions within the group. The one way to prove that I am the true heir is to hold the Spirit Banner and the Talisman. If I do, they will not question me, and we can concentrate on making the world a better place."

"I see." And he did. She rarely took the time to explain herself, and he was touched that she had done so now.

"Are you having doubts?" she asked.

For a brief moment, he wondered what would happen if he said yes, but he wasn't that stupid. And really, he wasn't having doubts. Just the personal toll was getting to him, clouding his mind. "Of course not."

"Good. Now I have to go."

He watched as she slipped out of bed and strolled across the floor, naked, her body slender and beautiful, and his heart ached.

In the end, the world would be a better, safer place.

He had to believe that.

CHAPTER THIRTY-TWO

Noah, Eve, and Zach talked for the rest of the night. Going over strategies, hitting dead ends, starting again. Until at least they had some idea of where to go next and a vague plan of how to get there. All they needed was a little cooperation from the star players.

While he still wasn't sure they could pull it off and save Harper, that had to be their main priority. And if he failed—presuming he survived that failure—he would go after those responsible and make sure they paid in blood.

The plan relied on convincing Peter that they didn't suspect him and that Noah needed his help.

He was still finding it hard to come to terms with Peter's involvement in all of this. The when and the how eluded him, but the more he thought about it, the more he was convinced that his uncle loved him. Just some bonds and beliefs were stronger.

How many governments were built on a foundation of blood? He'd always known there was a narrow line between terrorism and freedom fighting. Fighting for your beliefs.

Even if that was something as unbelievable as you were the reincarnation of Genghis fucking

Khan and were destined to rule the world.

He'd come across crazier things.

When the sky started to lighten, they tacked up the horses and headed out. Jochi had handed around strips of dried meat—presumably sheep, no one had asked—and they had eaten breakfast on the move. While his body still ached, his mind was clear. He felt better, and worse, than he had done in days.

Peter's betrayal bit deep, but at least he had hope again. And something to do. A plan to implement.

Eve was riding behind the guide, and Zach rode beside Noah, full of a restless energy that made his horse dance around beneath him. Noah knew how he felt; they'd both been focused on hunting down the person at the center of everything for so long. No one had believed them. Now he was sure Zach felt vindicated. As he did. He had found his target, and he wanted a shot at them.

"We're going to get the bitch," Zach said.

"Maybe."

"Definitely."

Noah didn't think it was going to be that easy. He pulled out his cell phone and tested for a signal. He'd been trying every ten minutes since they'd set off that morning. This time he saw the bars across the top of the screen. He was on.

"Eve," he called out. "Can we stop for a minute?"

She glanced over her shoulder. "You have a signal?"

"Yeah."

She called out something in Mongolian, and Jochi pulled up and turned his horse sideways across the trail. Noah reined his mount to a halt and swung down from the saddle. He threw his reins to Eve, who'd stopped just ahead of him. He didn't think Zach was capable of controlling two horses. Or one.

The temperature was warming up. Another clear blue sky and the chill of the night was giving way to the heat of the day. Sweat clung to his back. He walked a little away, back down the track. He didn't want Peter to hear the horses and guess where they were. It would take too much explanation that he wasn't prepared to give right now.

He worked out what time it was in the States, though he had no clue whether Peter was back there. Maybe he'd gone onto somewhere else after seeing Noah. Or maybe he had waited around in Russia for the summit. He was attending it, after all. He'd been a major proponent for the whole thing. Hell, he might have even advised the president to suggest the summit, which now took on a sinister aspect. Had he been putting more of those pieces in place? It was a hell of an opportunity to get all the world's major leaders in one room and take them out.

Never going to happen.

Whether they succeeded or failed, the summit was being canceled.

They just had to work out how. Noah was convinced that Peter didn't do anything with the information, which meant the summit would still be going ahead. And finding that out would put the final nail in Peter's coffin.

He pressed the personal number for Alex, who had been the second-in-command for Noah at Project Arachnid. He trusted Alex. Then again, he'd trusted Peter. Now, he no longer had faith in his own judgment. However, he had to tell someone to ensure that even if he failed, the summit would not go ahead.

The other man picked up after the first ring.

"Alex, it's Noah."

"What the hell are you doing calling at this time?"

"Just listen to me. This is for your ears only. Right now, this information goes nowhere else, not even the general."

"Okay."

"The security has been compromised, and the summit must be postponed."

"What's going on, Noah?"

"I can't tell you any more than I have. The intel is reliable. Keep it to yourself for now, but if you don't hear from me in forty-eight hours, you need to get that information to the president. I imagine you have a direct line."

As head of Project Arachnid, Noah had been able to circumvent the intermediaries and talk directly to the president in case of a time-sensitive emergency. Presumably, Alex would have the same access.

"I do."

"Good. Hopefully, I'll be in touch." He ended the call and glanced at Zach. "He'd heard nothing."

"So the general hadn't relayed what you told him about the summit?"

"No."

"I guess that makes it a definite, then."

"Yes." He bit out the word.

"You know, this is a good thing. We had zero leads. Absolutely nothing to go on. Now I'm guessing we have a direct line right to the top."

Noah silently agreed. That did nothing to erase the pain of betrayal, though. Peter had given him strength after his baby brother died and his whole family had fallen apart. He had inspired Noah to want to be a force for good in the world. Peter was the reason he'd joined the army. Peter, who'd always told him he saw things in black and white and that nothing was ever simple. Who had warned him that the day would come when he would compromise his morals for a result. And maybe he was doing that very thing now. Really, he should have made the intel regarding the summit known to all and everyone. Made sure that there was zero chance of it taking place. Except that would compromise their plan to free Harper.

Basically, he was putting the world's leaders in danger to attempt the safety of his child. A child who might very well already be dead.

He wouldn't think that. He had to believe.

He stared down at the phone for a minute, clearing his mind. He had to be convincing. Peter was clever and knew him better than anyone alive. He would see though him if he wasn't absolutely believable. But Noah was the best undercover operative Peter had ever worked with. Or so he'd told him.

He pressed his uncle's personal number. "Peter, it's Noah."

"Noah, I've been trying to get hold of you. What's happening? Have you heard anything about Harper?"

"Where are you?" he asked.

"London."

"I'm in Mongolia. Can you fly out here? Meet me."

"Of course. But why? Have you had more contact?"

"Yes. There was a message for me when I got back to the hotel the day we spoke."

"You didn't tell me."

"I was told they would kill Harper if I spoke to anyone. They wanted me to try and trace Eve's research. She was looking for the tomb of Genghis Khan."

"That's crazy. What does that have to do with the summit?"

"God knows. I have no clue. Except they were very clear: find the location within a week or Harper dies. That was two days ago."

"I take it you haven't found it. What can I do, Noah? I'll get everyone working on it. We'll find her."

The bastard sounded so convincing. "No, keep things quiet for now. I have the location."

"Of this tomb?"

"Yes. I found a satellite image Eve had hidden in a safety deposit box at the Marriott hotel the night before she died." They'd decided it was best to stick as close to the truth as possible. "I believe she was killed for that image, but I have no clue who did it. Anyway, I have the image, and I'm willing to trade it for Harper. What do I care about some eight-hundred-year-old dead guy? It's got no value—it doesn't make sense—but the hell with that. If that's what they want, I'll give it to them."

"How can I help?"

"I need back up, and I don't know who else I can trust."

Peter was silent for a moment. Hopefully guilt. He should feel fucking guilty. "Of course I'll come."

"I don't trust these people. In case anything happens to me, I want you there to get Harper out of harm's way. Take her home."

"I'll look after her. But are you sure you don't want me to bring the team? We'll take them down."

"I can't risk it."

"Okay. I'll organize a flight. Where do I meet you?"

"We'll be at the Holiday Inn in Ulaanbaatar. You can text me with your ETA to this number."

"I will. Be careful, Noah."

Noah ended the call. He stared at his phone for a minute while he waited for his heart rate to slow back to normal. The rage was building again, and that wouldn't help. When he was under control, he shoved the phone into his pocket and headed back to the others.

"Do you think he picked anything up?" Zach asked.

Noah thought back to the conversation, but he didn't think he'd given anything away. "No. I think we're on."

CHAPTER THIRTY-THREE

It was evening by the time Peter arrived in Ulaanbaatar. He had caught a commercial flight out of London, via Moscow. The whole journey had taken him eleven hours and given him too much time to think. Michaela would have provided him with a private flight if he'd requested it, but he hadn't. Nor had he told her where he was going. He would check in with her once he'd arrived. The truth was he hadn't wanted her to order him not to go, and there was a good chance she would have done exactly that. She believed he was too emotionally involved with Noah.

She was right.

He'd needed to be here because he'd told Noah the truth. He would make sure Harper was safe. Noah had sounded terrible on their last call. The whole thing had clearly taken a toll on him, which was hardly surprising.

Michaela had promised the girl was fine and would remain that way, whatever happened. Still, he couldn't quiet the niggling doubt. She had become so focused over the last few years and ruthless in pursuit of her ultimate goal.

The news that Noah had the location of the tomb had come as an enormous relief. Michaela would stick to her part of the bargain—that's how she worked. She would hand Harper back to her father in exchange for the location, and things could go back to the way they were. He would be rid of the awful burn of guilt that made him examine what he had become. He didn't like it.

Finding the tomb and the Talisman, fulfilling the prophecy. He'd begun to wonder if those didn't matter more to Michaela than the rest of the plan. A united empire that would span the globe. A chance for a unified world, with unprecedented peace and prosperity. A world without bias or prejudice.

That's how she had persuaded him all those years ago, and he'd wanted to believe her, because he'd always been a man who needed a cause. And he was in love with the passion she held for her vision of the future as much as with the woman herself. He'd wanted to be part of that.

Now he was forty-six and felt much older. The fires of his youth had burned out along the way, leaving a taste of ashes in his mouth and an empty space in his heart.

For years, he'd been finding it harder and harder to see through the blood and killings, but he was too far in now to back out. That wasn't an option. Besides, he still believed in her.

The world would forget the killings. Maybe he would as well, given long enough.

The one person he suspected would not forget was Noah.

Noah would never understand that sometimes the end did justify the means.

God, he was tired.

It would all be over in a few days, and their new world would finally be here. Except he was beginning to suspect that it would be just more of the same old shit. Humans were fundamentally flawed.

He pulled up in front of the hotel and switched off the engine. He'd sent Noah a text as he was leaving the airport, so he was expected. He just needed to give himself another moment to erase the guilt from his face before he faced his nephew.

Noah was bright, and he knew Peter too well. He would see straight away that something was wrong. Finally, when he couldn't put it off any longer, he got out of the car, handed the keys to the valet, and headed through the revolving doors into the reception area.

He glanced around, his gaze settling almost immediately on Noah's tall figure where he stood by the elevators. He walked over then stopped about a foot away, studying his nephew's face, not trying to hide the shock. "What the hell happened?"

He looked worse than when Peter had gotten him out of that Russian jail cell. Clearly, his nose had been broken recently, and new bruises were forming across his face. A deep cut bisected his left eyebrow. And there was the shadow of older bruises across his cheekbone.

"I'll tell you everything, but let's get somewhere more private first." Without waiting for an answer, Noah turned around and pressed the elevator button. The doors opened, and he stepped inside. For a moment, Peter hesitated, alarm bells ringing. Then he shook off the feeling—of course Noah felt off. His daughter had been kidnapped and he'd clearly been through some sort of trauma.

They got off on the fifth floor. Noah stopped in front of a door, put in a keycard, and stepped back to allow Peter to enter first. Peter looked into his face and knew in that moment that he'd made a huge strategic mistake. He glanced down the corridor, thought about making a run for it, then back at Noah.

He didn't say anything, just gave a small smile and gestured into the room. "We need to talk."

Peter took a deep breath then nodded, and with a sense of fatalism—maybe he'd always expected his secret life to catch up with him in the end—he stepped into the room.

He sensed a presence beside him. Before he could turn around, something swiped his legs out from under him, and he dropped to his knees. A kick in the center of his back sent him crashing to the carpeted floor. Pale cream and pink roses. Instinctively, his hands went beneath him to push himself up, and someone slammed into his back, hard, the weight driving him to the floor and keeping him there.

He relaxed his muscles.

A minute later, the pressure lessened, and whoever was kneeing him in the spine got off him. He didn't move, waiting for someone to speak.

"Get up," Noah said.

Peter pushed himself slowly to his feet. He took an internal inventory; he wasn't damaged. He hoped that was a good sign.

Maybe Noah didn't know. Maybe he just suspected that Peter had been involved in the death of his wife. The kidnapping of his daughter. He knew Noah had trust issues—hardly surprising after his childhood—just as he also knew that he'd always had Noah's trust. And his love. Noah was the son he and Michaela would never have.

Noah stood just inside the door, tension in every line of his body.

Another man stood by the bed, a pistol in his hand pointed at Peter. While he'd never actually met the man, he recognized his face. Zach Martin, an MI6 agent, and a thorn in Michaela's side for a long time. He'd been cut loose by his own people but somehow managed to elude every attempt to eliminate him.

"Hands in the air."

He raised his hands, and Noah moved behind him, frisking him quickly but efficiently, finding his cell phone. He had nothing else on him. "I'm not armed," he said.

Zach smiled. "Excuse me if I'm a little skeptical. You've clearly managed to successfully lie to the people closest to you for most of your life, so I'll not take any chances."

Peter shrugged. He was right.

Noah finished and stepped back. "Sit."

Zach gestured with the gun to an upright chair beside a polished wooden table. As he sat, Noah yanked his wrists behind him and tied them with something around the back of the chair. "There's no need," he said.

"Maybe I just want to do it."

He could understand that. "What now?"

"That depends on how much you're willing to tell us."

"You'd torture me?" Noah had never condoned the use of torture.

"I won't. But I suspect I know someone who will." He turned and called out. "Eve."

What the hell?

The bathroom door opened, and Eve walked through. Peter just stared, and then a slow smile spread across his face. He had really never considered this possibility. While he'd always known *they* hadn't killed her, it had never occurred to him that someone else hadn't. "You're alive."

She didn't return his smile. At first he thought her face was devoid of expression, then he looked into her eyes. Pure rage.

"Where's Harper? Where's my fucking daughter?"

Up until that point, he'd been considering his options, whether to deny any accusations thrown his way. He doubted very much that Noah had any actual proof. Now that possibility seeped away, leaving him tired and empty. The truth was he'd been battling feelings of defeat and futility since the moment Noah had told him that Harper had been kidnapped. His own niece. He'd thought Michaela cared for him in some strange weird way. That, on some level, he had meant something to her.

Now he knew how little he really meant.

That she would take his niece. Cause suffering to someone she knew he cared deeply for. Though, of course Michaela didn't like her people to have any other loyalties apart from her. This was probably a test.

If so, he suspected he was about to fail.

"I don't know," he said. "But I believe she's alive and unharmed."

"They sent me her goddamn finger," Noah said.

Shock crashed through him. Michaela had said the girl wouldn't be harmed. "Are you sure?"

"Yes, I'm goddamn sure. I saw a video."

Peter closed his eyes for a moment and focused on his breathing. His back ached where the knee had jabbed into his spine. He concentrated on that because it was easier than thinking about someone chopping off his niece's finger. Too bad he couldn't get the image out of his head.

This was a pivotal moment in his life. He could see that now. The last years had been leading up to this point. He took a deep breath, opened his eyes. "I'm sorry. I promise I didn't know. I had no clue it was planned until Noah told me she'd been taken."

"And you expect us to believe that would have made a difference?" Eve asked, incredulously. "Or that it would have been okay if it had been someone else? Someone else's niece or daughter that you took from her family and mutilated?"

She turned away, obviously unable to look at him any longer.

Would it have made a difference? The truth was, to him it would, but could he have shifted Michaela from her chosen path once she'd made a decision? A long time ago, maybe, but he had very little sway with her these days. No one did. She went her own way, and somewhere along the line she'd lost any form of compassion. Lost the ability to see the human race as individual people, just pawns to be used and then ruled. Collateral damage. She was obsessed with finding the tomb, and while he now understood the reason, it was still a part of her vision that he had never really sympathized with.

And he was no better than her. Worse maybe because he didn't have her absolute belief.

He could see now that Michaela had distanced herself from the harsher acts. He knew that she'd been responsible for the recent attack in Germany. Over ten thousand people had died, many of them children. She'd never asked him to be directly involved—she'd always been good at judging people. Knowing their strengths and their weaknesses. Maybe she'd known that he wouldn't have been able to stomach the actual killing. He was a soldier, and he'd killed before. That was different.

He'd become so good at turning a blind eye.

She'd told him to stay focused on the end game. These weren't acts of terrorism; they were legitimate strategic attacks on the enemy that would be forgotten in the years to come. How many more would die if the world was allowed to continue on its way, divided by race and religion? In her unified empire, minority groups would be supported, all religions accepted.

The only rule would be allegiance to the new order.

Shit. When had it all gone wrong? He looked around the room. Eve still stood with her back to him, hands on her hips, shoulders rigid. Zach Martin leaned against the wall, the gun no longer in sight. He appeared relaxed, though he didn't have the personal involvement of the other two. Noah stood to his left. He'd been staring out of the window; now he turned and caught Peter's gaze on him.

"I'm sorry," Peter said, because he was.

Eve whirled around. "Sorry isn't good enough. You have to help us get her back. You *have* to."

He glanced away. During his life, he'd betrayed everyone and everything. His country, his family, his men. He didn't expect forgiveness. And this was just one last betrayal.

What would they do if he said no? Torture him? Looking at Eve, so fierce, he thought it likely. She'd changed. The last time he'd seen her, she'd been diminished, suffering the lingering effects of PTSD he'd believed she would never recover from. Yet here she was, willing to do whatever was necessary to get her daughter back.

He thought of Michaela. She'd been unable to have children. It had been a bitter blow, and maybe that was when she changed. There would be no one to follow her. The next leader would be taken from the Descendants. They were probably already jockeying for power. Maybe that was when the hunt for the Talisman had taken over. She had to prove that she was the legitimate heir.

Noah moved to stand in front of him. "Can you get her back?"

Could he? Neither he nor Michaela knew where she was right now, but maybe there was a way. First, he needed to know one thing. "Do you have the location of the tomb?"

Noah pursed his lips, maybe deciding whether to tell him the truth or a lie. Then he shook his head. "No."

Shock reverberated through him. He'd been so sure that part was true. Instead, it was just a lie to get him here. "So it was never found?" He asked the question of Eve.

"We found it and then lost it again. Or, rather, Star found it. The real Star. I just showed her where to look and what to look for. I was given a shape and dimensions of an object they believed to be buried with Genghis Khan. It was distinctive and made of wood. It showed clearly on the high-definition satellite images." She sank down onto the bed, the strength seeming to go out of her. "It was all I ever wanted. The culmination of all my work, and I wish to hell I'd never started looking." She cast him an accusatory glare. "Did your people kill Star?"

He was beyond lies or prevarication. "I believe so."

"And torture her?"

"Maybe."

"Jesus. How could you be part of that?"

It was a good question. And one he didn't have an answer for. Or not one she would accept. That he'd wanted to be part of something bigger, something important. And Michaela was huge. Larger than life. A living legend. He forced his mind away—because even now, he could feel her pull—and back to the problem of how to get Harper out alive. They didn't have the location of the tomb, so the swap was not going to happen. If they got to that point and Michaela realized she'd been played, there was a good chance they would all die. He couldn't think of a way they could get to the swap and still come out alive—she had too many resources. So they couldn't let it get that far.

Yet if Noah told her that he had the location and wanted to make the trade, they would have to bring Harper here.

After he did this, he was a dead man. Michaela wasn't vindictive. She might be ruthless, but she didn't kill without reason. She would let Noah go—he had never given his allegiance. She wouldn't look on it as a betrayal.

Peter, she would hunt down to the ends of the earth.

It didn't matter. He deserved this. Looking back, he tried to pinpoint the moment when he should have turned back. When he should have realized he wasn't part of something bigger, he was part of something evil. One of the bad guys. Noah would have known. From an early age, he'd always been able to tell right from wrong. Peter had always considered it naive. Likely because in some part of his conscience, he'd always known he was "wrong."

"Peter?" Noah prompted.

He forced his mind to concentrate on the problem. He would do this one thing. Maybe gain himself a little redemption. It was good he didn't believe in Heaven or Hell. "Make contact," he said. "Tell them you have the location of the tomb and want to make the exchange. But first you want proof of life—that would be expected."

"You're sure she is alive?" Eve asked.

"Fairly certain." He couldn't say 100 percent. They'd cut off her finger. Jesus. "It would have been pointless to kill her. She's useful."

"So what happens next? We don't have the location. We can't make the trade."

"They'll have to bring her into the country. We'll find out where and when, and we'll take her back. Then you'll disappear. You'll get the hell away from here. Soon, Michaela will be too busy to worry about you."

Noah shook his head. "You really think we're going to let the summit go down?"

"You can't stop it."

"Maybe I can't, but you can. You have a direct line to the president. You're going to tell him everything. Once he pulls out, then the rest will follow."

Would it work? Probably. Though it would be a temporary respite. "While you might stop the summit, you won't stop *them*. They're too big. You have no idea of the resources they control."

"You do. And you're going to tell us everything you know." Noah turned away, crossed the room, and spoke quietly to Zach. The other man glanced between them all, then he nodded. He pulled the gun from the back of his pants and handed it to Eve, and then he left the room.

Maybe he would tell them. Or maybe he would take the coward's way out and find some way to end his life before he betrayed the woman he still loved. Or before she killed him. Or he killed her — that was the other option. He was maybe the one man who could do it, who could get close enough. First he had to help them rescue Harper. Anything else wasn't an option.

Noah came back to stand in front of him. "You can get the information as to where Harper will be?"

"I think so. Michaela will already know I'm

here. I'll contact her—tell her the truth, that when you found the location, you asked me to come as back up to look after my niece if anything happened to you. I'll tell her that as I'm already here, I can organize the trade from this side. Make sure the girl gets there safely. She'll believe me. She is aware I wasn't…happy with what was happening."

"You mean the kidnapping and mutilation of your niece?"

He winced. "Yes."

"You think the senator still trusts you?"

"I believe so. We extract Harper as soon as she's in the country. We'll need to be fast. Take out the team before they can report back. Hopefully, that will buy you time to get away with Harper." He looked to Eve, who was perched on the edge of the bed, the pistol on her lap, chewing her nonexistent nails. "I'll organize a plane back to England. You pick up your other two children and just disappear."

Eve nodded. He was guessing disappearing appealed right now. She wouldn't be the problem. He suspected Noah might not be so agreeable. While Eve had spent most of her adult life hunting for Genghis Khan, Noah—while he might not have been aware of it—had spent most of his life hunting for Michaela. Even when he knew nothing of the existence of the Descendants, he'd known that there was someone at the center of it all. It was uncanny how close his ideas had come to the truth. He suspected Noah wouldn't let it go. He'd want to end it. But it was futile. All he could hope was Noah's need to keep his family safe would supersede his wish to finally trap his spider. It was a gamble—Noah had always found it easier to walk away from the people he loved than to walk away from his enemies.

But all he said was, "When do we do this?"

"As soon as possible. We're running out of time. I imagine Harper is being held in the U.K. Even so, it will take at least twelve hours to get her here."

"Okay, then do it."

He moved behind Peter and unlocked the cuffs. Peter remained seated, rubbing at his wrists. Noah handed him back his cell phone. "Put it on speaker."

Peter sat for a moment calming his mind, deciding what to say. He had one chance. If she picked up anything in his voice, his attitude, then this was over before it began. Harper would die. His heart raced; his pulse throbbed at his throat. He'd been in combat and not felt this much fear, but he needed to do this one thing right.

He punched in the number then listened to the series of clicks as the call was rerouted through scramblers.

"Peter?" He could tell nothing from her voice.

"Michaela. I have good news. I heard from Noah. He has the location of the tomb."

"How did he find it?"

"Eve left the image in the safety deposit box in a hotel in Irkutsk."

"I knew she had it." He could hear the triumph in her voice, and even after everything that had happened, his heart ached at the thought of betrayal.

"He wants to make the exchange."

"You're with him now?"

"He called me. He wants me here so I can look after Harper if anything happens to him."

"He doesn't trust me. I'm hurt."

"He doesn't know you. But I can work the exchange on this end. Noah trusts *me*."

She was silent for a moment, though her breathing was fast. She was excited. "Darling, you're sure he doesn't know about us? He's not playing you?"

"No. He's too worried about his daughter. He wants her back in one piece. Well, two pieces. Apparently, they sent him her finger. There was no need for that. You said she wouldn't be harmed."

"I didn't order it. I just told them to make it convincing."

"Well, believe me, he's convinced."

"Okay, I'll wait for him to make contact. The

timing is close, but as long as we make it to the opening ceremony with the Banner and the Talisman in my possession, it will work. That gives us two days. You've done well, darling."

She ended the call. Peter handed the phone back to Noah.

"She called you 'darling.'" Eve's tone held accusation.

He shrugged. "We've known each other a long time." He sighed. He wouldn't ask for forgiveness. He knew it wouldn't be forthcoming, but he needed Noah to know one thing. "I didn't know about Harper. I would never have condoned it. I would have found a way to stop her. You have to believe me."

"Actually, I do. But Christ, Peter, how could you? How many innocent people have died? Over ten thousand in Germany." He ran his hand through his hair. "Why? Was it money? Power?"

Never money. Personal wealth wasn't something that interested him. Power, maybe a little. It was intoxicating, but not the truth. "Would you believe I wanted a better world?"

Eve snorted. Noah's expression didn't change. "I could believe that. What I find almost impossible to comprehend is that you stayed with them after they showed their true colors. How could you support an organization that killed so many indiscriminately?"

"It was never indiscriminate. You know that. You've always known it. You saw the patterns. Each attack was carefully thought out, with a purpose. They've been putting the pieces in place for eight hundred years. They might have killed, but it was never without reason. Is that so different than war? So different from the bombing of civilian targets during the Second World War? Than Hiroshima that killed thousands yet ultimately saved millions?"

It was an argument they'd had so many times. Trouble was he was no longer sure he was right. But he owed Noah to maybe try and explain. "I met Michaela Clayton when I was twenty-one."

Shock flared on Noah's face.

"We met at a political rally. I can't even remember what it was about. We were both at Harvard. She was studying political strategy. She had opinions about everything and a dream of a better world."

"Did she mention collateral damage at that point?" Eve asked, her voice dripping with sarcasm. "Torture? Mutilation?"

Strangely, he believed that Noah could forgive him, if they had long enough—say, a million years. However, Eve would never forget or forgive.

"No. We were lovers for two years before she told me about the Descendants. By then, I was sold on the idea. You don't understand how…

exciting it was. To have a direction, a goal, and it was so vast. A global empire."

"World peace?" Eve said.

He ignored the sarcasm, took the comment at face value. "Yes. And open trade. People could follow whatever religion they liked. Nobody would be hungry or go without medicine or education."

"Wow," she said. "You've almost convinced me. Maybe we'd better move on to the terrorism part. The part where thousands of innocent people die so your girlfriend can be ruler of the fucking world. You're unbelievable."

"I loved her." He shook his head. "If I'm honest, I still love her. But love is never enough. And it was only later when things got...bad. Michaela was hitting a lot of opposition within the group. She needed to prove that she was the legitimate heir. She needed the Banner and the Talisman. Once she had those in her possession, no one would question her right to rule. And there was a time frame, and it was running out."

"And that's where I came in. How convenient that I was already researching the tomb."

"I remember when you first mentioned it. Just after the two of you were married. At the time, I thought it amusing. Later, I thought it a way to get you...involved. To bind you to the cause. I'd always hoped that one day Noah would join us, so

I introduced you to Michaela. She liked you. That's how you got the funding to carry on your research."

"If she liked me so much, then why the hell did she send John Chen to kill me?"

"He was never there as an assassin. He was there to protect you. We knew the Darkhats were watching you. The minute they believed you were close, they would kill you. And that's exactly what we thought had happened."

"And yet here I am."

"I'm glad."

She snorted in disbelief. "You talk as if this is still happening."

"It will happen. Maybe not this year. Maybe not with Michaela. But it will happen. The Descendants are everywhere."

"You know I have to stop her?" Noah said. "I can't just walk away."

Peter had suspected as much. "Then you will die."

CHAPTER THIRTY-FOUR

Harper sniffed, a tear leaking from her eyes.

She couldn't tell whether they were moving or whether the motion was all in her mind.

Whenever she woke up they gave her a drink that tasted funny and made her sleepy. Now, though, she was awake, and her hand was one big lump of throbbing pain. She bit back a sob. She couldn't even look at the bandaged stump. If she did, then the sick crawled up the back of her throat.

How long since she was taken?

She'd lost track of the days.

She didn't know how long it was since they had woken her up and hurt her. They'd filmed it on a phone, said she had to smile for her dad, and then they'd chopped off her finger.

It hadn't hurt when they chopped it off, though she had screamed anyway. Things like that only happened in the movies. That had lasted all of about five seconds. Then it had hurt real bad, and she'd screamed again. One of them had stabbed her with a needle, and everything had gone dark.

It might have been better if she'd never woken up.

The one good thing was that her mom was

dead. She'd never thought she would think that. But this would have upset her mom if she wasn't dead already.

Her gran always said be thankful for small things.

Two men. A tall one and a taller one. Both dark haired and brown eyes. Round faces. Eyes like the pictures in her mother's books about Mongolia. She hated Mongolia. And she hated Genghis stupid Khan.

Was this something to do with her mom? She'd always known that something bad had happened to her. The last few times they'd spoken—they'd Skyped while her mom was in Mongolia—something had been wrong. Her mom had changed. She looked both better and worse. For as long as Harper could remember, her mom had been afraid. She often woke up screaming. She'd tried to explain. That something bad had happened to her a long time ago and that she was trying her best to put it behind her but didn't always manage to do a good job. After that, Harper had always been aware of the lingering fear in her mom's eyes. Those last times Harper had seen her, that fear had gone. Replaced by another.

And then she'd died.

Her dad had come for them. She'd thought he wouldn't. That they'd be alone. Or at least left with

Gran and Gramps. But he'd come, and while she hadn't let him see it — he *had* forgotten her birthday — she liked having him around. He was so big, and he made her feel safe.

She'd even liked the fact that her dad had a gun. That had made her feel safe as well. Whatever happened, he would look after them. And then her dad had disappeared. He'd promised them all he was going to be there for them. And then he wasn't.

For days, her few conscious moments had all been in the same room. An ordinary-looking bedroom, not much light, with shutters on the window. And a small bathroom that they had made her get up and use each time she woke. At first she hadn't been able to. Not with them so close. Then they'd said they would chop off another finger if she wet the bed, so she had forced herself. And then she'd thrown up.

Then last night everything had changed. They'd woken her up and made her get out of bed. Then they'd made her hold a newspaper in front of her and taken a photograph. And instead of the bathroom, they'd wrapped a blanket around her shoulders and half-carried, half-dragged her out of the room, down some stairs, and into the open air. She'd tried to look around, to get some idea of where she was, listen to the sounds, but she'd had only moments before they had shoved her into the back of a car. Then the stab of a needle and she had gone out again. When she'd woken, everything was different.

Except the pain.

She wanted to cry from the pain, sobs building up in her throat. She swallowed them down; she didn't want them to know she was awake. She tried to think of anything but her missing finger.

Lucy and Daniel. They'd lost their mom, then their dad, and finally Harper had disappeared. They'd be a mess. They were so little. Not like her. She had to be strong for them. Get back to them. Except she was pretty sure the bad men planned to kill her.

And she didn't want to die.

She bit back a sob and blinked a couple of times. She wasn't back in her room. She was laying on a row of seats, the blanket still around her.

Now there was a continuous low roaring noise in the background. And above that the sound of voices. The two men were somewhere behind her. She turned her head slightly, the movement jolting her hand, which was cradled against her chest, and she swallowed a cry of pain. She didn't want them to know she was awake.

The roaring changed, overridden by a whirring, clunking noise. And she realized she was in a plane. She'd only flown once before, when they'd moved from America to England. She'd only been five at the time, and she couldn't remember it at all. But she'd seen enough airplanes on the TV to recognize it. She was flying somewhere.

Maybe they were taking her to her dad.

The noise was growing louder, and then the whole plane jolted, and she reached out with her free hand to grab onto something and only just stopped herself from falling to the floor. There was a roar in her ears now. Were they crashing?

She didn't want to die, and the screams were building up inside her again.

But she could sense them slowing down, and finally, after what seemed an age, the plane stopped moving.

One of her guards stood in front of her. "Stay," he said. Like she was a dog.

As he walked away to peer out of the window, she pushed herself up so she was sitting, pulling the blanket tighter around her as though she could somehow stop the shivering. Her teeth were chattering.

He said something to the second man who was still behind her. He stood up and came around to her, grabbed her arm, and yanked her to her feet. She couldn't bite back the scream that was torn from her, and he shook her arm. "Shut up."

She bit her lip until she tasted blood and choked the scream to a whimper.

The first man was pushing open the door now.

Then he stood in the open doorway, watching something outside the plane.

Was someone coming?

Could it be her father?

She wanted that so much, her chest ached with the need.

Please, Daddy. Please, Daddy.

If he could just come through that doorway, then everything would be all right.

The man stepped to the side, and she squeezed her eyes tight shut. She couldn't bear it if she was wrong.

CHAPTER THIRTY-FIVE

The sun was just rising as they parked the vehicle at the edge of the airfield a few miles outside the city of Ulaanbaatar.

The plan was to get Harper and then get the hell out of there.

Part of Noah wanted to stick around, somehow get the senator to meet them and take her down. Alive or dead. She needed to be stopped.

They had talked and talked around it but could see no way to make it work if they rescued Harper. As soon as that happened, Clayton would realize Peter had betrayed her, and there was no way she would come to any meeting.

And rescuing Harper had to be the number one priority.

There would be time to go after the senator later. She would have nowhere to hide. And as soon as Harper was safe, Peter would contact the president and get the summit stopped. That would buy them more time. They would take down Clayton and then go after the Descendants. They had the knowledge to track them down now. To dig them out of wherever they were hiding. Peter would tell them everything they needed to know.

First: Harper.

"Where the hell are they?" he muttered. Had Peter lied? Betrayed them?

"There." Peter waved a hand toward the deep blue sky. Noah stared and finally made out the small speck of the plane, getting bigger by the second. Some of the tightness around his chest eased. This was going to work.

Eve and Zach were waiting at the hotel. As soon as Noah and Peter had Harper, they would meet them there. Peter had arranged to fly them all back to the U.K. in a plane belonging to the Descendants, which was ironic, but Peter claimed it was the one way to get out of the country undetected. And right now he had no choice except to trust his uncle.

The plane landed, taxiing to a halt at the far side of the runway.

"Okay, we're on." Peter drove across the grass toward the plane, Noah crouching in the back in case anyone was watching their approach.

As they pulled up beside the plane, his heart hammered, and his mouth was bone dry. There was so much that could go wrong with a hostage situation. They would likely kill Harper at the first inkling that anything was not going according to plan. Or she could be shot in the crossfire. They had to be fast and careful.

Noah focused on the cockpit, willing the pilot to move. They needed everyone in the same place.

Finally, the man got up and disappeared into the main cabin. Noah blew out his breath. "Pilot is moving."

"Give me thirty seconds," Peter said. "I'll keep them talking and locate Harper. Then you come in, and we take them down. They can't be allowed to get a transmission out or the country will be in lock down and you'll never leave."

Noah nodded. The plan depended on Michaela Clayton believing Peter was still loyal and that he had Harper. He would call the senator as soon as she was safe. While the ruse wouldn't last for long, it would hopefully be long enough to get them out of the country.

This would work. It had to work. They had given him proof of life, a short video clip of Harper holding up today's paper. She'd looked pale and fragile. Unlike herself, but alive.

As Peter climbed the stairs, the door opened, and a man appeared. He was medium height with short black hair and dressed in jeans and a gray T-shirt. He stood aside to let Peter pass. Noah counted the seconds. As he hit twenty-five, the roar of a gun exploded inside the plane, followed by a staccato rattle of shots.

What the hell had gone wrong?

He was out of the vehicle, pulling his gun from the holster as he raced up the stairs of the plane. He kicked open the door then crouched down.

The plane had gone silent.

He peered inside; Peter stood in the center of the cabin. Two men lay sprawled across the seats, bullet holes in their foreheads. A third lay in front of the door to the cockpit. He'd been hit in the chest. Harper was nowhere to be seen.

He searched the cabin frantically, with increasing panic, pistol held out, except there was no one left to shoot. Dropping his hand to his side, he turned back to Peter. "Where is she?"

"Not here."

The words didn't make sense.

"She's not here, Noah." Peter repeated his words. But they had to be wrong.

Harper had to be here. She was hiding. Or unconscious. Or…

A roaring filled his head. His chest tightened, and for a moment he struggled to breathe. He sucked in the air, concentrated on inhaling. Exhaling. Forcing down the panic clawing at his insides.

Turning slowly, he searched the cabin for anything that might make sense. That might give him a clue. Hope. Had they just got it wrong? She was never here?

Something on one of the seats caught his eye. A newspaper. He took the few steps and picked it up. It was the paper Harper had held up for the proof of life video.

She had been here on the plane, and now she was gone.

Had they done the video, sent him the proof he'd demanded that his daughter was alive, and then killed her? Dumped her body?

The adrenaline oozed from his system, leaving him weak and shaking. He sank to the seat behind him, paper still clutched in his hand, and closed his eyes. When he opened them, nothing had changed. He'd failed.

"They killed her. She's dead."

Somehow they must have discovered what he had planned. They'd told him Harper would die if he spoke to anyone. It had been a calculated risk involving Peter, and he'd lost.

A scream was building inside him.

They'd promised to send her back in pieces. Now the best he could hope was that she hadn't suffered. She was eleven years old. It wasn't fair. He almost choked on the words. Since when had life been fair?

"Noah, listen to me. She's not dead."

He stared into Peter's eyes. "You don't know that. Your fucking girlfriend killed my daughter."

"*My* niece. And Harper's not dead. There would be no point. They still need her. Michaela wants the location, and she's running out of time. She wouldn't jeopardize that."

He tried to find hope in the words, but his mind

was sluggish like trudging through thick mud. Drowning in it. Could Peter be right? But he'd been wrong about *this*.

"Unless they don't believe I have the location. Maybe she knows I was lying. Maybe someone told her."

"I swear I told her nothing." Peter sighed. He shoved his pistol into his shoulder holster and sank down into the chair opposite, running a hand around the back of his neck. "I told her nothing," he repeated. "This is a message to me. She doesn't trust me. I'm guessing Harper was on the plane, and they dropped her off somewhere on the way. Michaela set me up."

Noah concentrated on the words, trying to get his head around them. Could she be alive? If so, for how long? Because he didn't have the location. He had nothing to trade.

Peter had been his betrayer, but also his hope.

Now he had nothing.

"She believes you betrayed her?"

"I doubt that. If she believed that was the case, I'd likely be already dead. All the same, she doesn't entirely trust me on this. And it's too important for her to risk. I'm guessing I've been sidelined. I'm sorry, Noah."

"Sorry doesn't fucking help." He rested his head in his hands. "Sorry isn't good enough."

None of them would have been tangled up in

this were it not for Peter.

Clayton still believed he had the location. The only way forward was to make her believe that was the case. Lure her to a place and try and get Harper away. It was hopeless.

There was no way she would come alone. She'd likely have an army.

Plus he had been warned by the Darkhats that if he stepped within the Great Taboo again, he would be killed, and he had no doubt they would carry out their threat. Likely he'd be dead before he ever reached the meeting point.

He'd suggested they arrange the meet in a different area, but according to Eve, the Descendants already knew the general location of the tomb. There was no way they would believe it to be anywhere other than the Great Taboo.

At the same time, he had no choice except to try. Maybe with Peter's help, he could somehow get Harper away before Clayton realized she'd been double-crossed. Though how much help would Peter be if Clayton no longer trusted him?

"We'll go ahead with the swap," he said. "If you're right and Harper is still alive, then we'll try and find a way to get her safely away." Maybe that could be the agreement. Peter would take Harper while Noah went with the senator. How likely was she to agree to that? Right now, he couldn't come up with anything better.

"She's alive."

Something else occurred to him. "What about the summit?"

The plan had been for Peter to call the president as soon as they had Harper safe. They hadn't wanted to risk blowing Peter's cover before Harper was free.

The summit was only two days away. Soon they would all be in place. The world's leaders would arrive the day after tomorrow. They had to be warned.

"We can't take the risk that we die and there's nobody left who can stop the attack." Zach would try, but he had been blocked at every move. He was a rogue agent; no way would anyone listen to him. "I think you should make the call now."

"It will mean she definitely knows I'm working with you."

"I think we can take that as a given anyway. You've lost any strategic advantage you might have given us."

Peter didn't look happy, but he nodded and pulled his cell phone from his pocket.

"Put it on speaker," Noah said.

Peter pressed a series of numbers in, and it clicked through a relay.

"General Blakeley requesting a code red contact with the president."

"Access denied."

There was another series of clicks and then…

"General Blakeley, I'm afraid all your calls will be re-routed to this number in future. We've been ordered to bring you in for questioning."

That didn't sound good.

"To whom am I speaking?"

"I'm afraid that information is classified. If you will give us your current location, we will send people to pick you up."

"I have important information regarding an imminent terrorist threat to the president. As Commander of Project Arachnid—"

"Project Arachnid has been terminated and all personnel detained for questioning." And Noah was guessing they would be held somewhere out of contact until after the summit. "I suggest you give yourself up, general. Any further attempts to make contact will be re-routed here."

Peter glanced at him and shook his head. He ended the call. "We're cut off. Isolated."

A shiver ran through him.

Just how much power did these people have?

CHAPTER THIRTY-SIX

They got back to the hotel an hour later.

Noah was drained. Exhaustion tugged at him, mingled with despair.

The situation was hopeless.

He wanted to rage against fate, fight back, but he could see no way through.

The best he could hope for was to get Harper out of this alive. And maybe get close enough to Michaela Clayton to take her out. While that might not finish off the Descendants, it would maybe buy him some time to expose the organization.

It was impossible.

They'd tried to contact some of his old team, starting with Alex, and gotten nowhere. He could only assume that they had indeed been detained.

As he stepped into the coolness of the reception area, he came to an abrupt standstill. A woman stood at the desk, her back to him. Tall and slim, she wore khaki pants tucked into boots and a black tank top.

"What is it?" Peter asked from beside him.

He shook his head but didn't answer. Instead, he closed the distance between them. When he was a couple of feet away, she turned as though sensing his presence. For a long moment, she stared at him, her expression wary as if she was unsure of her welcome. Then her gaze flicked past him to Peter and back to him.

"What are you doing here?" he asked.

He wanted to hate her, though the truth was he couldn't. Sara hadn't betrayed him—she had betrayed her own people. She could have killed him that night, but she had let him live against direct orders, knowing she would be in dire trouble for allowing him to survive. Having said that, he was still pissed that she had lied to him. That she had lied to him and then slept with him. He'd thought there was something between them. It had all been an act, and he felt...used. Christ, he was pathetic. He hadn't allowed himself to care for anyone since Eve.

"I need to talk to you," she said.

"You do? What about?"

Her gaze flicked back to Peter. "In private."

Maybe she'd come to finish the job and kill him. She'd have to get in line.

He nodded and turned to his uncle. "Can you give us a moment?"

"Of course. I'll go get my things together and we can leave as soon as you're ready."

Noah waited until the other man headed toward the elevator and then steered Sara into the bar. It was empty at this time of day. They found a booth in the far corner. She slid onto the seat, and he took the one opposite.

"Was that your uncle, the general?" she asked.

"Yes. He came to…help me out." He couldn't tell her what they were doing. Likely she'd go straight back to her people and he would lose any chance of luring Clayton anywhere. "What do you want? I thought you made your position perfectly clear."

"I…" She shook her head. "Have you heard anything about your daughter?"

"Why?"

She closed her eyes for a moment. "I want to help, Noah."

"I thought you couldn't or wouldn't help."

Anger flashed across her face, then her eyes narrowed. "I'm going against everything I was brought up to believe here. Cut me some fucking slack."

"You were supposed to kill me. Don't tell me you didn't consider it."

"You're still here, aren't you?"

He sighed. "I'm sorry. You're right. Tell me why you came."

She took a deep breath. For a moment, she looked away. Whatever she had come here for, she wasn't finding it easy. "I memorized the GPS coordinates from the image file before I destroyed it. If you still need the location of the tomb to save your daughter, then it's yours."

For a moment, the words didn't make sense. She had the location. She would give it to him. Why was she doing this? Could she be trusted? Or did she have some agenda of her own? The questions were spinning in his head. "Why? Why the change of heart?"

"Because, the truth is *I've* changed. I grew up believing we had a purpose. That we were important. But really what are we doing? Keeping a meaningless secret. That's not worth killing for, and I don't want anyone else to die, either. Not your daughter. Not mine. Whatever is there, it's not worth it. It's just a tomb, a body probably turned to dust and ashes. We've spent our whole lives guarding the grave of a man who died centuries ago. I don't believe anymore. He's long dead, and that's not what's important. The living are what matters."

He sat back in his chair, and the tight band around his chest loosened. He hadn't even known it was there. Now relief flooded his system, and he could breathe again. There were good people in the world. He'd believed he was losing the ability to tell the difference. Or that they just didn't exist. Not in his world, anyway. Peter's betrayal had hit him hard.

But Star or rather Sara had hit him equally hard. Now she was here. Offering her help, though it would cost her dearly. And maybe there was hope again.

He studied her. She looked…earnest, caring even. But this was a woman who had managed to lie consistently to him for days. She was clearly a good actress.

The thing was he wanted to believe her. And she hadn't had to come here.

Who was this woman really? It was unlikely he'd have the chance to get to know the real Sara. He was running out of time.

Maybe she had some underlying motive, but he couldn't see the point. He needed time to think. Too bad he didn't have any.

"Let me help," she said, resting her hand on his arm.

What choice did he really have? He exhaled and then gave a short nod.

She closed her eyes for a moment. Clearly, she'd been in no way sure that he'd accept her offer. That made him feel a little better.

His mind was racing, trying to work how he could use this to his advantage. Would it make a difference? They could go ahead with the exchange. Get Harper out alive and then go after the senator.

Was Clayton aware he knew her involvement? She must have her suspicions. So even if she didn't kill him outright, there was a good chance she wouldn't risk leaving him free to try and stop her before the summit. But that was a risk they would have to take. They had the night to come up with a plan.

"So you'll make the exchange?" she asked.

"It's arranged for the day after tomorrow. We'd planned to use a bluff and hope to get Harper away. Though there's still the problem of getting into the Great Taboo without your people killing us before we get to the meeting place."

"I know. But I have an idea."

• • •

Sara studied him across the table. He looked terrible, worse than the last time they had met. Like he hadn't slept or eaten. The bruises had come out on his face, and he looked like a really crappy boxer.

She'd slipped away from the camp without telling anyone she was leaving. Although she was quite aware they could have stopped her if they wanted to because nothing moved in the Great Taboo without her people knowing it.

She'd argued with her father, trying to make him see that times were changing and they needed to change with them. She'd told him that she no longer believed that their cause was worth any more deaths. She was supposed to follow in his footsteps and one day become the next leader of the Darkhats, but how could she when she no longer had faith?

Despite that, for some reason, they had let her go, but then they weren't aware that she had the location of the tomb. If they'd known, things might have been very different. At best, she would likely have remained a prisoner. At worst, she would be dead.

While her father loved her, unlike her, he had never had any doubts as to their cause.

And she had no doubt that they would follow through on their threat to kill Noah if he returned to the Great Taboo unless she could persuade them otherwise.

"Go on," he prompted.

"You're right. Even if I give you the location, you won't make it. My people will kill you before you ever get there." She'd searched her mind for an answer, and she did have an idea. Though it was far from foolproof. So first she needed to discover if they had any other options. "Could you not arrange the swap elsewhere? Say the tomb was never on Burkhan Khaldun? Arrange the meeting somewhere far away." At least that way there would be one less group trying to kill him.

"No. Eve says they already know the general location. It was tied in with where the spear was found. Finding the spear is what allowed them to home in on the location of the actual tomb."

That wasn't good. She wished she could just go far away from here. Perhaps to some tropical island with Noah. Except that wasn't who he was. In his own way, he was as blinded as her father, totally dedicated to a cause. At least he had a genuine purpose—to save his daughter and stop a complete megalomaniac from taking over the world.

The only hope was to make a trade with her people. That she could convince them that there were bigger threats to the Darkhat's cause than Noah, that in fact he was fighting on their side. If the Descendants rose to power, her people were finished. If not now, one day soon the Descendants would find the tomb. They wouldn't back down if they failed this time. They would keep coming, and if all Noah had told her was true, they had the resources to finish this. An army at their disposal and her people would be decimated.

So she needed to make them see that times were changing and they needed to change with them.

But how?

"Do you have any clue who you're dealing with?" Maybe a concrete enemy would convince them.

Noah pursed his lips and didn't answer straight away. Maybe he didn't trust her. Could she blame him? He knew something, though; he was just weighing up what to tell her.

"It's Senator Michaela Clayton."

Noah's employer. Sara had done some investigation into the company when she'd been researching Noah, and it was vast, its resources almost limitless.

She remembered the woman from the cemetery the day of Eve Blakeley's so-called funeral. Tall, with dark red hair and green eyes. While there were no reliable images of Genghis Khan, many believed that rather than the typical Mongolian coloring, he'd had green eyes and red hair.

Christ, if only they'd known. "Are you sure?"

"My uncle confirmed it."

"How does he know? Has it just come to light?"

"Not really. You could say he had insider knowledge. He's been working with the Descendants since he was twenty-one."

She sat back in her seat. "You didn't know?"

A tic jumped in his cheek. "Of course I didn't fucking know. I would have killed the bastard. He's lied to me all my life. Shit, I believed he was one of the good guys. Hell, maybe the only good guy. Instead, he's been deep inside the very organization we were hunting. The organization that has caused thousands of innocent deaths, that took my daughter."

"His niece. Yet you're working with him now?"

"I didn't have a lot of options."

"And you trust him?"

"To be honest…I don't know. I think my finding out was in some way a relief for him. He's lived with doubts for so long."

Well, she knew all about that.

"And with guilt," Noah continued. "On balance, I do trust him, even though he's given almost a lifetime of loyalty to Michaela Clayton. And I think he loves her, even now. That's a hard thing to shake off. Maybe he's just biding his time. But, as I said, I don't have a lot of choice. And he also loves Harper. I think she was the final straw. Maybe blood is thicker than whatever he has with Clayton."

Michaela Clayton was a powerful woman. But there was never any indication that she wasn't exactly what she appeared to be. Would the information be enough to sway Sara's people into lending their support instead of killing Noah out of hand? Perhaps—though maybe it was wishful thinking—her people would not kill Noah straight away if she was with him. That would at least give them a chance to argue their case.

Then what?

Did they try and get them to agree to leading Michaela Clayton to the tomb they had guarded for centuries? Never going to happen.

There had to be a way. She just had to keep thinking until she found it.

"Are you married?" Noah asked.

Sara had been deep in thought, and the question came out of the blue. She shook her head automatically, partly in denial, partly to clear her mind. "No. Why?"

"I just wondered. You said you had a daughter. I assume she must have a father somewhere."

Why did he care? "We were never married and haven't been together for a long time." They'd met when she was nineteen and fallen in love, but he'd had a job to do. He'd been brought up in Russia and just back for a visit. He had no choice in where he went, just as she had no choice. "It was Yuri," she said.

He frowned. "The archaeologist who worked with Eve?"

"Yes. The man your ex-wife killed. At least we believe she killed him." Though only after he had no doubt tried to kill her. Would Noah deny or confirm it? But he said nothing. Her father had told her Yuri was dead, that he'd gone into the cave system—his job was to make sure Eve never came out with the spear. Instead, he had never been heard from again, and the guide who had taken them into the mountains had been shot dead. The spear was nowhere to be found; presumably, the senator had it now. She sighed.

"They'll never let you take her to the location."

"Eve says it's not the actual tomb that the senator wants, but this talisman that's buried with the body."

While her people had always known about the talisman, they'd considered it nothing more than a fairytale. A magical item that Khan had supposedly carried and that had been buried with him. Legend had it the Talisman and the spear had been with him through every battle. With them at his side, he was said to be invincible.

Obviously, her people had been wrong, and it was more than a fairytale. When she'd seen the image the real Star had sent to Eve, she'd known from the distinctive shape and size that she was looking at the Talisman.

"That's how she managed to locate the tomb," Noah said. "Apparently, the tomb itself would be almost impossible to identify alone. One of the reasons being that they know there are others buried in the same area. A tomb could belong to another family member, not Genghis Khan at all. But the box that holds the Talisman is a distinct shape, and the Descendants knew that. They gave the details to Eve. She had the shape and the size, the general location from the positioning of the spear when it was found. With those, she was able to give the real Star something to look for and somewhere to look. High-resolution imaging enabled her to see beneath the ground, and she found the Talisman."

Sara thought back to the image. She'd been picked for the role of Star because she had a computer/technical background, though she hadn't known anything about space archeology. But then neither had Noah, so it was considered the risk of him catching her out would be low. All the same, she'd done a lot of reading on the subject, and she'd been able to at least make sense of what the image showed. And recognize the GPS coordinates.

No one knew exactly what Genghis Khan had been buried with. Some said that he had wanted no pomp and ceremony, just to be made one with the earth. To go out as he had come in, with nothing. Others believed his family had buried him with huge amounts of wealth. That they had sacrificed his horses and surrounded him with their bodies, along with the bodies of the men who had dug his grave. Gold and jewels from his campaigns. The Talisman.

"Clayton wants the Talisman," Noah continued. "Actually, she needs the Talisman. According to Peter, there's some dissent in the group. Many of their people don't believe she's the true leader. Or do believe, but don't want her anyway. If she wants to unite the whole group, she needs the Talisman to show that she is the leader who was prophesied."

That made sense. Sort of. Yet she couldn't help but wonder how many within the group believed in the prophecy or how many were just in it for the money and the power.

Her people didn't care about the Talisman; they cared about the body. Their task had always been to protect the remains from desecration. They'd always translated that into keeping the location a secret.

However, if one person had found the tomb, then others would as well. Technology was too advanced now. She needed to make her people see that.

Her mind was churning. Would they listen to her?

So far they hadn't.

At that moment, Peter Blakeley appeared in the doorway with a bag in his hand. He stood for a moment looking around the bar before heading their way. His gaze flickered across to where her hand still rested on Noah's arm. She almost moved it but then tightened her grip. He looked so like Noah. She knew there was only ten years between them—they looked more like brothers than uncle and nephew. The likeness made her uncomfortable, probably because she didn't trust him. A man who could lie to his family for almost all his life. What was he hiding now?

"We have to go," Peter said.

Noah looked at her. "Well?" he asked.

He was asking if she would help. She gave a brief nod.

Too many had died. Somehow she had to find a way through this, a way for the killing to end. A way to make her people listen to reason and change the beliefs that had sustained them for centuries.

It wasn't going to be easy.

And there was a good chance they would all die before tomorrow was out.

CHAPTER THIRTY-SEVEN

Noah kissed Eve on the forehead. "Give Lucy and Daniel a hug from me," he said. "Tell them I love them."

"You can tell them yourself," Eve said. Then her face softened. "Find her, Noah. Bring her back to me."

"I will." Or he'd die trying. Which right now seemed the more likely outcome.

Eve wasn't happy with the arrangements; she'd wanted to stay, to go with them and help rescue Harper, but Noah needed her out of the country. Unless Peter had double-crossed them, the Descendants still believed Eve was dead. And they had two more children who needed her. She was going to get Lucy and Daniel and disappear for a while. Maybe forever.

He glanced over to where his uncle stood leaning against the wall away from the group. Eve hadn't forgiven him. Noah doubted she ever would.

Zach was going with her. Another who wasn't happy about the plans, but he saw the sense to it. They'd spent last night interrogating Peter, getting every bit of useful information from his head. The scale of the organization was terrifying. They'd had centuries to position themselves, and now they had people high up in every major government and industry in the world. Some of the names on the list had blown his mind. Even if they managed to take down Clayton—and right now it seemed highly unlikely—the infrastructure would still be there, hovering just beneath the surface, waiting for the right moment to strike again.

At least with Zach staying alive, someone would have the intel. Zach would wait to see the outcome, and then he'd have to decide how best to use that information. MI6 was compromised. It looked like Project Arachnid was no more. But Peter had also given them a list of names he believed to be untainted by the Descendants. Zach would try to approach them, get someone to believe in his highly unlikely conspiracy theory. All while staying alive.

He turned to Zach. "Look after her. Don't let her die. Again. Once was enough."

"I'll do my best." They shook hands, and Noah watched as they got into the waiting car.

Peter came up beside him and put a hand on his arm. "You can walk away from this. Go with them. There's still time. I'll do everything I can to get Harper back."

"She's my daughter."

"And you don't trust me."

It wasn't a question, so Noah didn't bother with an answer, just watched as the car pulled away and they disappeared into the flow of traffic. "Have you tried to contact Clayton?" Noah asked.

"Of course. But nothing. My direct link has been cut off. However, I did get a message with a meeting point."

"She knows you're working with me?"

"I doubt she *knows*. But likely she suspects."

"Maybe you're the one who should be leaving, then."

He snorted. "There's nowhere I can go. She'll hunt me down. You, Eve, the children—she'll let you go. Whatever you think, she's not a vindictive woman. You owed her no loyalty. As long as you don't get in her way, she won't come after you. Me? I'm a dead man walking. It's just a matter of time."

"Unless we kill her."

Peter winced slightly and wasn't quick enough to hide the reaction. "I doubt we'll get the chance. Not this time, anyway. She'll come with a small army." He sighed. "We need to go."

They headed toward the car. "Do you trust her?" Peter asked in a low voice, nodding toward where Sara stood by the vehicle, hands in her pockets, waiting for them to say their good-byes so they could be on their way.

Hell, Noah had no clue. He shrugged. "She can help." Maybe the only one who could.

"How?"

Peter sounded skeptical, but Noah wasn't about to reveal to Peter that Sara had the location. Not until he needed to, anyway. He still wasn't certain of where his uncle's loyalties would lie when put to the test. "We need to get into the Great Taboo. Without Sara, I doubt I'd get more than a few feet in without them putting a bullet in me. They sort of promised that would happen." Or a spear. Or an arrow. He'd prefer the bullet.

Peter nodded. Up ahead, Sara waited at the car, one eyebrow raised. She didn't like Peter. Didn't trust him, that much was clear. She was watching them closely and would likely protect Noah from his uncle if necessary. Which was sweet. He couldn't remember a time when someone had tried to protect him.

Yet unlike Peter, she hadn't tried to make him walk away. In the short time they had been together, he figured she had gotten to know him pretty well. Knew when something was futile.

"Peter wants to know if I can trust you," he said as they came to a halt. "If it comes to a choice—which side will you choose?"

She cast Peter a dirty look. "I've already chosen. And I'll do everything in my power to finish this."

"Good enough. Let's go."

Peter was driving. Noah sat in the back with

Sara. "Okay, what do you think?"

"Right now, if you step into the Great Taboo, you'll be killed before you can get a word out. They won't wait for your explanations. As far as they are concerned, by their standards, they already risked enough in letting you go."

"Why did they?" Noah asked. At the time, questions had not seemed a good idea.

"Because my father owed Tarkhan his life. He once told me that their friendship was the only thing that had kept him alive when they were in the labor camp. And he's a man who pays his debts. However, he will only bend so far for friendship."

"But with you along, they won't kill me straight away?"

"That's the theory," she said, though she didn't sound convinced.

"But they might?"

She shrugged. "They might. I left without telling anyone, but if they'd wanted to, they could have stopped me before I left the area, so I'm hoping they'll give me a chance to speak before they kill us both."

The plan was that Peter would drop them off at the point where they would have to change vehicles. They would go on to the Great Taboo. Peter would go to his meeting with Clayton. So he would be part of the swap.

"And if they do give us a chance to talk?"

"Then we ask for a meeting with the council. Not all of them are as entrenched in the old ways. Some may be willing to listen."

"And at the meeting?"

"We ask for their help. We tell them the truth, or at least some of it. The Descendants will never stop hunting, and next time, they will find the tomb, but that they actually want the Talisman not the actual remains. Maybe we can work with that."

"So how do we stay alive? Any advice?"

She smiled. "Genghis Khan used to pray to the eternal blue sky. Maybe that would be an idea."

He glanced out of the window. They were leaving the city now. Outside, the sky was a deep, overarching blue. It was the height of summer. Christ, he'd give anything a try right now.

He wanted this.

He wanted to stop Clayton so badly, it consumed his mind, and that was not good. He needed a clear head.

He stared again at the blue of the sky and prayed...

Let me stop her.

CHAPTER THIRTY-EIGHT

Sara leaned against the vehicle as she waited for Noah. He was talking to his uncle, presumably making the last arrangements. Both the same height, both lean with short dark hair.

How could they be so different?

But were they?

Was General Peter Blakeley a bad man?

Any more than she was bad?

He'd clearly believed in what the Descendants were doing. If they hadn't kidnapped Noah's daughter, would he have ever turned on them? Clayton had made a serious error of judgment because Peter clearly loved his niece as he loved Noah. Up until then, he'd been on Clayton's side. While he might have doubted that some of her ways were justified, he had never stepped out of line. Noah claimed that his uncle was in love with the senator. People did strange things for love.

She had gone against her own people to help Noah, because she couldn't bear the thought of him losing his daughter. She'd had doubts herself, hadn't liked the easy killing. But while she'd thought of making changes from within, she had never contemplated outright betrayal. Because that's what this was. It went against their most basic beliefs.

So really, she *was* like Peter. Both of them betraying their own sides for the people they loved.

There. She'd admitted it. She cared for Noah. Not that she would ever tell him that. It was definitely on a need-to-know basis, and he did not need to know.

It looked like they had finished talking. She climbed into the driver's seat. It made sense for her to drive. She knew the route—she'd driven it a hundred times.

Finally, with a last nod, Noah came over. He slung his bag into the back of the ATV and climbed in beside her. She pulled away as he was fastening his seat belt. She cast him a sideways glance. He was relaxed back in his seat and staring at the sky through the open top of the vehicle. Maybe he was praying after all. When she was a little girl, her papa had taken her up the sacred mountain, and she had prayed to the eternal blue sky.

She had believed back then.

Now she no longer believed.

Not in that, anyway, though she still believed in a better world. That it could be possible, but they had to fight for it. All it took for bad people to win was for good people to do nothing.

They had to do something or die trying.

They were driving along the banks of a river. As they reached the ford, she turned and drove into the water, over the rocks and up the steep bank on the other side. She could feel the vehicle straining, but it pulled through, and then they were into the forest, the track through the trees almost invisible unless you knew it was there. She weaved between the trunks.

"We just crossed the border into the Great Taboo," she said.

"So how long until they know we're here?"

"They already know."

She'd seen the spotter, sitting astride a horse, as they entered the area. He would have already contacted the camp. They could expect a welcome committee any moment now. Her skin prickled. She had no clue what form that welcome would take. They might just decide to take Noah out, and she'd warned him there was a chance, though he didn't appear concerned. In fact, he seemed more relaxed now. She reckoned he wasn't a man who did well with inactivity, and waiting was not a strong point. He was happier on the move.

No one shot them.

"This is as far as we go," she said, hitting the brakes and coming to a halt at the base of a steep incline. As she turned off the engine, a rider appeared over the first ridge, leading two saddled horses.

"That's a good sign, right?" Noah murmured from beside her.

"Yes. They might still decide to shoot you, but I'm guessing they'll listen to us first." Though she had an idea they weren't going to like what she had to say. She climbed out of the vehicle and waited as the rider approached. Noah grabbed his rucksack from the back and slung it over his shoulders.

The rider was armed, a pistol at his thigh, though it remained in the holster. He didn't speak, just stopped beside the ATV. Sara nodded then took the reins of one horse and led it to Noah before mounting the second.

Still without speaking, the rider turned and headed back up the mountain. Sara followed, Noah behind her. The track was too narrow to ride side by side. She glanced back over her shoulder. He seemed at ease on the horse, his position relaxed, moving easily, leaning forward in the saddle as they climbed.

A knot tightened in her stomach as they approached the camp. Would her people see this as a betrayal? While she had her doubts, it was all she had ever known. And she loved her father.

Darkness was falling as they rode into the camp. Her father was waiting, standing with the rest of the council, his face expressionless, and she had no clue what he was thinking.

Time to find out whether they lived or died.

• • •

The welcoming committee didn't look particularly welcoming.

It was a group of seven men. Sara had told him that while her father was the ultimate leader, all important decision were discussed and determined by a council of six men. The seventh he recognized as Tarkhan, still leaning on crutches. It was these men they would have to convince.

Sara didn't believe their chances were high.

He halted his horse next to hers and swung down from the saddle. Someone came up behind him and said something, presumably in Mongolian. He glanced at Sara where she still sat on her horse.

"They want to search you for weapons," she said.

He shrugged out of the rucksack and dropped it to the ground then held his arms out while they frisked him. He wasn't armed. He had a pistol in his bag. After checking him, the man searched through his bag, took the pistol and pushed it down the back of his pants, then nodded to the council members.

Sara dismounted and handed her reins to the man, who took Noah's horse as well and led them away.

"This is my father, Ulagan," she said to Noah, gesturing to the tall man at the center of the group. He spoke to her in Mongolian, and she answered in the same language. Then turned to him. "He wants to know why you're back when it was made very clear that you were to leave the country and never return."

"And what did you tell him?"

"That the enemy have your daughter. You are loyal to your family and willing to risk your own life by returning here in order to save hers. And that you have a proposition that you wish to share with the council."

He studied her father. He was tall, with sun-darkened skin and black hair, and clearly Mongolian, unlike Sara. Maybe her mother had been from somewhere else. He caught Noah's gaze and pursed his lips then nodded and turned. They followed the small group as they disappeared into a nearby yurt.

The yurt was empty except for one chair, which Tarkhan took with a sigh. Kerosene lamps hung from the ceiling, casting flickering shadows. The rest of them sat cross-legged in a circle, leaving the space farthest from the door and next to Sara for him. He sank down to the ground and composed himself, pushing thoughts of Harper to the back of his mind because he had one chance at this.

"So Major Blakeley, my daughter tells me you

have a proposition for us. Perhaps you could explain why we shouldn't kill you right now?" The man's English was perfect.

Noah took a deep breath. "I know where the tomb is."

Ulagan's eyes narrowed. "So you lied when you were last with us?"

"No. At that point, I didn't have the location."

"I gave it to him," Sara said.

Shock flashed across his face. "You had the location and you never told us? Instead, you gave it to this man. Why?"

"Because he needed it. The Descendants have kidnapped his daughter. They will only give her back in exchange for the location of the tomb."

"How was it found?"

"Eve Blakeley. We discovered an image in a safe deposit box in Irkutsk. I destroyed the image but memorized the GPS location. That's what I gave to Noah."

"So why come here? Why tell us when you know what the outcome must be?"

He figured that was him dying. While he didn't want to die, this had been a calculated risk. He would never have survived a trip to the Great Taboo anyway. If he had come without Sara, he would have never made it inside the area. They would have picked him off first. Then Harper would die. Christ, she would probably die anyway.

But this was her one chance.

"Because it's time for us to adapt," Sara said. "We've spent centuries protecting the location of the tomb, but times change. Technology moves on. How long do you think the secret will remain a secret? If one person found the tomb, then others will also find it. It's over."

"You're sure the location is real?"

"The image showed the Talisman. It's real."

"The people who have my daughter don't want the tomb itself," Noah said. "They want the Talisman—they don't wish to desecrate the body. And they won't give up. They have the resources to tear this place down around you until they find what they want."

"We can't risk that. We cannot risk our enemies knowing the location of the tomb. We cannot know their intentions for certain."

"Then move the Talisman. Take it to a new location."

CHAPTER THIRTY-NINE

Though it was close to midday, the air was chill, and Sara shivered, wrapping her jacket around herself. They were close to the summit of Burkhan Khaldun, and they were in the clouds. The air was damp against her face, her nostrils filled with the pungent scent of pine and damp earth.

The biggest hurdle was over, so why couldn't she shift the knot of unease that tightened in her belly?

She had expected more of a fight.

It had been a long night. The council had questioned Noah extensively then gone into a huddle. Finally, and to her surprise, they'd agreed to the plan, and much of the night had been spent discussing details and possible locations.

They'd finally slept on the floor of the yurt, wrapped in blankets, and then set off at dawn.

Beside her, Noah stood, hands in his pockets. Some of the tension had eased from him. She hadn't realized just how tightly he'd been wound until it was gone.

"Eve should have been here," he said. "She would have loved this."

The day had turned cloudy as they climbed until they were moving through thick white mist.

First on horseback and then on foot, her and Noah, plus her father and eight volunteers. They would have to dig, and they had only hours to complete the move if this had any hope of working.

The GPS coordinates had led them here, just above the tree line where the pine forest gave way to grassy scrub-land that would be deep in snow for most of the year. It was a beautiful spot, looking out over the vastness of the land far below them. She could imagine why Genghis Khan had chosen this place.

From her recollection of the image, Sara had told them where to dig.

Maybe her unease was simply that this was going against everything she had been brought up to believe. Her whole life had been dedicated to ensuring the sanctity of the tomb. She'd never balked at doing her duty, had considered it a sacred chore. Their one role in life was to ensure that the tomb was never found. And yet here they were, digging in the earth, desecrating the final resting place.

But if their actions saved one life, then surely it was worth it. The living had to be more important than the dead.

And what did she expect? A bolt of lightning from above to wipe them out?

She had no belief in divine retribution.

They were concentrating on the small area where she believed the Talisman would be buried. The image hadn't shown the location of the actual body. There was a good chance that he hadn't had any sort of sarcophagus. They liked to be at one with the earth, and there would be nothing substantial to show up on the imaging.

The area was small, and they worked in teams of four for half an hour and then swapped places with the second team. It was grueling work and the digging slow. They had to be careful they didn't damage anything that might be buried here. The sound of their harsh breathing filling the air mixed with the rhythmic sound of the shovels hitting dirt, the soft thud as it hit the ground.

They dug until the men vanished beneath the earth, only the sound revealing their continued labor.

Had the image been wrong? Maybe it was faked and never real, but she didn't think so. She bit down on her lip until she tasted the sharp metallic twang of blood on her tongue.

Noah edged closer and took her hand, holding it tight as if he could feel the sanctity of the moment. Or was he thinking about his daughter? Where was she? Was she afraid? So much hinged on this.

Finally, there was a cry, and the digging ceased. Noah made to move forward, and she stopped him with a hand on his arm. He wasn't to go near the grave—her father's stipulation.

Sara held her breath as they lifted out a box. Octagonal, it was about two feet across and heavy; she could tell by the way they lifted it then placed it gently on the ground.

At that moment, there was a break in the clouds, the mist seemed to melt away, and they stood under the deep blue sky as Genghis Khan must have done all those centuries past. She looked to the sky and prayed for forgiveness…and strength.

•••

Darkness had engulfed them by the time they came down off the mountain, though the horses seemed to know their way instinctively. Noah was alone with Sara, and they rode in silence. She'd been quiet since they had found the Talisman. Was she regretting her decision to help him?

They'd left her father and the others at the new resting place, ensuring there was nothing to give away the recent upheaval. They'd picked the new site carefully with certain conditions in mind, mainly that terrain and vegetation would allow them to conceal the digging. The exchange was set up for the morning. At least now there was hope that tomorrow, they would get Harper back. Peter would see her to safety, and Noah would attempt to take out the senator. It had to be done. He couldn't allow her to go on; she was responsible for too many deaths.

That was tomorrow. They still had the night to get through, and he found he didn't want to be alone. While he hadn't put it into words—even inside his head—he knew his chances of surviving the next day were almost nonexistent. As long as he got Harper out...

They rode into the camp and dismounted, took off the saddles, and released the horses into the corral. As they turned away, she slipped her hand into his and led him across the camp to a large yurt on the edge of the cluster of tents.

Inside was some sort of storage room, with shelves piled with goods. She grabbed a rolled-up sleeping bag from one and handed it to him then crossed to a huge industrial fridge. She filled a bag with food, added a few other things from the shelves, and slung it over her shoulder.

"Fancy set up for a camp site," he said.

"It's run on solar. Better than when I was a kid. We had to make do with warm yak's milk. Come on, let's get away from here."

He half expected the guards to stop them, but the place was quiet, only the stamping and nickering of the horses breaking the silence of the night. Sara led him away from the yurts, heading back along the route they had come, but just a short way. She stopped in a clearing in the pine forest and laid the sleeping bag on the ground. After the cold of the near summit, the night felt warm. She sank down gracefully and patted the space beside her.

As he sat, she pulled a bottle of wine from the bag. She opened it with her knife and drank straight from the bottle then handed it to him, and he drank deeply, feeling the warmth in his belly. She laid bread and cheese and some sort of roasted meat on a platter between them, and his stomach rumbled. He hadn't felt like eating in as long as he could remember. As he dug in, he concentrated on the food filling his stomach.

There was nothing left to think about. Everything had been done that could be done. Now there was just the night and Sara.

They finished the wine, and he swept the remains of their meal aside. Then he dragged her into his arms, took her mouth in a deep kiss, and pulled her down to the sleeping bag.

CHAPTER FORTY

Michaela Clayton peered out of the window and gazed down at the immensity of the empty land below her. They were flying over the lower slopes of Burkhan Khaldun.

Where had Noah Blakeley been since the call? How had he evaded the Darkhats?

She shifted in her seat and studied the two people opposite. Her attention landed briefly on Peter Blakeley—she'd lost him, and she couldn't believe how bad that knowledge made her feel. A tightness across her chest, but she couldn't hate him. She'd known how he felt about Noah Blakeley and his children, and somewhere—deep down where she wouldn't admit it—she'd hated that. She'd loved Peter most of her adult life, known her love was returned, but she'd wanted it all. So she'd tested him, needing proof that his loyalty was all hers. She'd lost. When this was over, she would have to deal with him.

She forced herself to catch his gaze—he was watching her, and he gave her a small smile, yet she could see the knowledge of his own death in his eyes.

She shifted her attention to his niece, Harper, sitting beside him, her good hand clutching his.

She was too young to understand that he had been, if not complicit in her kidnapping, at least in league with her kidnappers.

The girl looked so like her uncle, the same black hair and gray eyes, the same beaky nose dominating a face she still needed to grow into. If they'd had a daughter, would she have looked the same? Or would she have taken after Michaela? Perhaps she would keep the girl around afterward.

The plan had always been to bring Noah into the group, but Peter had said to wait—that the time wasn't right. Now it never would be. She was still unsure as to whether he knew her identity. She hadn't questioned Peter, not wanting any more lies between them. It didn't matter, anyway—Noah would know as soon as she stepped from the chopper. She could have sent someone else, but she had worked too hard for this. And he would never forgive the kidnapping and mutilation of his daughter and never forgive her.

Which meant he would also need to be dealt with, and she suspected he was aware of that. That's why Peter was here. To take the girl to safety.

Harper looked better than she had a day ago. When she had arrived yesterday, her skin had been leached of color, a combination of fear, pain, lack of food, and a low-level infection from the wound in her hand. Now she had some color in her cheeks.

Michaela's doctors had done a complete checkup. They'd given the girl medication for the pain and antibiotics for the infection, and she was already recovering. Strong genes.

She wasn't a monster. She didn't kill for no reason.

She looked away and out the window, searching the ground. Where the hell was he? They'd been circling the coordinates he had given them for ten minutes now. Had he double-crossed them in some way? Peter thought not. Maybe the Darkhats had intercepted him and he was already dead. They'd been a plague to the Descendants for centuries. Many times they'd tried to wipe them out, but they knew this area too well, knew where to hide, and after the purges, they'd always sprouted up again stronger.

Noah was a trained soldier, but he didn't know this land.

Her heart was beating hard and her breathing short and fast. She almost didn't recognize the feeling as fear. And desperation.

Damn, she needed this over with.

This afternoon was the start of the summit. Before it began, she had a video call with the leaders—she had to show them the Talisman and the Spear.

She needed this proof for her people and also for herself.

For the first time, she acknowledged her doubts. Doubts that they would find the Talisman, that it even existed. Doubt that she was the true heir to Genghis Khan. There had been others before over the centuries who had thought they were the one, and they had all failed.

Would she, too, fail?

At her feet lay the long case holding the spear. If she hadn't been the one, then she would not have found the Spirit Banner. She had to hold onto that fact.

They were nearly there.

"Ma'am, we have a visual. We're going in to land." She heard the voice through her headphones, and some of the tension eased from her.

She searched the ground and homed in on Noah. He stood on the grassy mountainside, hand shading his eyes as he stared up into the sky. The area was flanked by thick pine forest, but there was a flattish, clear area big enough for the helicopter to land. Close by, the ground fell away, dropping into a deep ravine.

This wasn't the actual location. He had said he would lead them there once he had seen his daughter. He didn't trust her. She'd actually expected the site to be higher up the mountain—

that was where they had concentrated searches in the past. Perhaps that was also why they had been unsuccessful.

The helicopter touched down lightly on the ground, and she was unfastening her harness within moments. Once free, she gripped the spear. Across from her, Peter unfastened the girl's harness before his own. Michaela pushed open the door and jumped to the ground then stepped away so Peter and the girl could get out.

Behind them, a second helicopter landed, and three of her bodyguards jumped out and came to stand around her, then the two helicopters rose into the air, the wind from the blades pulling at her.

She was wearing a tracker. The helicopters would follow and then pick them up after they had located the tomb and she had the Talisman in her possession.

Noah walked toward them. There was no surprise in his eyes; he'd clearly known who to expect. Beside her, Harper gave a cry and then ran toward her father, hurled herself into his arms, and buried her face against his chest. Noah stroked her hair, held her close while his gaze fixed on their small group. He gave Peter an almost imperceptible nod and then fixed his cold gaze on her. His eyes were without expression, but she got the impression of immense rage held in check. He looked awful, bruises marking his face, a new scar on his forehead.

Then he placed his hands on Harper's shoulders and held her away. He lowered his head and kissed her on the forehead then spoke to her quietly. She shook her head, and he spoke again. Finally, she nodded. Tears welled in her eyes as she stepped away, and the two of them headed toward her. They stopped in front of Peter, and he gave the girl a gentle push.

"You'll look after her," he said to Peter.

"She comes with us," Michaela said.

Noah shook his head. "She can't—she's not strong enough. We'll be climbing and no way will she make it with that hand. Peter can stay with her."

Her eyes narrowed, and her gaze shifted from him to his daughter. Her left hand was cradled against her chest. Damn. He was right. Had he planned it this way?

As if he could understand her thoughts, he waved toward the cliff's edge. "We're going down there. You couldn't have landed any closer."

She walked across and peered over the edge. Below was a narrow rocky ravine, too narrow for a helicopter to land. She turned back to Noah. "You have the image?"

"No. It was destroyed."

"Convenient."

His gaze flicked to where his daughter stood. "No, actually, it wasn't. But I'd memorized the GPS. You don't need to worry. I can find your tomb."

"Okay. Let's do this. But Peter goes with us. One of my men will stay with your daughter."

His lips tightened, then he nodded. He'd no doubt been expecting that. He knew how these things worked. Without another word, he turned and strode back to the tree line, returning with a coil of rope over his shoulder and two shovels in his hand. Crossing to the edge of the cliff, he dropped the shovels over the edge then tied one end of the rope to a rocky outcrop and threw the rest after the shovels.

She waved to one of her guards, and he crossed the short distance, took a hold of the rope, and disappeared over the edge of the cliff.

Noah reached out and touched his daughter's arm. "Keep safe, sweetheart. We'll be back soon." Then he followed her guard over the edge. Then Peter.

It was her turn next, and she swung the handle of the spear bag over her shoulder, moved forward, and grasped the rope. It was rough in her hands. She'd done this before, gone through rigorous training, just not for a while. The rock face was sheer. About a hundred feet below, she could see them staring up at her, squinting into the sunlight. Maybe they were hoping she would fall and kill herself.

She wouldn't fall.

Twisting her body, she slipped over the edge, her feet finding the rock face. For a moment, she hung there, then she slowly moved down, hand over hand.

For the last few feet, the rock face vanished, and she dangled in the air. She peered down; she could make it. Releasing her hold on the rope, she dropped, her ankle twisting and giving way beneath her as she crashed to the ground, the spear digging into her back.

A hand reached down for her, and her bodyguard pulled her to her feet. She glanced across to where Noah and Peter stood impassive, watching her, no doubt hating her. She could feel the intensity of their stares.

Once her friend, her lover. Now her enemy. Everything had a price.

As she took a step, pain shot through her ankle, up her leg, and she would have fallen if not for the hard grip of her guard. "Shit."

The second guard landed, took in the situation.

"Are you okay to go on?" Noah asked, his tone expressionless as if he didn't care. Of course he cared. If she didn't go on, then he wouldn't get his daughter back.

"I'm fine." She pulled free of the guard's hold,

ignoring the pain as she took another step forward. "Lead the way."

Sweat rolled down her forehead, stinging her eyes as she followed the two men, her guards bringing up the rear. They didn't look back once, just kept up a steady pace, winding around the narrow ravine. There were no plants, the ground bone dry, the footing sandy. She doubted anyone had been down here in years. Maybe centuries.

She gritted her teeth against the pain and kept walking.

Finally, they came to a standstill, and she halted behind them. Was this it? A smile tugged at her lips.

She stood for a moment, breathing deeply, ignoring the sharp pain shooting up from her ankle. Up above, a narrow blue strip of sky showed between the steep edges of the gorge. She'd expected more sky. And unease tugged at her.

Had he got it wrong?

"You want the Talisman, not the body? Yes?"

She glanced up at his question, eyes narrowing. "How did you know?"

"Eve left notes. We found them with the image."

That made sense. They'd given her the shape and dimensions of the box that contains the Talisman. She nodded. She had no wish to desecrate the body of her revered ancestor.

He stood for a moment, orientating himself. Then he turned so he was facing south and closed his eyes. Was he visualizing the positioning? He stood for so long that she had to clamp her lips to stop from screaming.

Finally, he waved a hand at an area that looked no different than anywhere else. A patch of clear, sandy ground. "According to the image, it's about six feet down."

She looked around, found a smooth rock, and walked over, refusing to limp, but a sigh of relief escaped her as she sank down. She watched them dig, taking it in turns. They dug until she could no longer see them, and then she listened to the rhythmic sound of the shovels.

She wasn't sure how much time had passed.

At last, Noah gave a shout from inside the hole. Peter, who'd been standing beside it, jumped down.

A rush of excitement filled her, and she pushed herself to her feet. She closed the space, her guards at her back, and came to a halt at the edge of the hole, just as they heaved a box to the surface.

Octagonal, smooth wood, dark with age, but perfect.

Ignoring the two men as they emerged from the hole, she sank to her knees. She reached out a hand, stroked her fingers over the smooth wood. It felt warm to her touch, as though it was a living thing, and sensations prickled up the nerves of her arm, settled in her chest.

She'd never believed in magic. Had always thought the Talisman was nothing more than a symbol. Now she was filled with a sense of limitless power. She would prevail.

Running her fingers along the underside, she searched for the catch that would unlock the box.

She'd won.

The Talisman was hers.

CHAPTER FORTY-ONE

Sara reined in her horse and sat for a moment, listening. Overhead, she could hear the drone of the circling helicopters.

She'd wanted to be there with Noah yet accepted that it wasn't possible. He'd been told to come alone, and he wouldn't do anything to risk his daughter's safety.

All her people had been ordered to stay away. They couldn't go up against helicopters. Sara alone had been allowed in the area. She knew the plan, and she was going to look out for Harper once the others left. There was another route into the ravine — one possible on horseback — but they'd gone this way to ensure Harper would be left behind. No doubt she would have a guard. If everything went to shit, then Sara's job was to kill the guard and get Harper to safety.

There was no reason anything would go wrong, except maybe the mad bitch would decide to kill them all anyway.

And she still couldn't get rid of the nagging feeling that had been dogging her since they'd dug up the tomb yesterday. That something wasn't right. That things had been too easy. The obstacles she'd expected to struggle with had fallen away effortlessly.

She was situated on a rise about fifty feet from where Harper huddled on the ground, arms around her knees. The guard was paying her little attention, pacing the area, peering over the edge. Occasionally, he tried his radio, but they would be out of contact. That was one of the reasons her father had picked the place. That and the sandy ground and lack of vegetation made it possible to hide the recent disturbance. Plus there was also a burial site already there. One of Khan's family. Many of them had been buried on the mountain.

She could take the guard out easily. She had a bow in her hand, the arrow already cocked. And a rifle in the holster in her saddle.

A noise sounded behind her. Hoof beats on the soft sand? She nudged her mount around, hand tightening on the bow. A horse and rider emerged from the trees. She recognized her father. Her nerve endings tingled with a warning.

He halted a few feet away then swung himself down from the saddle.

"Father?"

She glanced down, saw the pistol in his hand, hanging by his side.

He didn't speak, but his arm slowly raised until the gun was pointed at her chest. Her mind was blank, her body numb. Some part of her was screaming to run, but she couldn't move. She stared into his eyes, saw the sadness and the resolve.

She was going to die. Her gaze dropped, focusing on the pistol, the fingers tightening on the trigger.

Then her father dropped to the ground, an arrow through his neck.

And she sat staring, unable to move.

Tarkhan rode up, the bow still in his hand, pain etched on his face. He stopped beside her then glanced from her to where her father lay, blank eyes staring up at the blue sky. Back at her.

She swallowed. "Why?"

"They're all dead."

"Who?" Her thoughts were struggling back from the edge of death.

"The men who volunteered to move the Talisman. They're dead. Your father came here to kill you. And afterward, he would have turned his gun on himself."

Her brain scrambled to make sense of the words. But really, they made perfect sense.

Her father had believed them. That Michaela Clayton would keep coming. So they'd gone along with the plan. He'd never meant any of them to survive. The volunteers, her father, herself.

He had dedicated his life to the sanctity of the tomb. He wasn't going to allow any of them to survive. That just left Noah alive who knew the location.

What had her father done?

CHAPTER FORTY-TWO

Noah wanted to back away, but he couldn't get his legs to obey. Couldn't completely stifle the strange compulsion to move closer and run his fingers over the smooth wood as Michaela Clayton was doing.

To open the box and see what was inside.

As he'd lifted it out of the ground, shivers had prickled across his skin.

He knew he wasn't safe. That likely he'd never leave this place. That had always been an unspoken part of the bargain. His life for Harper's. And he could live with that. Or, rather, die with it.

He just wished he could be there to see the end. To see Michaela Clayton brought down. As she would be.

She was sliding her fingers along the edge of the box, searching for something. A way to open it maybe. There was a look of almost mystical reverence on her face. The spear lay by her side; she'd taken it from the case as they'd dug. It had survived eight hundred years. Maybe there *was* magic in the world. He almost smiled at the thought.

Peter stood close by him. Peter was another who was unlikely to survive. Maybe he'd last longer than Noah, hopefully long enough to get Harper to safety, but Clayton wouldn't let him live. He knew too much. And in the end, he had chosen his side, and it hadn't been the senator's. Despite the betrayal, a wave of sadness washed over Noah at the thought. The truth was he loved his uncle.

He looked into his face, gave a smile. "Thank you," he said. He meant for everything, for being there for him when he was a screwed up kid, then later, for guiding him, teaching him right from wrong. Ironic, really, but Noah's passion for justice and fighting against evil came from Peter.

A look of surprise flashed across his uncle's face. Then he nodded and glanced away, his gaze settling on something high above them, a frown forming between his brows.

Noah's attention was drawn back to the senator. She'd found whatever she was looking for, and she'd gone momentarily still, her eyes closed. Now she opened them, and a smile curved her lips. She slowly lifted the lid—

"Noah!" His uncle's tone was frantic, and Noah dragged his gaze away and upward. A rider was silhouetted on the cliff's edge above them. Sara. She was waving and shouting, but he couldn't hear. The wind had gotten up and snatched the words away. He concentrated on the shape of her mouth, translated it into words.

It's a trap.

His gaze jerked to the box.

The lid was lifting. He looked to Peter, saw the dawning understanding. He made to move. Too late. Someone crashed into him, and he was hurled across the space and he was falling. Something heavy landed on top of him, shoving the air from his lungs, and a moment later, the world erupted and darkness engulfed him.

Warm wetness seeped down over Noah's face. A heavy weight held him down. He blinked a couple of times, clearing the sand from his eyes. He tried to raise a hand to wipe his face, but it was pinned beneath him.

He lay for a minute, breathing slowly. He could hear nothing around him. Everything silent, a faint hum in his ears from the explosion. Finally, he took a deep breath and heaved the body from on top of him and scrambled up. Peter sprawled on his front, the back of his head caved in, a mass of blood and brains and bone fragments. Noah reached out a hand and felt for a pulse, knowing it was hopeless.

Peter had saved his life. He had hurled them both backward and into the hole they had dug to free the Talisman. Then his body had protected Noah from the debris that fell.

He dragged himself out of the hole and stood

staring around at the chaos. The two guards lay close together, unmoving. He crossed the space; they were both dead. Leaning down, he pulled the pistol from the nearest man's waist.

At first, he couldn't locate the senator. Had she somehow escaped the blast? Then he caught the flash of her dark red hair close to the rock wall, her body almost covered by rocks and sand.

She'd been at the very apex of the explosion. Likely, the force had hurled her backward, her body crashing into the unforgiving rock. The lid of the Talisman's box was embedded in her throat, the Spirit Banner of Genghis Khan buried deep in her chest.

It seemed somehow fitting.

"I guess you weren't the one after all," he murmured.

EPILOGUE

It could have all ended so differently. Closing his eyes, Noah relived the moment when Sara had come galloping around the corner of the ravine, Harper behind her. His girls to the rescue.

It had been touch and go.

Now they were all in hiding in a safe house organized by Zach in the Highlands of Scotland. Eve and the children. Sara and her daughter. Right now, they had to lie low.

They'd just eaten, and he sat on the sofa, a twin on either side of him, Harper at his feet, her head resting against his knee. While they were safe here for the moment, long term, they had to solve the problem. Too many people wanted him and the people he loved dead. If the Darkhats didn't get them, then the Descendants likely would—once they had gotten over scrabbling between themselves for a new leader.

So he didn't plan to stay hiding for long. Now was the time to go on the offensive, when the enemy was in disarray. The threat was still there, and he wanted to be part of the solution.

The first thing he'd done when they'd gotten out was contact everyone he could with a warning. The summit had been halted with only hours to go before the opening ceremony. The world's leaders had gone home, though it was to be rescheduled for a later date. They needed to work together now more than ever.

He understood the dangers the world faced better than anyone. Project Arachnid was to be reinstated, and he would take lead. Zach would be their U.K. liaison. And they were reaching out to other security forces across the world.

They had lists of names from Peter. He'd shared everything he knew. They were cleaning out the rot. Uncovering the bad guys, dragging them out of the darkness and into the light. It was going to be a long job.

He'd brought Eve a couple of souvenirs back.

A spear and the lid of the Talisman's box.

She stroked her hand along the shaft of the spear. "I don't suppose you would tell me where the tomb actually is?" Eve said.

He turned around and glared. "No."

"Hmm. Well, I could always move onto something new. I have a few ideas. Maybe the lost labyrinth of Ancient Egypt?"

Hell no!

Noah clamped his mouth closed on his instinctive reply to give himself time to come up with a more diplomatic approach. But really?

Because if there was one thing he'd learned through this whole mess, it was that the past shaped the future, and who knew what ancient evil lay buried beneath the desert sands, just waiting to be stirred...

ACKNOWLEDGMENTS

I want to say a huge thank you to everyone at Sideways Books for all their help with getting *The Lost Tomb* to where it is now. Especially my fabulous editor, Heather Howland.

A special thank you to my friend Andy, whose interest in space archaeology was an immense help and inspiration.

And finally, thank you to my wonderful critique partners at PC, who read my chapters and told me what they really think (as in—you're not *really* going to kill Eve, are you?)

ABOUT THE AUTHOR

After a number of years wandering the world in search of adventure, N.J. Croft finally settled on a farm in the mountains and now lives off-grid, growing almonds, drinking cold beer, taking in stray dogs, and writing stories where the stakes are huge and absolutely anything can happen.